THE AUTHORITY OF THE STATE

THE AUTHORITY OF THE STATE

LESLIE GREEN

CLARENDON PRESS · OXFORD

This book has been printed digitally and produced in a standard specification in order to ensure its continuing availability

OXFORD
UNIVERSITY PRESS

Great Clarendon Street, Oxford OX2 6DP

Oxford University Press is a department of the University of Oxford.
It furthers the University's objective of excellence in research, scholarship,
and education by publishing worldwide in

Oxford New York

Auckland Cape Town Dar es Salaam Hong Kong Karachi
Kuala Lumpur Madrid Melbourne Mexico City Nairobi
New Delhi Shanghai Taipei Toronto
With offices in
Argentina Austria Brazil Chile Czech Republic France Greece
Guatemala Hungary Italy Japan South Korea Poland Portugal
Singapore Switzerland Thailand Turkey Ukraine Vietnam

Oxford is a registered trade mark of Oxford University Press
in the UK and in certain other countries

Published in the United States
by Oxford University Press Inc., New York

Reprinted 2008

ISBN 978-0-19-827313-4

To my parents

PREFACE

This book undertakes the somewhat old-fashioned task of explaining and evaluating the state's claim to authority over its citizens. It has been said that, 'The issue of authority has such a bad reputation that a philosopher cannot discuss it without exposing himself to suspicion and malice.'[1] Perhaps I can avoid certain suspicions, though no doubt only by attracting others, if I say in advance that this is the book of a sceptic and not an enthusiast. It argues that modern states claim an authority which cannot in general be justified. But at the same time it is not the work of a philosophical anarchist; I contend that political authority is sometimes legitimate, although this stops short of what is suggested by the classical doctrine of political obligation. If I am right about this, then much of modern legal and political theory is based on a mistake. There is no need to explain how political institutions could be such as to ground a general obligation to obey. Like other failed transcendental arguments, these ones seek the possibility conditions of a premiss which is simply false: there is no such obligation.

An earlier version of this work was accepted as a D.Phil. thesis by the University of Oxford. I am grateful to Charles Taylor, who first introduced me to these problems and who, by example and instruction, made political theory important to me and then directed my research in its preliminary stages. Its supervision was later taken over by Joseph Raz, whose continuing encouragement and criticism were invaluable. I have learned much from our many discussions and from his writings; perhaps I should have learned more. I am also grateful to the Commonwealth Scholarship Commission in the UK, to the Social Sciences and Humanities Research Council of Canada, and to my parents, all of whom supported my work during my time at Nuffield College.

Among many others who helped with advice, and even more with criticism, I must thank especially John Finnis,

[1] Y. R. Simon, *A General Theory of Authority* (Notre Dame: University of Notre Dame Press, 1980), 13.

Steven Lukes, Neil MacCormick, David Miller, Patrick Nowell-Smith, and Jeremy Waldron. They saved me from many errors, but cannot be blamed for those that remain. My students at Lincoln College, Oxford and then at York University, Toronto also grappled with earlier versions of these arguments and helped improve them. And I am grateful to Shu-Yan Mok for his assistance in preparing the final manuscript. I owe Denise Réaume more than I can express here: she often took time out from her own research to discuss, encourage, and criticize mine, and in many other ways bettered my work and my world.

Portions of the following previously published papers have been reprinted here, usually with alterations: 'Law Co-ordination, and the Common Good', *Oxford Journal of Legal Studies* 3 (1983), 299–324; 'Support for the System', *British Journal of Political Science* 15 (1985), 127–42; 'Authority and Convention', *Philosophical Quarterly* 35 (1985), 329–46. I am grateful to the editors and publishers of those journals—Oxford University Press, Cambridge University Press, and Basil Blackwell—for permission to use that material here.

L.J.M.G.

CONTENTS

I

SOCIAL ORDER AND SOCIAL RELATIONS

1. THE PROBLEM OF POLITICAL AUTHORITY

ALL modern states claim authority over their citizens, and that is one thing which distinguishes them from bands of robbers. But the state's authority, unlike that of parents over their children, also claims to be supreme: even when it lacks a monopoly of authority in the society, when it shares it with other persons and groups, the state does so on its own terms. It claims to bind many persons, to regulate their most vital interests, and to do so with supremacy over all other mechanisms of social control. Sometimes these grandiose claims are hollow. In a society undergoing upheaval they cannot be made effective and quickly become legal fictions. Even when they are effective they may be unjustified, for legitimacy is not among the existence conditions for a state. However—and here is the real importance of Weber's celebrated argument—a belief in its legitimacy tends to increase its stability and effectiveness. It is therefore a crucial question in what circumstances, if any, such beliefs are justified.

So conceived, the problem of authority is a part of foundational political theory; one is tempted to say, the most important part. In the introduction to *The Social Contract*, Rousseau takes this for granted when he writes, 'I begin without proving the importance of my subject.' For us, however, it is not quite that easy. Throughout much of the world and certainly in those modern states which are the primary concern of this book, political order is now better established, more extensive, and more accepted than was Rousseau's *ancien régime*. Our states are less easily avoided and their claims have generally become larger and show few signs of retreat. The partisans of minimal government do not stand as a counterexample; they contend for the use of political power for different purposes than do those who favour state intervention, but rarely do they advocate less overall authority. In contrast with the eighteenth century, contemporary political life is more normal, more regularized—almost part of a natural external order. If no less questionable, the authority of the state is now at least less questioned. The consequences of this change of context are important for both theory and practice. Hobbes's fear of anarchy, for instance, now seems to be an absurd starting-point for a theory of the state: so far from being a constantly looming threat, the state of nature would be very difficult to reach from our present position. We have backed away from the precipice, and the stability of the modern state together with the increased scope of its claims mean that the consequences of being wrong about the nature and justification of its authority are more profound. In this respect modernity has increased the stakes in social and political theory. It is in this context that we begin our exploration. The problems facing us on the way are both descriptive and normative, questions of the nature of political authority and of the soundness of those moral arguments which are commonly marshalled in its defence.

Modern political theory gives us less guidance in these matters than one might hope; the general problem of political authority is rarely regarded as being of primary importance. There would not now be much agreement with T. D. Weldon's claim (made during the dark years for the subject) that, 'The aim of political philosophy is to discover the grounds on which the State claims to exercise authority over its members.'[1] Few of the most powerful contemporary thinkers, from Rawls and Nozick to Habermas and Luhmann, would accept this view. In one way, this is an advance; in another it is a retreat. Weldon's project was to produce a value-free analysis of the language of politics, one which was descriptively adequate for the complexity of life in modern society, but neutral on the question of how such life should be appraised. The revival of normative political theory is a great advance over this. Questions of justice, liberty, equality, and

[1] T. D. Weldon, *States and Morals* (London: John Murray, 1946), 1.

obligation are now properly given a central place as first-order problems of political morality: our contemporary classics ask what justice requires of us, not what the contours of our actual justice-talk are. Their spirit is critical in the best tradition of political argument. And with the revived attention to normative argument has come the recognition that many concepts important to the descriptive study of politics are at the same time partly concepts of appraisal, that there can be no purely value-neutral description of the political world in the way that Weldon thought. One's classification schemes (is this a political party or a faction? a democracy or a tyranny?) do not divide the political world at its natural joints, for it has none. They impose on it an ordering which can be evaluated as more or less accurately representing the way political actors understand their world or as being more or less useful for the descriptive and critical purposes of external observers. But neither of these guiding interests sustains the view that political theory can be a neutral linguistic inquiry. For that reason, a study of the authority of the state cannot be a study of the ordinary meanings of the words 'state' or 'authority'. Whatever the general merits of the linguistic approach in philosophy, it is of little use here. To explain the meaning of the word 'state', for example, we would have to account for its use in expressions like 'the state of Maine' or 'state enterprise' and these are irrelevant to our theoretical interests. The position of 'authority' is even worse, for that word covers notions of both expertise and rule, the connection between which is, to say the least, an open question. Moreover, it is unlikely that a clear and settled concept of authority is shared among citizens of modern states. Perhaps Hannah Arendt is right in thinking that the preconditions in shared religious and traditional beliefs have simply vanished and that for us the study of authority can only be archaeological.[2] Neither the historical nor the linguistic exercise is undertaken here, however. There is no abjuring the lessons of history nor appeals to linguistic evidence about how we would describe certain situations; but our approach must be cautious rather than programmatic. Our aim is to isolate a central case of

[2] H. Arendt, 'What is Authority?', in her *Between Past and Future* (Harmondsworth: Penguin, 1977), 91–141.

authority relations which seem both ubiquitous and problematic in politics. In doing so we must appeal not only to conceptual argument, but also to general empirical observations and considerations of political morality.[3]

While the revival of normative political theory provides some encouragement, the moral questions which have come to dominate contemporary writing are, however, of a recognizably narrower gauge than those which preoccupied earlier writers. We more often ask whether a planned economy is consistent with individual liberty, or whether private property is compatible with social justice, than whether there should be some state as opposed to none or whether political relationships should be counted among our most important interpersonal ties. Perhaps this reflects a realistic assessment of the likely avenues of progress, a healthy respect for problems of the middle range as opposed to the architectonic in political theory. It is also possible, however, that it has its roots in a failure of imagination and a dwindling inquisitiveness about the moral standing of the modern state, a willingness to take its existence and legitimacy more or less for granted. Even otherwise sophisticated social analysts fall prey to these vices. For example, Roberto Michels, not one generally disposed to a rosy view of politics, was strikingly credulous on this point: 'It is futile to discuss the *raison d'être* of authority', he wrote. 'Authority exists and will continue to exist as it has always existed in one form or another, because it has its basis in traits deeply rooted in the human mind and because it answers the practical needs of society.'[4] We are surely entitled to something more persuasive, some reasonably detailed account of such needs, and an explanation of why authority best serves them. How is it that otherwise careful thinkers can be so undemanding?

There are at least three pressures internal to political theory which lead us to underestimate the importance and difficulty of the problem of political authority. In the first place, it is

[3] See especially, D. Miller, 'Linguistic Philosophy and Political Theory', in D. Miller and L. Siedentop, eds., *The Nature of Political Theory* (Oxford: Clarendon Press, 1983).

[4] R. Michels, 'Authority', in E. R. A. Seligman and A. Johnson, eds., *Encyclopedia of the Social Sciences* (New York: Macmillan, 1930), ii. 320.

true that a state's authority cannot be justified if it rules unjustly. Questions of whether we should respect the law, of whether there is an obligation to obey, and so forth, are not well posed until we have some view of what political justice requires. It is true that the pressing questions of political morality concern the appropriate attitude to *unjust* laws, but these all presuppose some theory of justice. As Rawls rightly says, justice is the first virtue of social institutions.[5] But from the correct premiss that the legitimacy of authority depends on the justice of its use we must take care not to draw the false inference that the problem of justice is theoretically prior to the problem of authority in the sense that there is no point investigating the latter until we have solved the former, or that all interesting problems of authority will be resolved by a comprehensive theory of social justice. The relationship between them is more complex than that.

A state is legitimate only if, all things considered, its rule is morally justified. (It is absurd to say, as some political scientists do, that a state is legitimate if it is believed to be legitimate by its citizens; for what are we to suppose they believe in believing *that*?) This judgement may, in turn, be broken down into various departments: whether the various ends of social policy which it pursues are laudable, whether it assigns the correct weights and priorities to the goals, whether it pursues them through justifiable means. Only rarely will all of these evaluations stand or fall together; we often want to say that a government is pursuing suitable goals, but going about it in an unacceptable way, or that although it is carefully observing the rule of law and the rights of individuals, it is not seeking the right ends. The exercise of authority is among the means which states characteristically use to attain their objectives. It is a mode of social control, a 'specific social technique' as the jurist Hans Kelsen put it.[6] Like any other means, its value is conditional upon the ends it serves and, in this case, on the justice of those ends. But although that is so, we cannot assume that having solved the problems of justice

[5] J. Rawls, *A Theory of Justice* (Cambridge, Mass.: Harvard University Press, 1971), 3.

[6] H. Kelsen, *General Theory of Law and State*, trans. A. Wedberg (New York: Russel and Russel, 1961), 15.

we will have solved, without more, the problem of its authoritative imposition. Very often we face a choice among social techniques, and this choice turns partly on the nature of the techniques themselves. If an ideal distribution of income could be achieved either through voluntary exchange or authoritative imposition, it would not follow that we should be indifferent about which to use. Nor would it follow that any consideration of the merits of either method must attend a fully paid-up theory of economic justice. We might have a preference between two techniques, other things being equal. The problem of choice of technique retains a partial autonomy from the broader question. It is therefore puzzling that those who have spent the most time on the theory of justice have had the least to say about the various modalities through which it might be achieved, particularly when we consider the importance of authority in the political system. Political societies are organized pre-eminently by laws, commands, and rules and their special claim to authority distinguishes them from regimes of custom or terror. In ignoring or delaying consideration of the problem of authority, contemporary political theorists end up in the embarrassing position of lacking an adequate account of their own central concern. It is as if economists had studied production and distribution before giving any thought to the nature of exchange.

There is a second source of the contemporary neglect of authority in political theory. The most pressing normative question in the theory of the state has often been thought to be the *limits* of state action. The liberal tradition in particular has been preoccupied with the nature, justification, and preservation of limited government. And its opponents have contested the very same ground, seeking to redescribe or redraw those same limits. But it is clear that the scope of legitimate state action cannot in general coincide with the limits of justified authority, for the reason that not all state action is authoritative. J. S. Mill drew the necessary distinctions in a rough but useful way as follows:

> Government may interdict all persons from doing certain things; or from doing them without its authorization; or may prescribe to them certain things to be done, or a certain manner of doing things which is left optional with them to do or abstain from. This is the

> *authoritative* interference of government. There is another kind of intervention which is not authoritative: when a government, instead of issuing a command and enforcing it by penalties, adopts the course so seldom resorted to by governments, and of which such important use might be made, that of giving advice and promulgating information; or when, leaving individuals free to use their own means of pursuing any object of general interest, the government, not meddling with them, but not trusting the object solely to their care, establishes, side by side with their arrangements, an agency of its own for a like purpose . . .[7]

Authoritative state action is thus mandatory, prohibitory, or regulatory and typically enforced by sanctions. Only such action and coercive social pressure comes under the scrutiny of Mill's harm principle, that is, the principle that restrictions of liberty are justified only when they prevent harm to others. But it does not follow that because the non-authoritative, educative, and advisory activities of the state are not limited by this principle that they are morally unconstrained. Even here, state action must be justified by adequate considerations of public policy, in Mill's view, by general utility. A complete theory of state action will have to comprise both of these and attempt to integrate them in a coherent normative framework. But that large and important task cannot proceed without an adequate account of the nature of authority. For example, one cannot defend the thesis that authoritative state action should attract the stringent scrutiny of the harm principle without certain suppositions about the character of authority as a mode of social control.

In arguing about the limits of legitimate authority one can easily lose sight of the nature of authority. The notorious weakness of Locke's theory of consent, to consider another text central to the liberal canon, is almost entirely a consequence of the preoccupations of his argument. He is primarily interested in limiting authority by appealing to the limits on the validity of individual consent: no one can consent to be killed, and thus not to tyranny, and thus no tyrannical government enjoys legitimate authority, consent or no. We should not be surprised that this casts little light on the nature

[7] J. S. Mill, *Principles of Political Economy*, ed. J. M. Robson (Toronto: University of Toronto Press, 1965), 937.

of authority and consent. Locke does not need to explore these issues in order to set limits on state action. Unlike Hobbes, for example, he is more interested in the boundary conditions of authority than in its core. To look for a theory of authority in this would be like trying to derive a complete account of voluntary obligation from the premiss that we cannot contract to murder someone. This undoubted limit on our capacity to bind ourselves is not sufficient to explain the nature and force of those contracts which are permissible. Similarly, knowing that authority may not be used to worsen the position of the worst off, or to violate rights, or to diminish the level of general welfare, tells us little or nothing about its nature.

A final distraction may be attributed to the peculiar features of the context in which authority is usually discussed. The best modern writers on the subject are jurists, as we might expect, given the signal importance of the legal system in the modern state. Yet the notion of authority is more primitive than that of law. Law is both institutionalized and systematic in nature: there are specialized organs for the interpretation and enforcement of its rules. These features are very important to the study of legal authority, and there is therefore a temptation to dwell on them exclusively or, worse, to import them into the more general idea of authority relations. Yet this can mislead, for the justification of legal authority is bound up with the idea of the rule of law, that is, the virtue of the systematic authority of the legal system as a mode of social order. To assert that a given society lives under the rule of law is not just to make the descriptive claim that it has a legal system in force. It is to ascribe to it a certain degree of success in living up to a cluster of specific procedural ideals, for example, that laws are promulgated, consistent, clear, not retroactive, and that they bind citizens and officials alike.[8] These are clearly desiderata of any legal system, and perhaps of other uses of authority. But even a legal system which fails to live up to the rule of law claims authority, and that is the more basic notion. A defence of the rule of law would be too narrow as an interpretation of political authority.

Such are the main pressures which tend to distract contem-

[8] See L. L. Fuller, *The Morality of Law*, rev. edn. (New Haven: Yale University Press, 1969).

porary political theory from the problem of authority; doubtless there are others as well. However important the general problems of justice, the limits of state action, and the rule of law, they do not themselves settle the questions we address here. Entangled with these issues, though distinguishable from them, is the problem of the nature and soundness of the state's claim to authority.

2. SUPPORT FOR THE SYSTEM

There is a standing temptation to make this problem seem easier than it is by adopting a certain perspective in political theory. The most rudimentary reflections on the nature of human well-being support the view that some form of social order is a necessary condition of human flourishing. One need not be a Hobbesian to see that without this people will very often fail to attain their common interests owing to limited information, imperfect rationality, and restricted sympathies. Yet we should not be misled by the truism that social life depends on social order into thinking that the way we secure that order is a matter of indifference. Consider further the analogy introduced in the previous section. Suppose we favour some particular distribution of holdings among persons, a particular assignment of rights and duties. It is, I think, possible to say of such a distribution that it is good or bad, other things being equal. This is not the strong and false claim that all that matters is the shape of the distribution in question. No one favours an equal distribution of property if it comes about by theft. On the contrary, we are also concerned with what Robert Nozick calls its 'historical' features. Typically, for example, we prefer a distribution of goods that results from voluntary exchange to the same distribution resulting from force or fraud. In part, we make this judgement because we doubt that force or fraud will in fact reliably result in distributions of the sort that we favour. That is one argument for free exchange: it can, in certain conditions, be relied on to yield an efficient distribution of goods in a way that forced allocations cannot. But that is not the only or most weighty reason for preferring certain distributional histories to others: we also attach value to specific forms of human relationship, specific structures of interaction, in a way that is partly independent of the outcomes to which they lead. Thus, even where we can reach the same end via two different distributional means, we will often still care about which we choose. (Naturally I do not claim that we always have such a choice of means at our disposal; but it is incontrovertible that we sometimes do.) I will call this concern about the modalities of social order a *social relations* perspective, since it is one which values not merely the form of social order which is achieved, but also the way in which it is achieved.

The main argument for attending to social relations is that we have outcome-independent preferences for certain ways of doing things. That is a moral claim. But this perspective is also supported by the descriptive claim that social relations matter to political actors, even when we hold their preferences to be unjustified. Few would take the freedom to trade to be the sole or paramount freedom worth having; we can all think of cases in which we judge that it should give way to more important concerns—perhaps it should not regulate the distribution of medical care, or blood for the purposes of transfusion, of basic education, or of law and order. Yet for any one of these there are people prepared to disagree and to hold that this is indeed an area where market freedoms are vitally important. To accurately describe their views we will need sensitivity not only to the sort of social order we are trying to achieve, but also to the modalities through which it is pursued. As a matter of fact, people do care about means as well as ends.

One treatment of the problem of authority in modern political science merits attention at this point, partly because it may seem to belie my claim that authority is a neglected subject and partly because both its insights and errors show the importance of understanding authority as a kind of social relation. David Easton was the most sophisticated and influential of those who sought a general theory to integrate the fragmented study of politics and he was one of the few to take empirical research seriously. But for our purposes, the most important reason for considering his well-known writings is that he held the distinguishing mark of politics to be authority, that the political system is essentially involved, in his famous phrase, in the authoritative allocation of values for a society.

As is widely recognized, Easton's theory is mainly a set of analytical categories combined with some large-scale speculation about the vital processes of political life. The political system he takes to be an aspect of the social system. It is an open, transformational system which functions so as to turn inputs of demands and support into outputs of policies and allocations, the consequences of which then feed back into the inputs. Owing to the inherent scarcity of many valued resources (not the least of which is time) there is an inherent propensity to overload or stress which, if unchecked, could lead to the failure of the system to perform its characteristic function: the allocation of valued goods in an authoritative way. Political systems have the capacity, however, to respond to such stress through changes in both system structure and system states: both the constitutional order and particular policies are subject to change. But any system may fail to make such adjustments and may therefore fail to persist through time. Our interest in this possibility flows from the fact that, with the exception of certain small societies, all social systems require some way of authoritatively allocating goods, for there are distributional problems which neither the market nor social custom can satisfactorily solve.

Now this sets the agenda for explanatory political theory since, 'Political systems have certain properties because they are systems.'[9] These include boundaries and criteria of identity through time. Although Easton regards all social mechanisms as means for allocating valued goods, he distinguishes the political system from other sorts by its mode of operation (it allocates *authoritatively*) and by its scope (it regulates *the whole society*). These identify the political system and constitute its essential unity: 'All political systems as such are distinguished by the fact that if we are to be able to describe them as persisting, we must attribute to them the successful fulfilment of two functions. They must be able to allocate values for a society; they must also manage to induce most members to accept these allocations as binding, at least

[9] D. Easton, 'An Approach to the Analysis of Political Systems', *World Politics* 9 (1957), 384.

most of the time.'[10] In view of the manifest importance of political life, we therefore have a theoretical interest in discovering what Easton calls the 'vital processes' which enable the political system to persist in the face of the risk that demands on it could become too great, or there might not be enough support for the authorities, the regime (i.e. the rules of the game), or the continued existence of the political community as a whole. In other words, people may expect too much output from the political system, or may not be willing to contribute enough input for it to survive. The latter Easton considers to be particularly important: a decline of support for the system is inimical to the continued existence of political life, which in turn threatens the essentials of human well-being.

At this point, the complexities of the theory become labyrinthine and there is a risk that in tracing them we may get lost among the tortuous paths of the varieties, sources, and forms of support. But the notion of support in general will suffice for our purposes, and it is quite easy to grasp. Easton defines it in this way: 'A supports B either when A acts on behalf of B or when he orients himself favorably towards B. B may be a person or group, it may be a goal, idea or institution.'[11] This points us in the right direction, although there are some uncertainties hovering around the ideas of acting on behalf of someone, or orienting oneself favourably towards him. The problem is that what counts as a 'favorable' orientation will certainly depend on his wishes, and on certain social conventions. In a later essay, Easton recognizes this and claims that in order to correctly classify any political behaviour as supportive, one must first situate it in an appropriate conventional context of meaning: 'Violence and other acts of aggression directed at political objects, payment of taxes, service in the armed forces, migration from a political system, and the like, *in an appropriate context of meaning* may represent overt supportive or oppositional behaviour.'[12] Yet it

[10] D. Easton, *A Systems Analysis of Political Life* (New York: Wiley, 1965), 22–4.

[11] D. Easton, 'An Approach to the Analysis of Political Systems', 390. Cf. *A Systems Analysis of Political Life*, 159.

[12] D. Easton, 'Theoretical Approaches to Political Support', *Canadian Journal of Political Science* 9(1976), 438–9.

would seem that the only political system in which non-payment of one's taxes or conscientious objection to military service could count as *support* for the system would be one in which that behaviour contributes to the persistence of that system. (If it is thought that taxation conceptually requires that non-payment is not supportive, on the ground that a charge is not a tax unless so ordered by the government, then substitute 'participation in party politics' in the preceding sentence.) So the appropriate context is not simply a subjective one of what the socially recognized meaning of some action is, but also the objective one of whether it in fact helps the system survive. Let us say that this is a way of promoting the interests of the system or its officials and thus record the following loose but adequate definition:

(1) *B* supports *A* if *B* expresses a pro-attitude towards *A*, or if *B* acts so as to promote *A*'s interests.

Now recall that the political system is said to be demarcated by the fact that it regulates human behaviour authoritatively; this feature also enters into the existence conditions for political systems. The nature of authority is therefore crucial to political theory, and that would seem to be consistent with the argument of this chapter. But Easton's extensive studies of authority and its role in politics in fact lend little comfort to this view. One of his early formulations simply held that, 'A policy is authoritative when the people to whom it is intended to apply or who are affected by it consider they must or ought to obey it', that is, when it is 'accepted as binding'.[13] This is indeed part of the general concept of authority, as we shall see in Chapter 2. On what the crucial last phrase may mean, however, Easton equivocates. Sometimes, compliance resulting from threats or even the direct use of force is counted as accepting a policy as binding,[14] at other times it is held that it must be motivated by the belief that the requirements in question are somehow desirable.[15] In his most extended and careful discussion of the topic, Easton says that authority is a species of power (understood as causal influence over

[13] D. Easton, *The Political System* (New York: Knopf, 1953), 132.

[14] Ibid. 141.

[15] D. Easton, *A Framework for Political Analysis* (Chicago: University of Chicago Press, 1965), 50.

behaviour), exercised intentionally, of which the subject is aware, but distinguished from force or persuasion by the fact that it is 'taken as a premise' for the subject's behaviour, without further consideration of its merits: 'If A sends a message to B and B adopts this message as the basis of his own behaviour without evaluating it in terms of his own standards of what is desirable under the circumtances, we can say that A has exercised authority over B.'[16] Note that this is much narrower than the first general conception of authority: it further restricts it to a form of rational communication which attempts to influence behaviour in a particular way. What is so striking, however, is that Easton immediately widens the definition again by including as evidence of the recognition of authority *any* regular compliance behaviour, whatever its motivation: 'the fact that [one] does obey the other is sufficient evidence for describing the power relation as one of authority', and thus, unconsciously echoing Bentham and Austin, 'Anyone who is regularly obeyed is an authority'.[17] We are therefore left with an equivocation between two quite different definitions:

(2) *A* has authority over *B* if and only if *B* regularly complies with *A*'s requirements.
(3) *A* has authority over *B* if and only if *A*'s requirement that *B* ϕ forms a premiss for *B*'s ϕ-ing without *B* considering the merits of acting as *A* requires.

These are not intended to be jointly necessary conditions, nor are they so employed in his writings. Moreover, they are bilaterally independent; neither entails the other. Nor is (2) sufficient evidence for (3): the subject may regularly comply for the sole reason that what is required of him matches his own view of what ought to be done on the merits of the case. Finally, observe that there is a close relationship between (2) and the definition of support, (1), for supportive attitudes and behaviour will generate compliance. Indeed, given the broad definition of support, (2) amounts to little more than the claim that an authoritative form of social order is one which enjoys

[16] D. Easton, 'The Perception of Authority and Political Change', in C. J. Friedrich, ed., *Authority* (Cambridge, Mass.: Harvard University Press, 1958), 179.
[17] Ibid. 180.

regular support, and that any regularly supported form of order is authoritative. Thus the theory of systems persistence becomes a theory of supportive behaviour and attitudes, and this is indeed the focus of nearly all the theoretical and empirical work in modern political science. But to confound 'being authoritative' with 'enjoying support' is to abandon the view that politics is a distinctive system of allocation, that it is a bounded sphere of social life. If authoritative allocations are just those which enjoy regular support, then to say that the political system is that which authoritatively allocates goods for a given society is just to say that it is that society's stable, persisting system of allocation. And that is inconsistent with the boundary criteria of politics since all parts of the social system are said to be allocative and, when they persist and are stable, are supported. Something has gone deeply wrong with the theory.

Part of the blame may be due to methodology. The trouble began by abandoning (3) in favour of (2). Recall that (3), however, made the identification of authority depend upon determining the subject's reasons for compliance. We have not yet mentioned the most well-known feature of the systems theory research programme—that it sought to produce a purely behavioural, value-neutral science of politics. But (3) will be quicksand for anyone wanting to move in that direction owing to the many hard cases in inferring reasons from behaviour, so it is not surprising that Easton prefers the flat behavioural contours of (2).

The consequence of this is to blur the distinction between authoritative and stable social orders. Yet stability is neither a necessary nor a sufficient condition of authority. There is no reason to believe that political allocations are likely to be more stable than distributions based on widely held customary or ethical beliefs, or even the allocations of a perfectly competitive market. (Indeed, given an initial distribution of property rights the market tends to an efficient equilibrium—the very paradigm of stability.) In Easton's theory, authority and stability are confounded in the supposed functional requisite for systems persistence, namely, support. But whether authoritative social orders really are stable ones is surely an empirical thesis, and an important one if true. It is not to be allowed as a conceptual claim. For all the disparate sorts of compliance behaviour to be measures or indicators of some theoretical variable such as support we need not only auxiliary theories linking concepts and observables, but also consistency at the conceptual level itself. Support is not an adequate boundary marker for the political system, since many other forms of social organization, including religion, the economy, and the family also attract widespread positive attitudes and supportive behaviour. To conflate authority with general support therefore undercuts the very motivation for isolating the political system in the first place. There is nothing distinctive to persist through time, and thus the proposed identity criterion (continuity of the regime, or authorities, or political community) is unmotivated. Because, at base, the measures are not theoretically grounded—because there is no reason to believe that there is anything which they measure—the numerous studies associated with them are misguided. The systems theory which was once so popular in ordinary empirical work in political science is merely an overlay: at best a benign and dispensable decoration, at worst positively misleading and obfuscating.

3. ORDER AND STABILITY

What is the importance of this episode in political science and its failure to produce adequate categories for understanding the nature and importance of authority and stability? It shows how far astray we may go in emphasizing the importance of social order to the exclusion of the variety of social relations which sustain it. In some circumstances and with respect to certain problems the focus on support and stability is warranted. The following discussion from a good modern textbook in political science reflects just the sort of concerns discussed in the previous section, though without the overlay of systems theory:

> The institutions of the Fifth Republic appear to have that wide measure of public acceptance called legitimacy. The central institution of a strong and directly elected President is widely supported. Opinion surveys have shown that this is the type of regime people want and the enormous interest shown in presidential

elections bears this out. In 1974 the two principal candidates for the Presidency were addressing vast public meetings, and the electoral turnout reached a record 89%. In addition, the public for twenty years has continuously granted parliamentray majorities to a coalition which has made support for the Fifth Republic, its institutions and its government, the central point of its appeal.[18]

I have not selected this passage to discuss any faults it may have; its judgements turned out to be as secure as one could reasonably expect, given the nature of French politics. It is open to question how far the proposed indicators do in fact measure support for or acceptance of the regime, and even more questionable what this tells about its legitimacy. What is clear, however, is that it does make an important observation about the changed nature of French politics, that the instability of the Fourth Republic seems to have gone. From that point of view, the nature of support for the system is a primary interest; in that context the stability and popular acceptance of political institutions are of both theoretical and practical importance. But we must take care not to leap from such particular constitutional histories to the view that there is a general problem of order or stability in political institutions and that this problem should therefore set the agenda for a theory of the state.[19] The problem of stability is real, but limited.

Some forms of social order are indeed problematic, such as those beneficial social rules which are liable to free-riding. These have often been thought to figure prominently in the justification of political authority, and we shall examine such arguments in due course. But not all forms of social order are like this; some more closely resemble the conventional norms of language which do not need to be enforced in order to be in force. It is therefore a mistake to think that there is a single, dominant 'problem of social order' which authority must somehow solve. We are not in the possession of a general

[18] J. R. Frears, *Political Parties and Elections in the French Fifth Republic* (London: Hurst and Co., 1977), 9.

[19] Anthony Giddens cautions us against thinking that there is a general problem of order in social theory in his *Studies in Social and Political Theory* (New York: Basic Books, 1977), 208–12.

theory of social order, nor is there any good reason to expect one. If we allow ourselves to be hypnotized by such problems we will miss much that is of importance. In a way, that is the flaw in much of the writing in modern political science which has followed the lead of Easton and the other behaviouralists. They saw that authority has a central role in the understanding of politics, but studied the nature and sources of stability instead, justifying the leap with implausible accounts of the former in terms of the latter. But all such projects are doomed in advance to failure. Just as a theory of stable democracy is a theory of what makes *democracies* stable, a theory of stable authority is a theory of what makes *authority* stable. The conceptual work must come first.

There is, then, no necessary connection between stability and authority in political systems. And, more generally, there is no reason to think that a social order of a certain sort, say, one which is relatively stable and secures the expectations of its members, is necessarily connected to a certain form of social relations. But there may, of course, be other significant relationships between them. One important possibility is suggested by Max Weber at the outset of *Economy and Society*:

> An order which is adhered to from motives of pure expedience is generally much less stable than one upheld on a purely customary basis through the fact that the corresponding behavior has become habitual. The latter is much the most common type of subjective attitude. But even this type of order is in turn less stable than an order which enjoys the prestige of being considered binding or, as it may be expressed, of 'legitimacy'.[20]

Now Weber is not analysing the concept of authority here, but offering a theory of what makes certain authoritative orders (or more exactly orders of 'domination') stable: the fact that they are believed to be exemplary or binding. This, in turn has a number of possible sources, including three central cases or 'ideal types' which, for all their difficulties, must be among the most celebrated typologies in social science: traditional, charismatic, and legal authority. The possibility of such causal relationships between authority and stability is of great

[20] M. Weber, *Economy and Society*, I, ed. G. Roth and C. Wittich (New York: Bedminster Press, 1968), 31.

interest. If, as Weber says, they are positively correlated, then we have reason to regard the belief in legitimate authority as one of importance, for it will stabilize the political order. But that observation itself tells us nothing about the nature of authority nor the considerations which might warrant the belief in its legitimacy.

It is equally possible that there is a justificatory relationship between them. It may be that without authority some forms of social stability would be unachievable. That family of arguments does have a place in our discussion, and will be examined in some detail when we come to consider conventionalism and contractarianism. Each of those theories holds that a certain form of social relations is needed to secure a certain form of social order. But again, the truth of that thesis will not license the sort of connection that many have tried to draw between stable and authoritative governments.

Both the normative and the causal connections merit attention, but only after we have considered a prior problem: what *are* authority relations? What is it, in Weber's terms, for an order to be 'considered binding'? How should that natural metaphor be cashed? To this question Easton's criterion (3) offers a rough but, as I shall argue, substantially correct answer: it is accepted as binding only if it forms a premiss for the subject's action without his considering the merits of what it requires. That could reasonably be regarded, not as a form of social order, but as a particular form of social relations which may have special meaning, justification, and value for their subjects. If it is right to think of politics as the realm of the authoritative allocation of valued goods for a society, then support, stability, and compliance behaviour are much less important in its study than many have thought. Rather, the existence of authority in a society depends on there being standards such as commands, rules, and laws which figure in a particular way in the practical reasoning of its members, in their deliberations about what to do: they guide action without direct appeal to the subjects' own view of the merits of the case. To understand authority in this way, as a feature of practical reasoning, is to embark on a very different kind of political science from the one anticipated by systems theorists or even by most of their critics. Where it leads is in the direction of the traditional theory of the state as an institution which claims authority over its subjects and whose claims are made good when they surrender their judgement to its requirements. It leads towards a conception of politics as a certain kind of social relations—authority relations—rather than as a certain kind of social order. The analysis and justification of such relations is the central problem of this book. It also has good claim to be the central problem of political theory.

2

THE NATURE OF AUTHORITY

1. PRIORITIES

OUTSIDE political theory, interest in authority has taken many forms. Political sociology, especially of a Marxist and structuralist bent, is at least nominally concerned with the subject as it bears on the relationship between state action and social structure.[1] It asks: Is the belief in legitimate authority an ideological support for class rule? To what extent can the state act independently of the interests of the ruling class? But important as these questions are to the general theory of class conflict they do not help elucidate or evaluate the state's claim to the allegiance of its citizens, and the theoretical questions which dominate political sociology—the identification of social classes, the nature of their interests, the autonomy of political organizations—do not themselves adequately discriminate among different aspects of superstructure. There are, after all, equally pressing questions about the autonomy of its cultural, religious, and educational aspects. Many of these institutions also claim allegiance of their members and attempt to sustain it through similar devices. A complete theory of the state, however, must include an account of what it is for the state to exist as a differentiated form of social order and must seek to explain the characteristic social relations which distinguish it. Without some such account we have no theory of the state, but only a perfectly general theory of social development.

Another common approach differing from that taken here focuses less on social structure than on individual behaviour and seeks explanations for the acceptance and efficacy of authority in society. These include the debates about the

[1] See, e.g., N. Poulantzas, *Political Power and Social Classes*, trans. T. O'Hagan (London: New Left Books, 1973); R. Miliband, *The State in Capitalist Society* (London: Quartet Books, 1973); E. A. Nordlinger, *On the Autonomy of the Democratic State* (Cambridge, Mass.: Harvard University Press, 1981).

existence of an 'authoritarian' personality type, or the evolutionary sources of a propensity to obey commands.[2] Interesting though these speculations may be, there are two reasons for delaying consideration of them. In the first place, they tend to be consumers rather than producers of theories about the nature of authority. The ambiguities in interpreting Milgram's famous experiment[3] which found subjects surprisingly—indeed, alarmingly—willing to obey commands to cause others pain, lie largely in doubts about whether, in the social context of the experiment, the experimenter's requests were taken to be authoritative. The findings are relevant only to the extent that we are confident that the researchers are actually investigating the phenomena that interest us. Secondly, such psychological theories do not ground normative arguments, and we are concerned about political authority precisely because authority relations seem problematic and undesirable to many people, at best a necessary evil. It might be objected that some such theories do bear more closely on justification than I have suggested because they demonstrate psychological constraints on moral possibility: ought implies can. Moreover, there is a functionalist argument which begins with Freud's claim that 'Every individual is virtually an enemy of civilization', and moves to the conclusion that the latter can be sustained only through the renunciation of instinctual satisfaction. When examined, however, the actual mechanics of these arguments generally turn out to be ersatz social contract theories. In *Totem and Taboo*, for instance, the original act of parricide is claimed to create a need to replace the order destroyed; but the reimposition of Father's rules only gives rise to the dark ambiguities of love and hate, dependence and dominance. Here, the image of authority is one bound up with all our ambivalence to the repression of desire: its necessity, ubiquity, and harm. This is an irrationalist social contract, however, founded on universal but confused childish fantasies; not one illuminated by the light of reason nor even motivated by the barren consistency of self-interest. If contractarian arguments are thought to

[2] See T. W. Adorno *et al.*, *The Authoritarian Personality* (New York: Harper and Row, 1950).
[3] S. Milgram, *Obedience to Authority* (New York: Harper and Row, 1974).

justify authority then we should investigate their most plausible versions; that is a project for Chapter 5.

All such approaches miss the mark, for it is not possible to explain the nature of authority solely by reference to the causal conditions which maintain it or the social functions which it performs. Neither can one explain it solely through moral arguments which seek to establish the conditions under which authority is justified. As Joseph Raz argues, 'The analysis of authority cannot consist exclusively of an elucidation of the conditions under which one has either legitimate or effective authority. It must explain what one has when one has authority.'[4] Similarly, Richard Flathman correctly notes that 'The question of justifying *authority* can only arise if there is or at least could be authority to justify'.[5] The first task is therefore a conceptual one; we must seek to discover not how authority persists or how it is justified, but what it is.

2. CONSCIENCE AND COMMITMENT

Let us focus our inquiry by considering some common worries about authority relations. Many people believe that fidelity to one's own freely and deeply held moral beliefs is extremely important. How they choose to describe this sense of importance varies. Some see it as a question of identity: our values are not imposed on us from without; our adoption of them and our attachment to them is a valued expression of our moral self-conception, of standing up for the persons we see ourselves to be. It is true that our moral identities are sometimes in crisis and that they evolve over time but in general this self-image is important to us and rightly makes serious claims on our action. Others see the demands of conscience not so much as an aspect of self-expression, but as an instance of a more general duty of fidelity. We should remain faithful to our deepest commitments, either for our own sakes or because we interact with others who naturally and legitimately come to rely on us. Or again, one might see the appeal of conscience as one of self-respect. In betraying

[4] J. Raz, *The Authority of Law* (Oxford: Clarendon Press, 1979), 7.

[5] R. Flathman, *The Practice of Political Authority* (Chicago: University of Chicago Press, 1980), 182.

our convictions we show ourselves to be less virtuous than we could be, and thus weaken the grounds for legitimate self-approval. We become the sort of persons we would not want as friends. Finally, in its most historically significant version, conscience is sometimes seen as that radically private knowledge people claim to have of God's will or the law of nature—an inner supreme court against which social rules and conventions are to be tried without hope of further appeal.

If valid, these provide compelling reasons for obeying the commands of conscience, and to them we might add the more simple comforts of peace of mind. It is not difficult to see then, why the claims of conscience are sometimes thought to be all important, to have enough claim to moral sovereignty that we are tempted to say, with William Godwin, that, 'There is but one power to which I can yield a heart-felt obedience, the decision of my own understanding, the dictate of my own conscience.'[6]

There is of course a trivial sense in which it is always the subject who decides, even when he decides to obey another. In this sense one cannot help yielding only to the dictates of one's own conscience. But this is not what worries those sceptical of authority relations. They reject even a freely taken decision to substitute for one's own conscience the will of another and to become, in Kantian language, heteronomous. In an important and justly famous essay, Robert Paul Wolff puts the case that the claims of conscience entail that the very concept of legitimate authority is a contradiction in terms, that it is of the nature of authority relations that they are unjust. Following Kant, he argues that people enjoy dignity because they are endowed with reason and free will. They are thus in fact responsible for their choices, and their primary moral obligation is to take responsibility for them; they have a duty to be autonomous. This requires not merely choosing as one thinks best on balance but also using all available information in making up one's mind about what to do.[7] It is therefore the primary moral duty of each to form his own judgement on

[6] W. Godwin, *Enquiry Concerning Political Justice*, ed. I. Kramnick (Harmondsworth: Penguin, 1976), 229.

[7] R. P. Wolff, *In Defense of Anarchism*, 2nd edn. (New York: Harper and Row, 1976), 46.

moral matters. But as Wolff properly observes, to recognize the authority of another is to surrender one's own judgement to his: 'Obedience is not a matter of doing what someone tells you to do. It is a matter of doing what he tells you to do *because he tells you to do it*.'[8] To refrain from theft because one sincerely believes it to be morally wrong is not to obey the law, but one's conscience. Only when the fact that an action is legally required, prohibited, or permitted itself counts in one's practical reasoning does the law make its authority felt. But this seems to lead immediately to a dilemma, for moral autonomy requires that each form his own judgement in moral matters and act on it, while authority requires the surrender of that judgement: 'If the individual retains his autonomy by reserving to himself in each instance the final decision whether to cooperate, he thereby denies the authority of the state; if, on the other hand, he submits to the state and accepts its claim to authority then . . . he loses his autonomy.'[9] The rational and moral person will not ignore the state's commands, but neither will he treat them in the spirit in which they are issued. They will be considered as requests or as advice, but not as authoritative requirements prescribing action. 'The responsible man is not capricious or anarchic', writes Wolff, 'for he does acknowledge himself to be bound by moral constraints. But he insists that he alone is the judge of those constraints. He may listen to the advice of others, but he makes it his own by determining for himself whether it is good advice.'[10]

Wolff has moralized this dilemma, by postulating a primary duty to be autonomous. Not everyone, however, thinks of autonomy in this way, as a duty. More often, it is seen as a capacity or skill for significant self-determination. However, to see just how deep Wolff's problem runs, observe that a non-moralized version of the dilemma remains even when autonomy is given a weaker interpretation of this sort, for the source of the problem is not the duty to be autonomous at all but rather the underlying conception of rationality. Reason itself seems to require that we always do what is best on the balance of reasons as we see them, whereas authority claims adherence

[8] Ibid. 9. [9] Ibid. 40. [10] Ibid. 13.

contrary to the balance of reasons and thus seemingly contrary to reason itself. It has even been suggested that this tension is part of the very concept of authority: 'An appeal to authority —to requirements imposed by authority—is an *alternative* to an appeal to reasons—to requirements based on reasons for acting.'[11] If so, then the claims of conscience are such that no requirement should ever be treated as more compelling than a piece of advice: information worth considering but to be relied on only to the extent that one judges it sound and then only for the reason that one so judges it.

The oddity is that this does not accurately describe authority relations as understood by those who either accept or reject them. A parent does not intend to make the same sort of claim when advising his child to put on a coat before going out as he does when requiring the child to do so. A member of the bar does not conceive of her role when advising clients on a point of law in the same way she does when adjudicating a claim after being appointed to the bench. The distinction between advice and authority is revealed both in the intentions of its subjects and in their different reactions to non-compliance. One may regard someone who fails to act on good advice as imprudent, but not as insubordinate. An adequate view of authority must give some account of this distinction.

3. ADVICE AND AUTHORITY

It is true that we sometimes use the word 'authority' to mean 'expert' and to designate someone of special knowledge, insight, or wisdom. Burkhardt, for instance, was an authority on the Italian renaissance. And certain works are called 'authoritative' when they are thought to possess some special reliability or value (such as the Bible, or Kemp Smith's translation of Kant's *Critique*). Modern states do generally claim to be authoritative in this sense and, as Weber recognized, with the increased power of the bureaucracy these claims become more common and perhaps even more plausible. Yet, thus understood, authority seems to be not so much

[11] D. Gauthier, *Practical Reasoning* (Oxford: Clarendon Press, 1963), 139.

contrasted with advice as dependent on it. Knowledge may well give power as Bacon thought; should we also say that it gives authority?

It is, of course, open to dispute whether there is any relevant expertise in political affairs. It seems unlikely, for example, that economic policy is wholly a matter of technical expertise—distributive questions plainly are not. And even in those areas where expertise is both possible and relevant, and where it should be decisive in determining policy, there is little plausibility in the view that the bureaucracies of most modern states have greater reserves of it than do universities or private research organizations. There is indeed one subject on which officials are always more expert than the rest of us, and that is in reports and predictions of their own behaviour. This is a crucial variable in determining the success or failure of many policies and, because of real or imagined needs for official secrecy, sound information on it is unlikely to be available from other sources. Of course, this is not what those who identify authority with expert advice have in mind, and it goes no way towards justifying the authority of the state.

Expert advice gives reason for belief, not action, and thus is authority only in the theoretical rather than practical sense. 'An authority' on some matter is someone whose judgements about it are reliable, not someone whose utterances demand compliance. Richard Flathman has tried to minimize this difference, suggesting that in the case of a theoretical authority they command, if not obedience, at least respectful audience.[12] But this is misguided. Although we ignore the advice of such authorities at our peril we are in no way bound to attend to it or follow it. Perhaps it is unseemly or beyond the bounds of conventional morality to fail to accord such respect to the opinions of the wise, but that could be so only in virtue of some further binding principle about the way we ought to treat such people. Possession of the appropriate knowledge is indeed relevant to our respecting them, but only because it serves to identify a particular person as worthy of that respect, as one to whom the principles apply. It is none the less the principles and not the knowledge which bind us.

[12] R. Flathman, *The Practice of Political Authority*, 96.

Political authority is not mainly a matter of such theoretical authority even where it does exist. Failure to recognize this spoils Peter Winch's analysis of authority. He contends that the idea of social criteria establishing a correct way of acting is essential to the normative nature of authoritative commands, and hence, 'someone who is *in* authority is always an authority *on* something.'[13] That this is false may be seen by considering the case of the law courts. All courts claim authority in the realm of their adjudicative competence, but it does not follow (and is not required) that the judge on the bench is 'an authority' on any particular area of law. Indeed, in most jurisdictions there are certain judges whose opinions are notorious for being theoretically unsound. There may well be barristers or university lecturers whose views in that area of the law are generally more reliable; even the plaintiff's judgement in a particular matter may be superior to that of both bench and bar. But of all these only the judge can offer an authoritative decision on the case, a decision which is binding *whether or not* it coincides with the best available legal advice. It might, in some cases, be preferable to have a scheme for arbitrating disputes according to the best available advice and the determinations of which were inherently open to reversal by anyone demonstrably in possession of superior information or judgement. But that only shows that in some cases it would be best not to settle disputes in courts of law.

Many others have been led astray by seeing theoretical rather than practical authority as the centre of political relations. Often, this is encouraged by holding the normative thesis that expertise is an appropriate ground of practical authority, that the wise should be obeyed. Godwin, for example, feels constrained to deny that anyone has valid claims to superior moral wisdom for fear that such claims would create grounds for their practical authority over others. It may be true, he argues, that some do have special insight about building houses or educating children but this is not so 'in those cases of general justice which are equally within the province of every human understanding'.[14] He thus takes

[13] P. Winch, 'Authority', in A. Quinton, ed., *Political Philosophy* (Oxford: Oxford University Press, 1967), 101.

[14] W. Godwin, *Enquiry Concerning Political Justice*, 245.

unreasonable confidence in the opinions of others to be 'the strictest and most precise meaning of authority' and hence is led to predict that, 'In proportion as weakness and ignorance shall diminish, the basis of government will also decay.'[15] If, however, authority and advice are to be distinguished as suggested above, then 'true euthanasia of government', of whose prospect Godwin was so sanguine, will not come about by such means. A body of wise persons or a committee of experts does not necessarily constitute a state. The latter is extinguished only when it ceases to claim practical authority or cannot get its claim recognized as valid; whether it also ceases to claim technical expertise, or whether it ever did, is only one possible cause of this.

4. THE VALUE OF AUTONOMY

How then should authority in the practical and non-advisory sense be understood? How do we cope with Wolff's argument that *either* we comply with authoritative requirements because we judge that to be the best course on balance and thus deny their authority *or* we comply against our own best judgement and surrender our autonomy and perhaps our rationality as well? Let us begin by setting aside the issue of whether the state's authority claims to bind its citizens prima facie, or whether its claims are absolute. In one sense of that slippery term, no authority can be prima facie for no authority presents itself to the agent as merely one consideration among the many he is entitled to weigh up. Authoritative injunctions purport to be categorical, to bind. But that does not entail that authority must be absolute, since it does not entail that it purports to defeat all other considerations. Authority may be prima facie in the sense that it is capable of being overridden though not ignored, provided that what is overridden is a categorical requirement. Whether a certain form of authority is absolute or not is central to the question of whether it is justified, but it is irrelevant to the nature of authority and to the dilemma we currently face. Even a weak claim to prima-facie authority will, if accepted, skew the burden of proof in a

[15] Ibid. 243, 248. And cf. G. Cornewall Lewis, *An Essay on the Influence of Authority in Matters of Opinion* (London: John W. Parker, 1849), 7.

way that Wolff's autonomous person would find repugnant. If it is irrational to act contrary to the balance of reasons as one sees it, then it is irrational to count in that balance, even as a single consideration among others, something in which one sees no merit.

The resolution of this dilemma is best approached by considering the single case in which Wolff thinks that the incompatibility of authority and autonomy does not obtain: unanimous direct democracy.[16] If each person votes directly on every measure, the argument runs, then each will be governed only by those policies which he himself supports. Is this solution satisfactory? The disadvantages of a unanimity rule for social decision making are well known: it imposes huge transaction costs on those bound by it, and it entrenches the status quo. Unanimity requires all the eligible voters to be in favour of a proposed change in order to shift from the starting position, whatever that may be, and only one opposed vote to stay put. But what is there in either rationality or autonomy that so favours the status quo? Surely we should weigh the benefits of a decision rule against all its costs.[17] In general, these include:

transaction costs: a measure of the difficulty of getting the people required to participate as well as the costs (in time, information, foregone opportunities, etc.) of securing their agreement, and

externality costs: a measure of the harm that can be done by a decision imposed on those who oppose it—the familiar problem of tyrannized minorities.

Now, as the decisive fraction, D, of the total population, N, needed to take a decision rises, these two costs move in opposite directions. Transaction costs, T, are an increasing function of D: they are trivially small when one person can bind the rest and extremely large when unanimity is required. Externality costs, E, on the other hand, vary inversely with D. The unanimity rule ($D = N$) guarantees each person a veto over what others can do to him or her, while dictatorship ($D = 1$)

[16] Wolff so argues only in the first edition of his book.

[17] On this point I follow J. M. Buchanan and G. Tullock, *The Calculus of Consent* (Ann Arbor: University of Michigan Press, 1962), ch. 6.

makes it more likely, on fairly plausible factual assumptions, that his or her interests will be adversely affected. Hence, the total costs of a decision rule are the sum of both of these and the optimal decision rule is the one which minimizes this sum. If the cost curves resemble those in Fig. 1, then the optimal decisive fraction, D^*, is the point of their intersection.

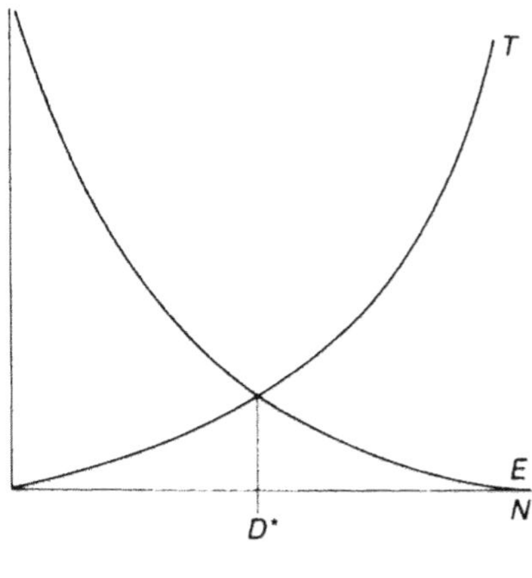

Fig. 1

Wolff supposes that the unanimity rule is optimal because only it is consistent with autonomy. But for this to hold, the externality cost function must have a radically different shape from the one in Fig. 1. If D^* can never fall below N the avoidance of externalities must take lexicographic priority, such that we do not even consider the question of transaction costs until our autonomy is secure; it has an infinitely great relative value.[18] Unanimity would then always be the optimal decision rule.

As Wolff's critics have observed, however, this argument is wrong-headed, for the unanimity rule does not in any case model authority, even by his own account of what that

[18] Wolff does argue that unanimous direct democracy is in fact becoming more practical as technology improves, but this claim is otiose if transaction costs are to be regarded as insignificant in the total package. If our autonomy is both so sacred and so vulnerable then we should be willing to put up with the inconveniences of that regime, even if it requires much smaller-scale living.

requires: 'A person who "obeys" a command *because* it coincides with his autonomous decision is not obeying authority.'[19] Authority binds us to act even when we disagree with its requirements; unanimity makes our compliance conditional on our agreement. Wolff concedes, or half concedes, this point in the second edition of his essay, writing, 'It may be that men are bound by the collective commitments they make, but such commitments do not create the sort of political authority I was attempting to analyze.'[20] The half concession that is missing is that people could not be 'bound' at all in such circumstances. However desirable, the unanimity rule provides no account of how commitments come to bind. It does not explain what it is to have a settled commitment to act in a certain way in response to certain circumstances. There is no reason why any measure which enjoys unanimous agreement at this moment will continue to do so later and therefore no reason in general why any decision taken in the past should bind us to act in a certain way in the future. Autonomy in Wolff's sense requires the permanent possibility of changing one's mind, and hence that decisions are not binding over time.

By far the commonest commitments we undertake are those which bind us for limited purposes to other persons. Promises are the paradigm here. Wolff holds that 'A promise is an act, not the mere expression or summation of an existing obligation. It creates a new obligation where none existed before.'[21] But he also argues that if a promise to obey is the sole ground of our duty to comply with the state then we are no longer autonomous: such a promise does bind, but only by surrendering our autonomy.[22] Yet this is not a feature only of the promise to obey the state. Given the view that promises create new and independent obligations, it follows that *any* promise is a surrender of autonomy. By promising to obey, 'I have ceased to be the author of the laws to which I submit and have become the (willing) subject of another person', Wolff writes.[23] By parity of reasoning, however, in promising to pay

[19] J. Reiman, *In Defense of Political Philosophy* (New York: Harper and Row, 1972), 11.

[20] R. P. Wolff, *In Defense of Anarchism*, 88.

[21] Ibid. 41 n. [22] Ibid. 41. [23] Ibid. 29.

a worker an agreed wage in exchange for a day's labour, a capitalist has also become a willing subject in respect of the activity governed by that promise, for it is no longer his will alone which is sovereign over the outcome. He may be released from the shackles of his promise, but only the promisee has the power to do so. It is true, as Wolff recognizes,[24] that most promises only surrender one's autonomy in a piecemeal way. (The traditional marriage vows which bind for life are a possible exception.) And it is also true that Wolff is inclined to approve these lesser surrenders; but why? The natural response—because the benefits are worth the costs—opens a dangerous line of reasoning since it concedes that autonomy is, after all, commensurate with convenience. And that in turn leads to a straightforward instrumental argument for the authority of majority rule procedures. Wolff's objection to the authority of the state is not merely that its scope is too broad, but that it is a form of authority and thus inherently a surrender of autonomy. It is that attitude which recommends assigning an absolute priority to autonomy with respect to convenience and thus to minimizing externality costs before considering transaction costs. Now observe that there is no practical difference in terms of such costs between binding oneself to a social decision rule requiring a plurality of $(N-1)$ as the decisive fraction and binding oneself to obey a single person over a narrow *scope* of activity. If near-unanimity is disqualified because the risk or indignity of surrendering even that much control is too great, then most normal promises will also be disqualified for they too are only partial commitments. (In case this does not seem plausible, increase N by a few powers of ten.) Is it not as great a surrender of autonomy to promise to meet a friend for dinner as it is to be bound by an $(N-1)$ rule in a direct democracy of around fifty million? The chances of one's interests being seriously harmed as a result of the control given to the promisee cannot be much less than the chance of finding everybody else in the polity united against you. Indeed, in many circumstances the expected loss in the latter case must be smaller than in the former. If the objection is that anything less than complete control of one's moral

[24] Ibid. 15, 29.

world is incompatible with the dignity and status of free and rational creatures, then the promises also seem at risk.

Thus we have the following result. To be consistent, an anarchist of Wolff's persuasion would have to abjure promising as well as authority. And some have indeed done so. Godwin denies that promises bind. According to his rigorous utilitarian ethic we must always act so as to produce the best net consequences, and no action is morally indifferent; since each has some 'tendency' to good or evil consequences—however long and elaborate the chain of causation—each is either prohibited or required. Thus, argues Godwin, 'Previously to my entering into a promise, there is something which I ought to promise, and something which I ought not',[25] so either I have adequate reasons for promising to ϕ or I do not. If not, then promising cannot provide them. On the other hand, if I do, then promising provides an 'additional inducement' to do what ought in any case to be done. But moral virtue requires that we act for the right reasons, and the additional inducement is at best a temptation to do what is right, for the wrong reason. Moreover, in shifting moral concern from the natural consequences of our actions and focusing instead on the formalities of promising, we are likely to miscalculate and act wrongly as well. Not only is it therefore wrong to keep a promise for the reason that one promised, but this delusion is likely to cloud judgement about what in fact ought to be done. Hence, Godwin concludes, 'promises are, absolutely considered, an evil, and stand in opposition to the genuine and wholesome exercise of an intellectual nature.'[26] Thus, authority and promises are both immoral, and for the same reasons.

Let us recapitulate the argument to this point. The claims of conscience, when understood as the absolute demands of autonomy, appear to conflict with authority in any non-advisory sense. Thus authority relations appear irrational and immoral. But autonomy in this sense, of always acting on the balance of reasons as one sees it, is also incompatible with other forms of commitment including promising. If for the sake of consistency the anarchist abjures promising as well,

[25] W. Godwin, *Enquiry Concerning Political Justice*, 218.
[26] Ibid.

however, he will find himself in a difficult position. It is characteristic of the anarchist temper that it seeks to replace external commitments with internal ones wherever possible. From this point of view the ideal model of human organization is the voluntary association. There may be sound instrumental justifications for increasing the scope of voluntary commitment (it may be more efficient, less likely to impose harsh external costs, etc.), but these must count for little against the principled objection to all such commitments: they are a perverse form of social relations which inherently sacrifice autonomy or moral virtue. Yet this objection applies to any relationship, even one entered into voluntarily, which binds the agent to the will of another. Since that is the very aim of promising, promises too must be undesirable. And we can strengthen the conclusion yet further: *all binding commitments are irrational and immoral.* Either they are intrinsically open to revision by the subject (in which case they are not binding) or they are not (in which case he is heteronomous).

The difficulty lurking in this view should now be apparent. An anarchist favours the voluntary association model of society, but in such an association binding commitments are essential. First, they may be constitutive of membership in the association: members are those who promise to be bound by its decisions. Secondly, the voluntary association needs to rely more often on certain kinds of commitments than do alternative forms of society. In the modern state, which is decidedly non-voluntary in character, the fact that many people treat the law as authoritative or fear its sanctions ensures that some valuable forms of social co-operation will not be frustrated by self-interest or short-sightedness. Through taxation, for example, the state secures certain public goods like national defence. But the anarchist renounces such measures and must therefore rely *more heavily* than others on promises, contracts, and other forms of self-assumed commitments. To reject authority relations on the ground that they are binding commitments and as such irrational is therefore to undercut a major alternative to that authority in supplying certain goods which even anarchists may value.

This should call into question the conception of autonomy at issue here. To the extent that it excludes all forms of binding commitment as derogations from autonomy it is without value and takes on the guise of purely abstract freedom, in Hegel's words, 'this unrestricted possibility of abstraction from every determinate state of mind which I may find in myself or which I may have set up in myself, my flight from every content as from a restriction.'[27] In contrast, autonomy as a human ideal, as the power to assume and undertake important projects and to establish valuable relationships with others, requires the capacity to commit oneself to certain courses of action. If autonomy is conceived in a purely negative and abstract way it is not even compatible with the idea of autonomy conceived as the pursuit of a 'life plan' in Rawls's sense or what Bradley called 'the systematization of the self'. Plans, projects, and relationships all require the capacity to place some restrictions on abstract freedom. No analysis of autonomy as a moral ideal which has the consequence of rendering these unintelligible should therefore be accepted.

5. CONTENT-INDEPENDENT COMMITMENTS

Standing back now from the anarchists' dilemma, we may notice one perplexing feature of the argument strategy. It seems a gross case of overkill to deny the *sense* of binding commitments in general when one really only wants to challenge their *use* in a particular case. What one should argue is not that justified authority is a contradiction in terms, but that to believe in it is a moral mistake. Non-anarchists are surely not just guilty of abusing words, but of abusing power. We need therefore to analyse authority relations in a way which shows them to be a form of binding commitment but not just for that reason objectionable. A satisfactory account should restore sense to the issue by locating the properly moral, substantive disagreement between anarchists and their opponents and should explain the apparent binding force of various forms of commitment in a way consistent with their rationality. The solution I propose is one whose elements appear first in Hobbes and which is elaborated with greater

[27] G. W. F. Hegel, *The Philosophy of Right*, trans. T. M. Knox (Oxford: Clarendon Press, 1958), § 5, p. 22.

sophistication in the writings of modern jurists including H. L. A. Hart and Joseph Raz. I shall argue that we can act *contrary to the balance of reasons* without thereby acting *contrary to reason*.

Many have noted that recognition of authority involves, in some way, a 'surrender of judgment'.[28] It is just this feature which distinguishes authority from the standard case of advice. An early attempt to make systematic this distinction appears in *Leviathan* pt. II, ch. 25, where Hobbes notes that, 'COMMAND is where a man saith, *Doe this* or *Doe not this*, without expecting other reason than the Will of him that sayes it.' In contrast 'COUNSELL is where a man saith *Doe*, or *Doe not this*, and deduceth his reasons from the benefit that arriveth by it to him to whom he saith it.' Both are thus forms of imperative utterance, but the expression of an authoritative command *itself* purports to be a reason for the subject to act, and it is a reason flowing from the will of the commander and displacing any other reasons the addressee might have.[29] Now Hobbes was an absolutist about authority, and it might be thought that this doctrine is peculiar to that context, but that is not so. Even a moderate like Locke describes the nature of political authority in similar terms. In the *Second Treatise* (§. 87) he says that in civil society, 'All private judgment of every particular member being excluded, the community comes to be umpire, by settled standing rules; indifferent and the same to all parties.' Locke's notion is clearly much richer than Hobbes's for it includes the central characteristics of the rule of law: its generality and equality. Yet even in this richer view we find the idea that the political order claims to exclude private judgement and to replace it with public and authoritative reasons for acting.

Joseph Raz has offered an explanation of this feature which

[28] For an especially helpful account, see R. Friedman, 'On the Concept of Authority in Political Philosophy', in R. E. Flathman, ed., *Concepts in Social and Political Philosophy* (New York: Macmillan, 1973), 127–31. See also J. Raz, *The Morality of Freedom* (Oxford: Clarendon Press, 1986), 38–42.

[29] I owe this interpretation to H. L. A. Hart, *Essays on Bentham* (Oxford: Clarendon Press, 1982), 253–4. Hobbes further claims that counsel always purports to be in the interest of the counselled, but command in the interest of the commander. This point follows from his general theory of moral psychology; it is not an essential feature of authority. The truth of the matter is that commands need not serve the interests of their subjects in order to be binding; but they may do so.

is both elegant and substantially correct.[30] According to him, the dilemma of authority is an illusion created by an over-simple view of practical reasoning in general. Although we often talk metaphorically about balancing considerations as if we had in mind a single clear metric on which we perform an arithmetic of consequences, our actual reasoning patterns are more complex. The considerations relevant to a practical decision are sometimes structured in an important way—we might say they are organized into different kinds or levels. *First-order* reasons are ordinary reasons for action such as ideals, desires, interests, or needs. Conflicts among such reasons are resolved (if they can be) by comparing their relative weights, by balancing the different considerations. A reason at this level is defeated by another reason at the same level only if it is outweighed by it. This is a familiar and common view and its centrality underscores its importance. But it is not the whole picture, for just as there are reasons for acting, we also recognize reasons for and against acting on such reasons. In Raz's terminology, these are *second-order* reasons. For example, a temporary incapacity such as a headache or a sleepless night might give you a reason not to act in a way that seems right on balance regarding a business decision, even when to refrain from accepting the deal is to reject it. The incapacity does not, however, weigh on one side of the decision or on the other; it does not count in favour of the investment or against it. The conflict between this second-order reason and the first-order reason is not resolved because the former outweighs the latter; the incapacity is no reason to decide one way or the other. Rather, it excludes action taken on the first-order balance of reasons alone and is thus an *exclusionary* reason.[31] Such reasons exclude those they defeat by kind, not weight. A similar feature is found in certain kinds of decision. When a post office clerk announces at some point, 'I'm sorry, we're closed', his utterance closes the wicket; it is performative and not simply descriptive. But as anyone who

[30] J. Raz, *Practical Reason and Norms* (London: Hutchinson, 1975).

[31] Ibid. 37ff. This gives a systematic account of a commonly observed feature of the role of rules in practical reasoning. As Warnock says, 'What the rule does, in fact, is to *exclude* from practical consideration the particular merits of particular cases, by specifying in advance what *is to* be done, whatever the circumstances of particular cases may be'. G. J. Warnock, *The Object of Morality* (London: Methuen, 1971), 65.

has ever just missed closing time knows, it is generally useless to attempt to get the clerk to consider the merits of one's own need for a stamp. The clerk does not take the view that the desirability of closing outweighs that of staying open for another moment, he simply refuses to consider the issue further. Binding commitments, such as obligations, can be understood to have a similar practical force: they are cases in which a person has a reason for ϕ-ing and an exclusionary reason not to act on some of the reasons for not-ϕ-ing. Such reasons may be both prima facie, in the sense that they are not conclusive about what ought to be done, and at the same time categorical. The fact that they exclude and not merely outweigh reasons for not-ϕ-ing makes them categorical; the fact that they may not exclude all contrary reasons makes them prima facie. Thus the force of such commitments depends both on the weight of the reasons they offer in favour of ϕ-ing and the scope of the reasons against ϕ-ing which they exclude.

This account has two desirable features. First it explains the nature of binding commitments in a way which leaves open important evaluative questions. Secondly, it accounts for the common view that binding commitments have a categorical force which does not depend on their weight. Not all authoritative requirements are equally forceful. Yet orders seem categorical in a way that considerations of self-interest do not. This is true even though few would hold that every order is weightier than every consideration of self-interest. On the present account, this is explained by the fact that the former but not the latter are exclusionary reasons. The dilemma of the anarchist can thus be understood as resulting from a view that either ignores the structured character of practical reasoning or denies that second-order considerations are ever valid. If it is ever rational to exclude certain considerations for performance of an action, then authority may be justifiable. The anarchist may now dissent on this point: he may argue on substantive grounds that the considerations which an authoritative command purports to exclude should not be excluded. Since the argument is a substantive one, it need not damage other forms of binding commitments, such as promises. The anarchist may therefore accept the proposed analysis of what it is, in Weber's language, to regard some requirement as binding, while discriminating among forms of binding commitment on other grounds; he can hold that some are immoral without holding that all are irrational.

We are now in a position to explain what it means for some requirements to be 'regarded as binding' and this is a crucial step in developing a test which identifies a given social relation as one of authority:

(1) *B* regards the fact that *p* as a binding reason to ϕ only if *B* regards *p* as providing reason to ϕ and a reason not to act on some of the reasons for not ϕ-ing.

Now, although authoritative requirements purport to be binding, not all binding commitments result from authoritative requirements. We have already noted that promises also create binding commitments, and this is also true of some decisions. What distinguishes authority from these? Authority is interpersonal in a special way. We do sometimes speak of individuals having authority over themselves and their own affairs, but this is parasitic on the standard notion of having authority over others. Likewise, authority to act in a certain way is the power so to act as against the claims of others. One person has authority over another only if he or she can make, vary, or extinguish binding commitments for that person. As an example of such commitments we may think of obligations. Anyone can undertake obligations for himself, say through promises or vows, and he can commit himself to a course of action by deciding to exclude further deliberation. Only an authority, however, can bind others. Thus:

(2) *A* has authority over *B* only if the fact that *A* requires *B* to ϕ gives *B* a reason to ϕ and a reason not to act on some of the reasons for not-ϕ-ing.

Having sketched the rationale for these conditions, I move to a third, and then to some general remarks in defence of the entire analysis.

Reflecting further on Hobbes's characterization of commands, we notice another feature. Commands purport to give reasons for acting which not only exclude deliberation of their subject, but also function in a way independent of what they are commands to do: it is not the nature of the action commanded but the *fact* that one is commanded to do it which is intended to be taken as a reason. But this seems to have nothing at all to do with the merits of so acting. It is a consideration of an entirely different sort, which has been called a 'content-independent reason'.

According to Hart's analysis,[32] a commander intends that his subjects respond to the fact that he expresses an intention that they should so respond, and he also intends that this response be independent of the content of his intention. The idea is that if a subject were to comply with the command only because he regarded it as having substantive merit, he would not be rendering obedience in the sense demanded. He would be doing what was commanded, but not even partly for the reason that it was commanded. This is inconsistent with the nature of commands as a way of guiding behaviour. Commands claim to be reasons for acting, not merely indications that there are other, and better, reasons for acting.

Again, this is a feature common to other areas of practical reasoning. When we keep promises, obey commands, or stick by decisions, we often feel that the force of the reasons on which we act does not wholly depend on the content of the specific promise, command, or decision which was made. A promise to read a friend's manuscript, for example, only partly derives its claim from the fact that it would be desirable to do so; a more important part of its force derives from the fact that a promise was made, the content of which could have been different, which might have been made to a different person, or which might have been made for a different reason. Likewise, the fact that one has firmly decided in advance to go jogging every morning at 7.00 provides some reason for not considering the issue further when the time comes and this reason is partly independent of the content of the decision taken, including whether that time was on balance the best one.

Thus, we may finally characterize authority relations in this way:

(3) *A* has authority over *B* if and only if the fact that *A*

[32] H. L. A. Hart, *Essays on Bentham*, ch. 10.

requires B to ϕ (i) gives B a content-independent reason to ϕ and (ii) excludes some of B's reasons for not-ϕ-ing.

Authority is thus a triadic social relation among a superior, a subject, and a range of action. Anyone who has practical authority has it over certain persons, and with respect to certain matters. A priest, for example, has authority over his parishioners in matters of cult; a teacher over pupils in matters of discipline, and a judge over all within the jurisdiction of her court. Of course, the fact that it is a triadic relation itself explains nothing; the nature of authority is explained by the fact that it gives some the power to create binding, content-independent reasons for others to act. To emphasize its relational character only serves to remind us of the different directions in which authority can be, and characteristically is, exercised and limited.

Let us now examine some familiar views about the nature of authority in the light of this conception.

5.1 *Institutions*

It is clear that political authority is generally exercised in the context of institutions: courts, legislatures, and bureaucracies. This has led some to suggest that authority is essentially an institutional phenomenon. It is true that content-independent reasons are especially prominent in institutional contexts. For example, an executor's duty to execute a will does not depend on its terms. To show that he has the duty one need only show that the usual validity conditions for such instruments have been satisfied, for example, that it has been signed and witnessed. One need not show that it distributes the testator's estate in a desirable way. In this sense, a valid will generates duties which depend on its form and not on its content. Similarly, a contract under seal derives its validity solely from the form in which it is expressed and not from any consideration which may exist for the promises of the parties, nor even from the fact of their agreement. Hans Kelsen suggested that this is a distinguishing feature of the concept of law itself, and not merely of concepts within the law such as wills or contracts. He wrote, 'A legal norm is not valid because it has a certain content . . . but because it is created in a certain way. . . . Therefore any kind of content might be law.

There is no human behavior which, as such, is excluded from being the content of a legal norm.'[33] That is simply the general form of the claims about wills and contracts which I considered above.

In such cases, there are recognized and reasonably settled institutions which constitute the activity in question: the law of wills, of contracts, or even the legal system as a whole. But not all binding, content-independent considerations are this formal. There is no single form of words or special document which must be employed in order to promise or decide something. (The oddly legalistic notions that promises do not bind if said with crossed fingers, or unless the word 'promise' is used are, significantly, characteristic of the child's view of morality.) This is not to deny that these notions are dependent on the existence of certain conventions, but these are of a much looser and informal nature.

The case of authoritative commands might suggest the contrary, for they are often set in the context of hierarchical institutions providing explicit criteria of validity and change, for example, in military or bureaucratic contexts where there is regular reliance on commands to guide conduct and where the stakes are high. Indeed, Flathman has suggested that it is 'a tautology' that authoritative orders must meet institutional criteria of validity: 'they must be shown to be valid in the sense of consistent with the "constitution", the "grundnorm", the "rule of recognition" or whatever, that is the source of authority they are alleged to have.'[34] Yet these very examples suggest that institutionalization of authority is specific to certain contexts only. The institutional validity of a requirement is a necessary condition of its authority only if it forms part of a normative system and the authority of norms in the system is transmitted from top to bottom, from more general to particular norms. Now this is a fairly good picture of the authority of law, but it is insufficiently general, for it cannot explain the validity of authoritative norms which belong to no normative system, nor of those normative systems in which validity is transmitted upwards (e.g., a rule of recognition which merely summarizes a list of independently valid

[33] H. Kelsen, *The Pure Theory of Law*, trans. M. Knight (Berkeley: University of California Press, 1967), 198. [34] R. Flathman, *The Practice of Political Authority*, 105.

norms). Singular commands detached from any formal institutional framework are possible and in primitive political systems are reasonably common; often no more than the leader's word is needed. Similarly, a motorist who gets out of her car to direct traffic around a road accident may do so by commanding, but there are no special institutions which she must invoke to do so. It is true that in order to use a particular gesture as a signal for one direction rather than another there are more general behavioural or linguistic conventions on which one must rely (e.g., the palm towards the motorists means 'stop'). However, these are simply the conventions which make communication possible; they are not unique to commands. They are informal and global rather than formal and local. This suggests that the institutional nature of authoritative reasons is inessential. When the practice of promising becomes institutionalized in the form of contracts or rules or commands in the form of law, the process consists partly in the emergence of explicit criteria of validity which are applied by the officials of the institution in question. An agreement is only a contract under certain conditions, which reduce uncertainty about the existence, scope, and weight of our voluntary obligations. But it is therefore clear that the idea of an institutionalized system uses rather than explains the notion of binding, content-independent reasons. It is these features and not the undoubted fact that in the modern state authority typically takes an institutional form which explain its nature.

5.2 *The Practice Theory*

Similar considerations establish that one cannot explicate the nature of political authority solely in terms of the philosophical notion of a social practice.[35] In his well-known essay on legal and moral obligation Hart says that such practice-dependent reasons are 'principles which would lose their moral force unless they were widely accepted in a particular social group',[36] whose violation warrants a coercive response, and

[35] In addition to H. L. A. Hart, this thesis has also been advanced by R. Flathman in *The Practice of Political Authority*, and by P. Winch in 'Authority'.

[36] H. L. A. Hart, 'Legal and Moral Obligation', in A. I. Melden, ed., *Essays in Moral Philosophy* (Seattle: University of Washington Press, 1958), 101.

which have a 'possible independence of content'. The last feature is explained for the case of promises in the following way:

> the obligation springs not from the nature of the promised action but from the use of the procedure by the appropriate person in the appropriate circumstances. This independence is further manifested by the fact that the obligation thus deliberately created may also be deliberately extinguished by the promisee.[37]

There are essentially two claims here: (1) content-independent reasons are practice-bound: it is the fact that a procedure or social practice is invoked which gives them their normative force; and (2) the application of such reasons is within our volitional control. Are these essential features of practical authority?

What is it, in the first place, for some reason to be practice-dependent? Let us begin by considering promising which shares certain important features with authority. Although one could not have promising without having some social practices, it is controversial whether its validity, that is, its obligatory force, derives from this fact. It is vital to distinguish the thesis that certain obligations can only be incurred through specified conventional means, from the thesis that the normative ground of the obligations is conventional. The latter is true only if the obligation would lose its force if it ceased to be practised among some group; the former is true whenever members of the group must invoke a convention in order to be bound. One could consistently believe, with Kant, that the ground of promissory obligations lies in the categorical imperative, and also that no such obligations are incurred except by invoking a certain social practice, for example, a certain form of words. Hart accepts the stronger thesis that the ground of such obligations is conventional. But content-independence is not a feature of the normative ground of the promising principle: it is not the thesis that promises bind *because* they are content-independent, but a thesis about the *way* in which they bind, that is, independently of their content. It is a feature of promises to be accounted for by any competent theory of their ground, whether it be convention,

[37] Ibid. 102.

the categorical imperative, the right of the promisee to performance, or the value to the promisor of the power to create special relationships with others. Promises bind, not in virtue of the content of the promises made, but of the sort of thing which the practice of promising accomplishes or expresses. Similarly, it may be true that some kinds of authoritative guidance can only be given by invoking certain conventional social practices. A bill must be passed, for example, according to the conventional manner and forms of parliamentary procedure. But this is consistent with it being the case that the normative force of legislation derives from a God-given power to legislate, or from the fact that the legislators are guided by the common good, or whatever. Content-independence acts only as a constraint on any acceptable theory of promises or authority. It requires that we explain or explain away that common view that such reasons have this feature. It lends no special support to the practice theory.

Let us turn now to Hart's second claim, that the content-independence of promises is manifest in the fact that they are subject to our voluntary control. Whatever that means, it cannot be (nor does Hart suggest) that such control is a necessary condition of content-independence. Consider the case of the 'positional duties', such as the duty of parents to care for their children. Hart says, 'The independence of content that these duties have is . . . rather different in that they are conceived as *assumed* by entry upon the particular role . . .'[38] the content of which is determined by conventions which vary from society to society. But if that is so, then these duties are not fully within our individual volitional control, for social conventions are not. Moreover, some of them (like the duties of a parent) adhere even when one does not enter the role voluntarily. Hart recognizes that not all commands are either voluntarily activated or practice-based. One who accepts the validity of God's commands believes that they create obligations independently of their content. It is the fact that God commands us that creates our duty, not the content of what is commanded. But those who accept this do not think

[38] Ibid. 103–4.

that they only apply to us as result of our voluntary actions. Whether this is also true of political authority is a matter of controversy to which we shall later return. Classical consent theory claims that political authority can bind only with the agreement of its subjects, but its many competitors deny it. It is certainly true, however, that modern states claim authority over some who have not consented to it.

There is a final difficulty with the practice theory which calls into question even its compatibility with the content-independence of authority. Content-independence must be construed so as to be compatible with the substantive truth that grossly immoral promises do not bind.[39] A promise to murder, for example, creates no prima-facie obligation to murder which is then outweighed by the enormity of the act; it is simply void *ab initio*, in the way that a contract may be void on grounds of public policy. The same is true of a command to murder. But why is this so? On the practice theory, we would say that the content-independent force of promises extends only as far as the practice and no further, and that there is no practice of demanding the performance of immoral promises and, indeed, a practice of prohibiting it. These limitations are thus among the practice rules constitutive of promising.

Some limitations on promising do have this character: I cannot promise that a third party will act in a certain way unless I already have authority to do so; I cannot promise that the sun will rise tomorrow unless I thereby purport to have it within my control. It is in such cases that we are most tempted to express the limits of promising in linguistic terms, to say that utterances purporting to commit others to certain actions or warranting that the world is a certain way are not just 'promises' at all. We have a lesser though still present tendency to treat procedural defects such as mistake, duress, and insanity in that way as well. (There is, however, more room for doubt here.) But whatever the linguistic facts of the matter, there is a difference in kind between the defects in such cases and those present in grossly immoral promises, such as a promise to commit murder. The impropriety here does not seem linguistic but moral. A sincerely made promise

[39] Ibid. 102.

to murder which does not otherwise misfire may be a promise, but it is an invalid one. It would seem odd to say that we have a *practice* of excluding such promises, for there are no marks of procedural failure such as occur when one mistakes another's words, or agrees only as a result of duress. It is not among the correct performance conditions for promising. Rather, such prohibited promises are defined by certain moral principles which do not themselves depend for their validity on the fact that they are enforced by certain social practices. Even if promising is practice-based, its normative limits are not. The principle that grossly immoral promises do not bind is not one which would lose its force unless widely accepted in some social group. Indeed, if a practice of enforcing murder contracts were to emerge this would strengthen and not weaken our denunciation of it. If this is correct, however, then the fact that immoral promises are void is an embarrassment to the practice theory for it suggests that no promises are content-independent. One may partition the set of possible contents into the prohibited and the permitted such that the force of a promise depends on its content being in the latter set.

These points about Hart's example of promising can be extended in fairly obvious ways to the case of authoritative requirements. Authority binds only over a certain range of action. Completely unlimited authority, in whatever sphere, would be even more undesirable than an unrestricted power to contract. Authority would be intolerable if its validity had no limits: the claim of superior orders is never a good defence to a charge of gross immorality. But our revulsion here is not itself part of a practice of regarding such commands as invalid. It may be that a given authority has never before issued such a grossly immoral command, so that a practice of resisting such commands could hardly have been incorporated into our rules. If the content-independence of authority is to be explicated by relying on the notion of a practice, then no authority is content-independent, for social authority—whether of parents, schools, or states—is limited by principles which are identified by their content. Authority is not therefore, an inherently practice-based notion.

5.3 *Generality*

Hart's latest writings characterize authoritative legal reasons as reasons which are peremptory, in the sense that they claim to set aside the subject's own assessment of the merits of the case, and content-independent. Now, however, this feature is attributed to the generality of such reasons and not to any alleged connection with a social practice:

> Content-independence of commands lies in the fact that a commander may issue many different commands to the same or different people and the actions commanded may have nothing in common, yet in the case of all of them the commander intends his expressions of intention to be taken as a reason for doing them. It is therefore intended to function as a reason independently of the nature or character of the actions to be done.[40]

Hart comments that this differs from the standard cases where there is a connection of content between the reason and the action, for example, where the reason is a valued consequence to which the action is a means. And he applies the same analysis to promises: 'Since we may promise to do very many different sorts of actions in no way related to each other, the giving of a promise regarded as a reason for doing the action promised has also the feature of content-independence.'[41] This idea is a familiar one; many have remarked that there seems to be something inherently general in the ideal type of law.[42] Hart appears to suggest that this generality is what accounts for its content-independent validity: a commander may issue many different commands to different people and yet the actions commanded may have nothing in common.

What is it, in fact, for actions to have nothing in common? In the first place, there are generally some descriptions under which they do have something in common. In the present example, for instance, they all share a common history: they are all commands of a particular commander. Perhaps that is

[40] H. L. A. Hart, *Essays on Bentham*, 254.

[41] Ibid. 255.

[42] See, e.g., J. Austin, *The Province of Jurisprudence Determined*, ed. H. L. A. Hart (London: Weidenfeld and Nicolson, 1954), 18–24. Cf. F. A. Hayek, *The Constitution of Liberty* (Chicago: University of Chicago Press, 1960), 148–61.

a matter of form rather than content. But they are also all commands to act or refrain from acting rather than commands governing belief. Does this not give them something in common? Perhaps the key is not the idea of actions having nothing in common, but rather the fact that the commander can issue many different commands to many different people, or that one can promise to do many different things. To speak in this way supposes that we have some idea of how to begin individuating commands and promises, or their possible contents. This is certainly a complex matter, but quite possibly it is also senseless. How many things can one promise to do? Are a promise to meet for lunch and a promise to meet for lunch unless some emergency arises two different promises or one promise, stated with and without an exception? The notion of how many different things one can command or decide seems equally obscure.

Even if some account could be given of these matters, two considerations establish that generality is not the essence of authority. One can only command those over whom one has authority, and one can only prescribe those actions which are *intra vires* the authority one has. If one's authority has a very limited range, like that of a parent over his or her child, or a very restricted scope, like the authority of certain regulatory agencies, then one's commands will lack the requisite generality. But to have authority over only a few people or for only a few purposes is none the less to have authority, and to command is even in these circumstances to claim that one's utterances provide binding and content-independent reasons to act.

At the limit, the generality of a command may be nil: the final chain of military command may include the authority of *A* to order only *B* to push or refrain from pushing the button, but no authority to command *B* to do anything else, nor to countermand any other order which *B* might receive. Here, it is true that *A*'s command functions as a reason for *B* to act even though it is such a reason for no one else, and for no other action. This is the vanishing point of generality, and yet it is none the less true that if *A* has authority over *B* his utterance is a reason for *B* to act independently of the nature or character of the action to be done. Such restrictions on generality are not special features of the institutional context of authoritative commands. I have already said that promises need not be institutionalized in this way, and yet they too lack full generality, because immoral promises do not bind. It is characteristic of all content-independent reasons that they are subject to such limits, and the existence of limits often plays an important part in our normative attitudes: unlimited authority, omnipotent promises, and unrestricted decisions all seem very undesirable.

One might reply to this criticism as follows. Content-independence is a matter of degree. The fact that immoral commands do not bind only shows that there are some things which cannot be commanded; but many things can be. A very content-independent reason is thus one which is valid for a large set of contents; a slightly content-independent reason is valid only for a small set. Apart from trading on an unexplicated theory for individuating contents, however, this reply is liable to an earlier objection to the practice theory. The boundary of the permissible set is marked off in terms of content. If the only promises or commands which failed to bind were ones in which there had been some procedural failure, say, mistake or duress, then the point might be sound. This is not so. Generality is a matter of degree; but content-independence is not. Like institutions and social practices, generality is very often associated with the exercise of authority, particular in its legal forms. But it does not help explain its nature either.

The rejected views all direct our attention to the wrong place. Binding, content-independent reasons are not a species of the genus reason, distinguished by being institutions, practices, or reasons of general application. All such accounts fail, for it is possible to think of authoritative reasons which are not institutionalized, practice-based, or general in scope and yet are binding and content-independent. The special features of authoritative reasons are not to be found in such considerations but in the way they function in practical reasoning. And it is these features which best explicate the sense in which legitimate authority is accepted as binding.

6. SOME OBJECTIONS

This analysis seeks to explain the nature of authority as a potentially problematic form of social relation which is central to political life. While it tries not to stray too far from common usage, it would not be correct to think that we need it to account for the ordinary use of the terms 'to be bound' or 'to be committed' or even 'to be obligated'. It does not purport to give the ordinary meaning of these or other notions intimately associated with authority; it aims at resolving certain problems which seem to be connected with the ordinary notion of authority: that somehow it is a surrender of judgement and yet is at least sometimes a candidate for rational justification. Nor do I claim that the theory is needed to explain all the attitudes and behaviour that are of interest when people claim to bind themselves to act in a certain way, or regard themselves as so bound. Perhaps some of this can be accounted for by assuming that people are trying to change their preference orderings, or the likelihood of various outcomes occurring. A smoker trying to break the habit may thus seek to pre-commit himself by locking up the cigarettes and throwing away the key, or paying the tobacconist not to sell him any more, or just by telling his friends that he has quit and thus increasing the social sanctions against backsliding. Such phenomena are not uninteresting, and a complete understanding of them is not simple. But this is not generally how those who claim and recognize authority understand themselves and their actions.

Secondly, it might be objected that this is little more than the familiar distinction between act- and rule-utilitarianism in new dress and therefore must fall to the same objections. These are now almost legendary:[43] understood abstractly, AU and RU are extensionally equivalent; where the former recommends breaking a rule, the latter recommends changing it and thus both end up making the same prescriptions. Understood empirically, the two levels tend to come apart entirely and become two ways of thinking, or two sorts of person: rule followers who do not attend to the net consequences of rule-following, and rule-breakers who do. But this account need

[43] D. Lyons, *Forms and Limits of Utilitarianism* (Oxford: Clarendon Press, 1965); but cf. J. Mackie, *Ethics* (Harmondsworth: Penguin, 1977), 136–40.

not be committed to any version of utilitarianism. It is true that reasons of the first order share the same formal structure as AU: there is a binary relation, 'is weightier than', which is complete in the domain of first-order reasons and over which a utility function can be defined. But the distinction between levels is one of kind and not weight and hence that relation is incomplete over the whole domain and no overall function can be defined.[44] This offers no solution to the outstanding issues between AU and RU. But those issues arise out of the attempt to account for categorical rules along utilitarian lines; the present theory simply offers an alternate explanation of their possibility.

A third objection is more troublesome. Within this general view of practical reason, there is an unexplained gap on which critics have rightly focused their attention. It may be conceded that it is a consistent structure, but denied that it is practically coherent. That is, the notion of binding content-independent reasons may be an intelligible one, yet the set of such reasons be empty.[45] Who would ever exclude a *valid* reason to act? One plainly needs no special theory to account for failure to act on invalid reasons for acting. Why then shouldn't the various incapacity cases just be treated as expressions of doubt about the validity of one's assessment of the balance of reasons? Isn't that just what it means not to trust one's own judgement? And how can something which is independent of the matter at hand be a reason for acting at all?

Nothing I have said thus far shows that authoritative reasons are ever valid, that, having this structure, they have the normative force they are sometimes felt to have. This causes a particularly acute problem for the analysis of authoritative commands. As Hart asks,

How can an artefact of the human will such as a command, or

[44] Strictly speaking, for this to be a utility function we need to interpret 'is weightier than' to mean 'is preferred to' in some sense which measures human welfare. On the existence conditions for utility functions, see J. Henderson and R. Quandt, *Microeconomic Theory*, 2nd edn. (Tokyo: McGraw-Hill, Kogakusha, 1971), 13–14.

[45] See R. Flathman, *The Practice of Political Authority*, 110–12; D. S. Clarke, Jr., 'Exclusionary Reasons', *Mind* 86 (1977), 252–5; C. Gans, 'Mandatory Rules and Exclusionary Reasons', *Philosophia* 15 (1986), 373–94.

compliance with a legislative procedure, either in itself be or be believed to be a reason for action. Surely, the critic may urge, such products of the human will could only be such a reason if there were some non-artificial ulterior reason for taking the former as guides to action . . .[46]

What we need is a way of showing how content-independent reasons can have practical force even though they are not ultimate reasons.

7. VALIDITY

7.1 *Indifference*

What could justify acting on the formal rather than substantive features of some requirement? How can we validly consider the mere fact that a command was given, or a promise or decision made, as a reason for doing what it requires? One might suggest that the force of such reasons is limited to cases where the substantive considerations are irrelevant, where they are a matter of indifference.

Let us begin with the most plausible case for the argument from indifference and work towards the harder ones. Certain kinds of decision may validly be regarded as having content-independent binding force just because they settle some matter about which we are indifferent. The virtue of decisiveness is, as Sidgwick saw, a minor one, but it is of general value, for people are liable to 'an irrational impulse' of 'continuing to some extent in the deliberative attitude when they know that deliberation is no longer expedient, and that they ought to be acting.'[47] Clearly, deliberation is inexpedient when the feasible options are all equally good, and in such a case the fact that one decides on a particular option can settle the issue and preclude further thought about it. How far can this be generalized? Must we be indifferent between options before we can reasonably regard our decision as binding in itself? Here, we must first draw a distinction. Alternatives A and B are subjectively indifferent to some individual only if he regards A as at least as good as B and B at least as good as A.

[46] H. L. A. Hart, *Essays on Bentham*, 265.

[47] H. Sidgwick, *Methods of Ethics*, 7th edn. (London: Macmillan, 1930), 236.

They are objectively indifferent only if he would, counterfactually, regard them as subjectively indifferent under conditions of perfect information and rationality. Now, objective indifference is not a necessary condition of deciding in favour of *A* over *B*, for the reason that it may not be worthwhile deliberating about the truth of the complex counterfactual. Indeed, we may legitimately bring deliberation to an end without forming a view on its truth at all. The 'irrational impulse' to which Sidgwick refers is thus not restricted to cases of objective indifference. What about subjective indifference? This is not necessary either, for I may be unable to assent to the conjunction of preference relations on whose truth it depends. For example, *A* and *B* might be subjectively incommensurable as such that I do not regard *A* as at least as good as *B*, nor *B* at least as good as *A*. Although I am therefore not indifferent, neither have I any preference. And yet this may equally be a case where it would be rational finally to settle on something rather than dither among incommensurables.

Now consider the more complicated case of promises. Some have suggested that promises turn indifferent choices into morally compelled ones.[48] And recall that Godwin held that because there are no indifferent choices, the scope for promising is nil. Once again, it seems reasonable to suppose that assuming voluntary obligations can settle certain indifferent matters. But the value of being able to assume such obligations cannot be wholly justified by its capacity to do this. Even when I have an antecedent obligation to ϕ (and thus it is far from indifferent whether or not I ought to ϕ) I may none the less wish to promise to do so, in order to show that I subscribe to that norm. Even if I injure you and thus acquire an obligation to compensate, I may promise to do so to thereby indicate that compensation is due as a result of a civil wrong, rather than as a tax on conduct. If we think that the scope of voluntary obligations is restricted to the set of indifferent choices, we must believe that they adhere only to moral trivia. This is not plausible. Not only does a choice become non-trivial after a promise is made, we often use promising to underscore its prior moral importance, as in the

[48] See, e.g., C. Fried, *Contract as Promise* (Cambridge, Mass.: Harvard University Press, 1981), 8; and W. Godwin, *Enquiry Concerning Political Justice*, 218.

exchange of marriage vows or when witnesses promise to tell the truth.

Finally, let us examine the case of authority, using as our point of reference once again the idea of a content-independent command. Sometimes it is indifferent what is done and authoritative utterances may be used to settle on a common way of acting. For example, we must all drive on one side of the road or another; it doesn't matter which, and the Highway Code can settle it for us. But the validity of authoritative commands can not be restricted to such cases of indifference. When a judge decides a case at law, she settles the dispute in a way that is binding even if wrong. But the justification for this can not be that it doesn't matter who wins, or even that who wins matters less than having some final settlement of the dispute. It is that such a procedure is thought to promote, though imperfectly, a correct settlement of the dispute. Thus, although indifferent choice may sometimes play a role in explaining the validity of binding, content-independent reasons to act, it cannot do so in general.

7.2 *Indirect Justifications*

When it is not a matter of indifference how we are to act, the validity of content-independent reasons is most plausibly explained by the fact that acting on such reasons may indirectly produce conformity with content-dependent reasons of the ordinary sort. For example, following orders may, in the circumstances of imperfect motivation and information which usually characterize military life, better secure our ultimate aims than would any alternative system.

It is initially plausible that acting for content-independent reasons may be consistent with the requirements of morality. Thomas Nagel writes:

> Sometimes a process of decision is artificially insulated against the influence of more than one type of factor. This is not always a good thing, but sometimes it is. The example I have in mind is the judicial process, which carefully excludes, or tries to exclude, considerations of utility and personal commitment, and limits itself to claims of right. Since the systematic recognition of such claims is very important (and also tends over the long run not to conflict unac-

ceptably with other values), it is worth isolating these factors for special treatment.[49]

Related arguments have often been made about the practical force of promises and decisions.

Most sophisticated utilitarians would be willing to go even further and to concede that utility must sometimes be pursued indirectly by reliance on social norms. In some cases, acting for content-independent reasons is not only consistent with the requirements of utility, but actually promotes them. That *direct* consequentialist arguments (such as act-utilitarianism) cannot justify authority follows from the nature of authority as a social relation. Direct consequentialism prescribes that we always act so as to maximize the net benefit on each occasion, but the binding and content-independent nature of authority precludes any perfect correlation between maximum benefit and obedience. As noted above, second-order reasons have a different role in practical reasoning and the idea of an overall metric of weight does not apply to conflicts between them and first-order reasons. Since the ranking of all reasons is therefore incomplete, transitivity will fail and no overall utility function can be defined. For that reason, direct utilitarian justifications for authority must fail. Indeed, as we have seen, Godwin takes the natural view that act-utilitarianism leads away from authority towards philosophical anarchism. For the strict act-utilitarian, authority will always have the stench of rule-worship.

Now this is just to put in more technical language what is recognized by most utilitarians and nearly all of their opponents: there are special difficulties in accounting for obligations and other forms of commitment along act-utilitarian lines. The most plausible forms of utilitarian argument for obligations and so on are indirect ones, which appeal to utility to justify the general practice of, for example, promising, and then justify specific acts of promising by the rules of the practice. Clearly, this is a plausible strategy also in the justification of political authority: one would try to show that a general practice of surrendering judgement to the state is optimal, and

[49] T. Nagel, 'The Fragmentation of Value', in his *Mortal Questions* (Cambridge: Cambridge University Press, 1979), 136.

justify individual attitudes and behaviour by reference to the constitutive features of that practice. The general line should be familiar enough.

So far, however, this is only a promissory note and not an argument. We cannot be satisfied with any indirect arguments lacking a specification of why a particular indirect strategy is the optimal one. Some reasonably specific account is needed before we are entitled to any confidence in the ultimate results of the indirect approach. If the conditions rendering indirect strategies optimal are variable, we need to keep track of whether and in what conditions they hold. If, for instance, indirect strategies seek to remedy inadequate information by relying on the morally relevant expertise of the authority, we would need to ensure that such information is in fact available to the authorities, that their judgement is reliable, and that they can be trusted to act in good faith. Whether or not authority can be justified indirectly is thus a complex matter which cannot be decided in advance without considering the precise sort of indirect argument offered.

It is too much to hope, however, that the validity of all content-independent reasons can be explained in this way. A non-partisan observer would have to admit that, over the range of the many reasons commonly regarded as having content-independent force, there is not yet a fully satisfactory account of the way in which they indirectly satisfy the demands of utility. There is an obvious though often neglected distinction between an argument that an indirect justification of some norm is possible, and an indirect justification for that norm. The latter makes complex factual and psychological claims, whereas the former is merely conditional on the truth of such claims. Even the case of promising is far from being settled and our commitment to the promising principle seems stronger than would be warranted by the cogency of any indirect arguments for it. Still, there is no denying that some content-independent reasons are susceptible to these accounts. Sidgwick's analysis of decisions, referred to above, is a likely candidate. We are thus left without a general theory of the validity of content-independent reasons. Although we cannot eliminate Hart's worry, we can perhaps live with it by noticing that it is not really a consequence of content-independence at all. What seems preposterous about authority is not the fact that it is content-independent, but that it is, as Hart says, peremptory, by which he means deliberation-excluding. It is intended, he writes, 'to preclude or cut off any independent deliberation by the hearer of the merits pro and con of doing the act.'[50] At least, it is intended to break the link between deliberation and action, to make compliance not conditional on the results of deliberation about the merits. Now these merits seem like content, so it naturally seems that content-independence is the threat. But that is not so. Decisions and promises are also both content-independent and peremptory. It is of the essence of promises that they exclude in advance consideration of certain reasons for non-performance, and it is analytically true that one who is still deliberating has not yet decided. But to cut off deliberation in these cases does not seem preposterous and has natural justifications, certainly in cases of indifference and perhaps more generally along the lines of the indirect arguments mentioned above. The case of authoritative commands is felt to be different simply because the power to cut off deliberation is in the hands of *another* person. This leaves one vulnerable to others; in the case of the modern state, to the requirements of a large and bureaucratic organization. How these can ever have the force they claim for themselves is indeed a pressing question, but not because of some obscure truth about the nature of practical reasoning. The authority of the state is problematic in large part because it is the state's.

8. LEGITIMATE AUTHORITY AND POWER

The analysis of authority relations proposed here is in one sense morally neutral: the correct identification of a person as having authority over others depends only on certain facts about the practical reasoning of those who make or accept such claims. It does not depend on whether they reason well in so reasoning. To accept this does not require any special commitment to the fact–value distinction, for it leaves open the question of how we are to determine the character of

[50] H. L. A. Hart, *Essays on Bentham*, 253.

people's reasoning; I make no assumption that this can be done in a purely naturalistic way. And it is consistent with my claim in Chapter 1 that there can be no value-free description of the social world since our conceptual frameworks all follow the patterns of our practical interests. But one can express an evaluative stance in ways other than endorsing or rejecting a claim to authority.

It is a consequence of this view that authority may exist without being justified. It has often been claimed, however, that 'legitimate authority' is a pleonasm and that relations of subordination which are not legitimate are relations of power and not authority.[51] If this is so, then it would threaten the neutrality of the proposed identification, for to recognize a relation as one of authority would be to impute to it legitimacy. The best solution here is a perspectival one. As a social relation, authority is to be identified from the point of view of those who participate in it and for whom the relation has a special meaning. Someone *claims* authority when he makes requirements of another which he intends to be taken as binding, content-independent reasons for action; his authority is *recognized* when another so treats the requirements; and, in the standard case, authority *exists* when its claims are generally recognized. From either point of view, the authority is regarded as legitimate, and this is a privileged point of view in its identification. In this sense only is 'legitimate authority' primary: one has *de facto* authority only if one claims or is recognized as having legitimate authority. Obviously, this carries no moral presumption in favour of authority relations. Indeed, in view of the special features we have identified, producing a satisfactory justification for political authority is a more demanding matter than is sometimes assumed. It is not equivalent to a justification for social order, since even an anarchist can admit there are strong prudential and even moral reasons to do what the law requires. What he cannot accept is that among these reasons is the fact that the behaviour in question is required by law. In contrast, a justification for authority offers a theory of social virtue which claims that a certain attitude towards the law and other

[51] Cf. the symposium with R. S. Peters and P. Winch, 'Authority', *Proceedings of the Aristotelian Society*, Supp. Vol. 32 (1958), 207–40.

political requirements is of moral value and is required of the good citizen. The attitude in question is that of regarding the state as authoritative, as having the power to alter one's commitments by excluding certain reasons for action. It is not, of course, presumed that political authority must claim or enjoy maximal exclusionary scope, ruling out of court all reasons but those which the law sanctions. The authority of the state may well be, and had better be, limited. Within those limits however, it functions to control the commitments of its subjects. To justify its authority is therefore to justify this structure of practical reasoning and this kind of social relation, and not some other one.

The related issue of whether political authority should be regarded as a species of social power thus turns out to be much less important tnan many have thought. They feel that to see authority as a form of power will demystify it and thus provide the only sound basis for a scientific understanding of the state. This view rests on a dual misconception. First, it is a reaction to a mistake about the sense in which legitimate authority is primary. To understand authority, we must understand the way it functions for those who regard it as legitimate. There is no more mystery here than there is in saying that the existence of a social rule can only be understood from the point of view of those who follow it; in neither case is any moral presumption established. 'Illegitimate authority' is no more a contradiction in terms than is 'invalid proof': considered as a social rather than abstract object, any proof purports to be valid, but may in fact be invalid. Likewise, it is of the nature of authority that it lays claim to legitimacy or is so taken, but nothing more.

This view rests on a second misconception as well, about the nature of social power. Authority is demystified only if, in reducing it to power, one reduces it to a simpler phenomenon free of the problematic aspects of authority. The most serious of these is the intentional concept of 'reasons for acting' and its various cognates. But it has been persuasively argued that social power itself cannot be identified without reference to such concepts, since power ascriptions must make reference to the interests or desires of those affected;[52] and there is not yet

[52] S. Lukes, *Power: A Radical View* (London: Macmillan, 1974).

any satisfactory account of either which does away with its intentionality. A purely behavioural account of power is no more available than is one of authority, so the reduction leaves us no further ahead.

The contrast between power and authority does not seem fruitful for one further and perhaps conclusive reason. Even within the general concept of power as influence over action, there is a family of conceptions of power. One way of exerting influence over another and thereby promoting or harming his interests is by changing the sorts of reason for which he may act. One may expand or contract his set of feasible options, one may alter his preferences over that set, or one may restructure his reasoning by requiring, prohibiting, or permitting him to act in certain ways. For example, a promise creates a power to demand or waive the action promised, and this power is itself created by a general power to bring such obligations to be. Exercising either of these *normative powers* can directly affect the interests of others. By definition, anyone in authority has normative powers since his requirements change the binding commitments of all who accept his authority. The idea that power may influence others' interests either causally or normatively is not mysterious and has a long pedigree, beginning with the ancient distinction between *potentia* and *potestas*. Distinctions among sorts of power are more important than is the supposed distinction between power and authority. Until we have a fuller analysis of the nature of power and its forms, it is likely that little will be gained by exploring the latter.

3

THE SELF-IMAGE OF THE STATE

In the last chapter, we identified some of the special characteristics of authority as a social relation and noticed the way they impose certain constraints on how it might be justified. But our subject is the authority of the state rather than that of the family, school, church, or army. The state shares with these social institutions its character as a *de facto* authority: like them, it claims and is generally recognized as having the power to alter the commitments of its subjects. Political authority, however, has other special features as well, and these pose further constraints on justification.

Consider that authority can be used to establish certain allocations of goods among persons. An alternate means of doing so is the market. This sometimes presents us with a choice between two allocative techniques without, however, a fully general rule for choosing between them. The fact that free markets tend to produce efficient allocations of resources is a general consideration in their favour, but there are also times when they fail to do so, and times when we wish to compromise efficiency with other values whose attainment cannot be guaranteed through market allocations. Thus, one might coherently favour market mechanisms to distribute automobiles while rejecting them for law enforcement. Now the same holds for authority systems. Here, however, there is an additional variable to consider, owing to the fact that authority is relational. Even over that range of cases where we hold authority to be a desirable allocative technique, we might favour granting authority to certain persons only. For example, we might hold that parents, but not the state, should have authority over children's education, or that the church but not the state should have authority in religious matters. Judgements about what is desirable in such cases depend on the distinctive features of the authority holder. The aim of this chapter is to isolate the most important of these in the case of the state.

I. STATE SCEPTICISM

How should we go about it? Ideally, we would first fix a set of necessary and sufficient conditions for the existence of a state in a given society. Some of these conditions would themselves point to distinctive features, and the totality would narrow the range of cases which we had to consider. Objections to this approach have, however, been common among political theorists. They complain about the diversity of definitions of the state that have actually been proposed: an instrument of class oppression, the ultimate sovereign power, a maximally comprehensive associational group, the national legal system, the concrete expression of a transcendent moral unity, etc. One patient scholar counted 145 different definitions;[1] even if his conceptual accounting were not completely accurate, the diversity is warning enough.

Such considerations have often generated scepticism about the utility of 'state' as a theoretical concept. In the fifties and sixties, political behaviouralists championed the view that the fundamental units of political analysis must be operationally definable, value-free, and cross-culturally applicable. The state was given failing marks on all three tests and was therefore jettisoned in favour of some more neutral, sanitized concept such as 'the political system'. Moreover, this was also consonant with a pre-existing tradition of scepticism in the English-speaking world. In contrast with Germany or France where critical reflection about political life tends to begin with the notion of the state, our first thoughts run to 'politics' or 'government'. Perhaps there is a lack of cultural resonance between our liberal, empiricist, and pragmatic political culture and a concept which sometimes seems authoritarian, metaphysical, and ideological.[2] Or perhaps weaker central governments and the common law tradition make state

[1] C. H. Titus, 'A Nomenclature in Political Science', *American Political Science Review* 25 (1931), 45–60.

[2] Cf. K. H. F. Dyson, *The State Tradition in Western Europe* (Oxford: Martin Robinson, 1980), ch. 1.

institutions appear less visible. Whatever the explanation, these related tendencies conspire to create a climate of opinion in which the idea of the state becomes mainly pejorative and is therefore discredited as a descriptive concept except among those who wish to appropriate the pejorative connotations. I do not wish to join them; if we should be sceptical about the moral standing of states, let that emerge through an assessment of the arguments which seek to justify their authority. There is no point in foreclosing debate by insisting on a view of the state which is inherently unattractive.

Two other sources of scepticism remain to be addressed. The first is the familiar charge that all talk of the state is reification, attributing existence to something which is no real part of the social universe; it treats the state as if it were 'out there' whereas in fact it is nothing but the ideological shadow of realities of a simpler nature. Often, this objection has oddly contradictory sources. While it is powered by scepticism about certain abstract entities, it is often held in conjunction with a view that we should replace the state with *other* abstract entities, such as social structures and classes. But if one has metaphysical scruples about talking about the state, I can see no reason to entertain other things whose status can be subject to similar doubts. It is open to a consistent methodological individualist, however, to have done with all such concepts and insist in talking only about individual political agents who are natural persons, together perhaps with their mental states. The difficulty here is that we cannot usefully describe the simplest features of political life in this spare vocabulary. First, these individuals are only relevant when acting in their political roles; it is trite learning to distinguish the public and private capacities of members of parliament, for example, and these roles cannot be described in purely individualistic terms. Secondly, many of the actions of politically relevant individuals can only be described in terms which are inherently institutional and therefore abstract: we talk of citizens voting and thereby make implicit reference to the various rules which constitute voting and without which their actions would just be the stuffing of bits of paper into a box. But once one allows political roles, rules, and other institutional facts into one's vocabulary, individualist rigorism looks less well motivated and the door opens to talk of political parties, courts, nations, and even states. Having conceded this and then to insist, with Stanley Benn and R. S. Peters, that ' the state is not a "thing", but a system of rules, procedures, and roles operated by individuals'[3] seems rather pointless. A state is as much a thing as a church is.

A related objection is that talk of the state is misleadingly anthropomorphic. Is it not a dangerous metaphor to speak of the state 'acting' and 'making claims' on us and is this not the sort of mistake which is encouraged by talk of the state in the first place? Not all metaphors are dangerous, however, and this one has utility in avoiding cumbersome circumlocutions about the activities of the officials of the state, in particular its legislative and executive officials. Of course when we say that the state claims our allegiance we are only summarizing certain politically relevant actions of officials: that they have passed a law which purports to impose obligations on us, that the police and courts regard these obligations as binding and will enforce them, and so on. In principle, we could replace talk of the state as an agent with a more convoluted vocabulary of individuals, officials, and social rules; but there would be little profit in it.

The real worry of those who object to anthropomorphizing the state is a moral one. They suppose that to indulge in such personification is to risk committing oneself to the thesis that the state can not only act, but has interests which must be counted when considering questions of political morality. The objection fails, however, because the inference is invalid. While it is true that the state has interests it does not follow that we must give consideration to these interests and doubly false to think that they outweigh the interests of individuals. It is a major normative assumption of democratic political theory that the state is not entitled to protect its interests as ends in themselves; it must act so as to protect the interests of its citizens. On occasions when protecting the interests of, for example, state officials will be a means to protecting the interests of its citizens then the interests of the state do count. But in cases of conflict they do not. This view finds expression

[3] S. I. Benn and R. S. Peters, *Social Principles and the Democratic State* (London: George Allen and Unwin, 1965), 253.

not only in philosophy, but also in the common law. The *de facto* doctrine, for instance, provides for the legal recognition of illegitimate authorities acting under colour of right, and validates the official acts of such persons in which the public have an interest, but only where to do so will benefit the public. The real interest which the authorities themselves may have in the validity of their acts is simply not counted. We naturally criticize public officials who devote their energy and resources to maintaining their positions, enriching themselves, or securing their re-election at the expense of those whose interests they properly represent. It is a moral mistake to think otherwise, but it is not a mistake encouraged by personifying political authority.

Finally, let me concede to those inclined so to object that this concept of the state is historically bound. This is as it should be, for unlike 'the political system' it aims to pick out an historically and culturally limited phenomenon. It is true, as Engels reminds us, that the state is a 'product of society at a certain level of development', or, as Hobhouse says in a different tone, 'the distinctive product of a unique civilization'.[4] It is that state and that civilization which form the background to these arguments. I am not investigating the nature of authority in other sorts of political organization. That there have been and still are stateless societies can scarcely be doubted. This is not to deny that primitive tribes, for example, had forms of social order, means for arbitrating and settling disputes, and so on.[5] But these lack the distinctive features—and problems—of the modern state. While nearly all of us now live in states, this is a matter of historical accomplishment rather than natural necessity. Until the seventeenth century it was not clear that reasonably unified, territorially based, secular authorities would successfully come to divide up the world among themselves. But this has happened and in consequence the moral situation of members of face-to-face societies, of tribal groups, and even of city-states is for us mainly of comparative and historical interest. These may in various ways be preferable to the forms of social order with

[4] L. T. Hobhouse, *Liberalism* (London: Williams and Norgate, n.d.), 7.

[5] For a useful introduction to these issues, see S. Roberts, *Order and Dispute* (Harmondsworth: Penguin, 1979).

which we are more familiar, but it is the latter that we must seek to understand.

2. FUNCTIONALISM

It is natural to suppose that one might characterize the modern state by enumerating the various social functions that it performs and contrasting these with those of other organizations. It is by appeal to their functions that we distinguish hammers from screwdrivers, or credit cards from identification cards. Can the state be understood in a similar way? It would not be much use, of course, to focus on very localized or detailed functions; we would not understand much about the nature of the state by knowing that in one country it regulates the price of milk, in another it enforces certain religious beliefs, and so on. We would need to look to broader and more general functions such as settling disputes, or stabilizing the dominant mode of production, or securing patriarchy. One might have general doubts about such an approach in the social sciences based on worries about the validity of functionalism. Is it ever an adequate explanation of the presence of some social institution to know that it promotes a certain outcome or state of affairs? For example, we say that the bones of birds are hollow because they are good for flight, but the explanatory power, some may object, is wholly contained in the theory of natural selection. Until we have discovered an underlying causal mechanism of the ordinary sort, our observations about functions provide agenda for explanation, perhaps, but not a complete explanation.[6] Fortunately, we may prescind entirely from this dispute. We are not trying to explain the origin or persistence of the state, but rather identify its distinctive features. We must not confuse a functionalist explanation of the emergence of the modern state with the theory of the state's functions. In the case of intentionally designed things, such as carburettors, their distinctive functions also figure in the best theory of their origins: they were built for a certain job. But the state was not.

The real difficulty with functionalist accounts of the state

[6] On functionalism generally, see G. A. Cohen, *Karl Marx's Theory of History: A Defence* (Oxford: Clarendon Press, 1978), 249–96.

lies in another direction. To be successful, they must identify some function (or set of functions) which are common to all states and unique to them. Yet none of the proposed general functions have this feature: other institutions maintain order, regulate the class war, secure patriarchy, and so on for all the plausible general functions. And at the level of particular functions, such as settling private disputes or providing a standing army, there is too much variation among states. There is in fact no non-trivial social function which is performed by all states and only states. The point was put well by Max Weber:

> What is a 'state'? Sociologically, the state cannot be defined in terms of its ends. There is scarcely any task that some political association has not taken in hand, and there is no task that one could say has always been exclusive and peculiar to those associations which are designated as political ones: today the state, or historically, those associations which have been the predecessors of the modern state. Ultimately, one can define the modern state sociologically only in terms of the specific *means* peculiar to it, as to every political association, namely, the use of physical force.[7]

We will delay until the next section assessment of Weber's positive proposal to characterize state action. For the moment let us consider his negative point against functionalist accounts: no function is universal or unique. The state is thus to be identified not functionally, by its ends, but modally, by its means. Political organizations characteristically serve a cluster of purposes, and their members contest which of these are the most important. The mistake of functionalism is just to think that any of these purposes are distinctive. This is not the strong and false claim that the state has no function—the Kafkaesque nightmare of a meaningless but oppressive bureaucracy is just a case of the state serving internal ends rather than the ends of its citizens. It is simply that we cannot identify the state by the functions it has.

Hans Kelsen made the same case in considering nature of law. 'It is the function of every social order', he writes, 'of every society—because society is nothing but a social order—to bring about a certain reciprocal behaviour of human

[7] M. Weber, 'Politics as a Vocation', in H. H. Gerth and C. W. Mills, eds., *From Max Weber* (New York: Oxford University Press, 1958), 77–8.

beings.'[8] But such orders differ according to how this behaviour is brought about: it may be done by threat, offer, command, advice, persuasion, and so forth. Law is distinguished as a 'specific social technique', meaning that it is distinctive as a means, in form and not in content. Law might have relatively limited aims, as do those canon courts which regulate only the religious activity of their subjects; on the other hand it may have comprehensive ones, as the domestic legal systems of modern states normally do. But these differences in social function do not cast much light on the nature of law. Many Christian sects lack a system of canon law even though they subject the religious behaviour of their members to the strictest customary regulation. Similarly, the free market could regulate many of those areas of social life now controlled by the state. When we take an interest in law as a specific social technique, we are interested in it as a means.

What role then does social function play in understanding the state? It is connected to normative arguments about the state's authority. It might be that certain ends can only be served by certain means, or that certain means are incapable of producing certain ends. A general argument to this effect has been put by Charles Lindblom. He characterizes political and economic systems according to a set of variations on two ideal types of social control: exchange and authority. The elementary distinction is that to control a person's behaviour through exchange mechanisms requires bribing him and thus using up scarce resources, and sometimes he cannot be bribed at all. However, once a person has recognized others' authority over him, nothing more than a valid order is needed to exercise control. Hence, the marginal cost of using an established authority system is nearly zero, and its repeated use may even increase its stability. Lindblom writes:

> A market system is a limited-use institution. Some tasks no market system can attempt or achieve. In simplest and very rough form, the distinction between what markets can and cannot do is this: For organized social life, people need the help of others. In one set of circumstances, what they need from others they induce by benefits offered. In other circumstances, what they need will not willingly be provided and must be compelled. A market system can operate in

[8] H. Kelsen, *General Theory of Law and State*, 15.

the first set of circumstances, but not in the second. Its limitation is conspicuous when compared with an authority system. Although authority is not required in the first set of circumstances, it can be used for both.[9]

In such ways, we may link function and means by showing how means are well or ill suited to certain functions. But this linkage is not tight enough for us to conclude that there are certain social functions uniquely suited to specific techniques; and because that is so we will not be able to identify the state as an institution by reference to a particular social function.

3. COERCION AND AUTHORITY

We return now to Weber's positive proposal: the state is distinguished not by its ends, but by its peculiar means—the ultimate use of physical force. 'Force is certainly not the normal or the only means of the state', he reminds us, '—nobody says that—but force is a means specific to the state.'[10] And Weber is joined in this view by Kelsen, who holds that the specific social technique of the legal system is coercion: every complete law is a conditional order to the officials of the state to apply force to its subjects if they commit an offence.[11]

As a psychological or sociological thesis about the sources of compliance, the view that the state is essentially a coercive order is unsupported by the evidence. As Weber saw, many people are motivated to comply by other things, and a state which had usually to rely on force to maintain order would not survive long. In normal circumstances many people accept the state as legitimate, others are attracted by the facilities it provides, and still others obey habitually. In none of these cases do coercion and fear of sanctions figure prominently among their motivations. At most, coercion has an indirect and secondary effect: it offers assurance to those who are law-abiding that they will not be taken for suckers and thus reinforces their primary motives for obedience.

Sometimes, the claim that the state is essentially an

[9] C. Lindblom, *Politics and Markets* (New York: Basic Books, 1977), 89.

[10] M. Weber, 'Politics as a Vocation', 78.

[11] H. Kelsen, *General Theory of Law and State*, 58–61.

apparatus for general coercion is offered as a thesis about the consequences of the political order: it replaces free, anarchic association with an order of organized domination. Grant for sake of argument that law is coercive at least in the sense of offering standing threats as insurance against recalcitrance. Yet the net consequences of such threats may still be to reduce the total amount of coercion in society. Just as the rules of debate, by restricting the momentary power of each to speak his mind, may increase the chance of each being effectively heard, the fact that threats are issued to all means that fewer are coerced than otherwise would be. Its net effect may thus be to reduce coercion.

Finally, as in the hands of Austin or Kelsen, this may be a thesis about the nature and individuation of laws: nothing is to count as a complete law unless it is related in a certain way to coercive threats. But when distinguished from the two claims rejected above, there is little driving us to reduce the variety of laws to a single normative type. The view that all laws are essentially coercive has been adequately refuted by modern legal theorists and it is not necessary to rehearse their arguments here.[12]

Force will not therefore suffice to distinguish the state from other institutions. Private security agencies and gangsters also apply force. Does it help to qualify this, as Weber sometimes does, by saying that only the state has the monopoly of the *legitimate* use of force? If 'legitimate' means morally justified then it is false, for force may also be legitimately applied in stateless societies, at least in cases of self defence. 'Legitimate' might, on the other hand, be taken to mean accepted, or regarded as morally justified. But this will not do, for related reasons: force is regarded as legitimately applied in other contexts as well. There is a standing temptation, against which I wish to guard, for political theorists to treat the problem of legitimate authority as if it were identical with the problem of the legitimacy of coercion. That these are co-ordinate issues is not in doubt. One reason it is often thought that the state is justified in coercing people is that it is thought to have authority over them. But it is possible for someone to

[12] See N. MacCormick, *Legal Right and Social Democracy* (Oxford: Clarendon Press, 1982), ch. 12.

have authority to require another to act in a certain way yet lack the authority to coerce those who will not comply, and it is possible to be justified in coercing someone without having any authority to do so. Soldiers fighting in a just war do not have authority over the enemy although their actions are justified. Perhaps it is fair to say, with Locke, that they exercise the executive power of the law of nature and that this law authorizes their actions. The whole point of that analysis, however, is to distinguish the sort of power one has within the authority system of political society from the real but quite different forms of justification available independently of it. It is just arguable (though I do not regard it as plausible) that whenever one is justified in *punishing* others one has authority over them, on the ground that coercion can only properly be regarded as punishment when meted out in accordance with some system of rules and by someone in a position of authority under those rules. If sound, that thesis establishes something interesting about the practice of punishment and the family of concepts to which it belongs. It cannot be regarded as providing independent grounds for the thesis that any justifiable coercion is an exercise of authority.

There is, however, something in the thought that the state's control must be largely efficacious for us to accept that it has authority. There is no point in claiming a monopoly of the legitimate use of force if no one pays any attention. Robert Nozick correctly notes that the claims of the state are never sufficient to secure its existence: '*Claiming* such a monopoly is not sufficient (if *you* claimed it you would not become the state), nor is being its sole claimant a necessary condition.'[13] The existence conditions for states also include the attitudes and dispositions of their subjects. In particular, it seems plausible that there must be some kind of acceptance of the claims. H. L. A. Hart suggests that this truth changes fundamentally the character of the social order: 'If a system of rules is to be imposed by force on any, there must be a sufficient number who accept it voluntarily. Without their voluntary cooperation, thus creating *authority*, the coercive power of law and government cannot be established.'[14]

[13] R. Nozick, *Anarchy, State and Utopia* (Oxford: Blackwell, 1974), 23.

[14] H. L. A. Hart, *The Concept of Law* (Oxford: Clarendon Press, 1961), 196.

This may be doubted. In the first place, it is not a conceptual truth that not everyone may be coerced. A tyrant with a nuclear device, say a doomsday machine, might secure the compliance of his population without anyone accepting his legitimacy. The fact that *he* accepts it is not to the point, for his commands are not directed at himself, but at the rest, and their compliance is secured only by fear.[15] Nor need we depend on our sometimes hazy intuitions about such science fiction cases. Even in actual societies where rule is indirect it does not follow (though it may be true) that all or most officials accept the rules. Coercion and acceptance are not the only springs of compliance. The modern state has other means at its disposal: it can also pay people. Some, perhaps many, officials will apply rules not because they accept them or are under threat to do so, but just because it is a good job and they are paid to do it. The practical impossibility of a completely venal system is due to the size of the modern state. It claims to regulate the behaviour of a great many people, so that many officials are needed even in present circumstances. Without some voluntary compliance on the part of subjects it would be just too expensive to run. This is clear enough from the fact that in most countries very little force is actually needed to induce large numbers of people to pay taxes. It might be thought that the threat of force is needed, but no such threat would be credible in the face of massive tax evasion. The present executive and administrative machinery could not cope with it and they could not be extended without more taxation. The credibility of most threats in the modern state depends precisely on their being unnecessary for most citizens. Though not impossible, rule by fear would almost always be too expensive.

There is a further flaw in Hart's claim. At best, it establishes that some must be willing to *comply* with the state in order for others to be coerced. But it does not show that those who comply must *accept its authority* nor does it show that their compliance is what constitutes its authority. It may be true that for a *legal system* to exist the officials must not only comply with but adopt an internal attitude towards the

[15] An illuminating discussion of the problem is found in G. S. Kavka, 'Rule by Fear', *Nous* 17 (1983), 601–20.

fundamental rules of the regime and treat them as standards of correct behaviour. If that is so then not every forcibly imposed system of rules is a legal system. One complies provided that one does what is required; one accepts authority, as I argued in Chapter 2, only if one takes the requirements as giving binding and content-independent reasons to act.

Coercion secures authority and makes it efficacious, but it does not constitute it. Coercive threats provide secondary, reinforcing motivation when political order fails in its primary normative technique of authoritative guidance. In documents and utterances and especially through legislation, the state exhibits its reliance on the primary technique by purporting to command rather than simply to advise, threaten, or bribe. Its officials intend that their requirements be taken as binding on their subjects irrespective of their content. The claim to authority and the willingness to enforce it, although not unique to the state, do set it apart from other aspects of the social system such as the sphere of custom or the market. This may seem like smoke and mirrors. How can it be that a set of *claims* distinguishes the state? Because political order is governed by rational appeals to people, and seeks to influence their behaviour through their beliefs. One thing (though not the only thing) that distinguishes the state from a band of robbers is that the state does not *admit* to being a band of robbers. An extremely powerful group of persons who guide the behaviour of others, who are able to enforce social peace and to provide other public goods but who do so without appeals to authority, would not be a state. If international peace and some measure of world order were secured though a concatenation of deterrent threats it would not follow that a world state had been born. Furthermore, it is a matter of fact that all modern states do claim authority, particularly through their legal systems; even the most brutal and direct application of physical violence is, when done under orders, gilded with the claim of authority.

4. THE PLACE OF LAW

Having said that authority and not coercion is the state's characteristic means, it may seem that we have adopted a legalistic view of government. It may be true, one might say, that legislation and its execution claim authority in the way suggested, and are reinforced by coercive threats, but this is to place too much emphasis on law and law-making in the political process.

From time to time purely legalistic theories of the state have been advanced. Kelsen takes the extreme view and denies that there can be any non-legal or sociological conception of the state.[16] He holds that the notion of state presupposes the notion of law, that the state is in fact nothing but the national legal order, and that to think that a useful distinction can be drawn between law and the state is to be in the grips of an 'animistic superstition'.[17] This is Kelsen at his most dogmatic. The identification of law and state itself has some queer consequences, such as the necessity that each state have only one valid legal system, or that a state persists as long as there is continuity of the constitutional order or its territory thus making the peaceful accession of former colonies to independent status a legal impossibility. Moreover, for many purposes of descriptive social science it is not even necessary to discuss the legal system at all. A sociologist is perfectly free to argue the case that so far from being a fundamental ordering framework, the legal conception of government is but another explanandum.

This does not quite dispose of the problem, though, for however we pick them out those individuals claiming political authority will die, emigrate, or otherwise leave that society. Since we do not wish to say, for example, that the American state changes when the membership of the Supreme Court does, we need some other way to account for the identity of the state through time. In his well-known criticism of Austin's theory of law, Hart argued that such considerations show that we need to introduce the concept of a *rule* determining who is sovereign and that with this emendation we are able to see that sovereignty does not after all provide the key to legal theory; that law must be, in some sense, a system of social rules.[18] Similarly, one might contend that a group of persons constitute a state only if they are acting in official capacity and

[16] H. Kelsen, *General Theory of Law and State*, 189.

[17] Ibid. 191.

[18] H. L. A. Hart, *The Concept of Law*, ch. 4.

that continuity of the state is thus ensured only by rules governing who is to count as an official and, more exactly, by a system of such rules, that is, by law.

We must take care not to fall prey to the vice of legalism. On the nature of the state, the classical positivists, Hobbes, Bentham, and Austin, are more reliable guides than are most of their modern heirs. Both Bentham and Austin ground their concepts of law in the prior concept of the state or, in Austin's language, of 'an independent political society'. It is true that Austin's conception of a group of people united under a single sovereign is ill suited to define what such a society is; but that does not show that some such notion is dispensable. Surely the concept of authority is more primitive than that of law. We do, after all, encounter authority first in the family and classroom and only later in the political arena. The notion of law itself is the notion of authoritative rules of a particular sort. The legal system is only one form of political authority. Despite his legalistic view of the state, Kelsen's theory is soundly anchored at one cardinal point. 'Law is not, as it is sometimes said, a rule. It is', he reminds us, 'a set of rules having the kind of unity we understand by a system. It is impossible to grasp the nature of law if we limit our attention to the single isolated rule.'[19] But the systemic nature of law is not a feature of authority in general. A rule of law is or claims to be an authoritative rule which guides the behaviour of its subjects by providing them with a binding reason to act, but not all such reasons take the form of law and probably no state could function if law were its only resource in guiding action. Besides imposing authoritative requirements through the legal system, the state may also make singular claims which do not derive their validity from any legal system at all. Weber's notion of the authority of a charismatic leader is a case in point, and there are less dramatic examples as well. In some circumstances, non-legal requirements may even be preferred where legal regulation would be inefficient, self-defeating, or symbolically inappropriate. A system of prices and incomes restraints, for instance, might only be justifiable in the absence of administrative costs associated with its legal

[19] H. Kelsen, *General Theory of Law and State*, 3.

imposition; and a system of voluntary restraint cannot be legally imposed. In choosing an extra-legal mode of guidance the state might simply be opting for exhortation and persuasion, but there is no reason why this must be so. Leaders can appeal directly to their subjects, relying on their personal authority and purporting to obligate them in the name of fairness, or solidarity, or the nation. At the bottom of the contrary thesis may lie the normative view that the state *ought* not to regulate behaviour except by means of the legal system. It is widely believed that there is special virtue in regulating conduct by law, because of certain procedural values which the legal system secures. The extent to which this is true depends on one's conception of the rule of law, and that is an issue which cannot be discussed here. Suffice it to say that, even if the rule of law is preferable to the rule of man, this does not deprive the latter of its capacity to claim and exercise political authority.

None of this is meant to deny the extraordinary position of law as the most important means of claiming authority in the large, bureaucratic state. It may even be the hallmark of modernity. Singular appeals from leaders are now much less important, even in an age when mass media make the communication of such appeals easier. Although the importance of law as a way of exercising political authority is real, it is tied to certain historical conditions. As John Plamenatz accurately puts it, 'The idea of law-making as the prime business of government is peculiar to societies which are changing fast and are aware that they are doing so. In Europe it became a commonplace among political theorists only in the seventeenth century.'[20] It is because this pace of change has not slackened nor our consciousness of it dimmed that law remains the primary—but not unique—expression of the authority of the state.

5. SUPREMACY AND MONOPOLY

Thus far I have argued that the state is distinguished from other social institutions not by its functions, but by its

[20] J. P. Plamenatz, *Consent, Freedom and Political Obligation*, 2nd edn. (London: Oxford University Press, 1968), 178.

authoritative means of acting, which are expressed primarily though not exclusively through law. But this does not yet adequately distinguish it from other social authorities. Some churches even have their own legal systems. What is different about the state?

Intuitively, it seems that the state does stand in a special position among other authorities, in some way superior to them. It is often argued, for example, that a necessary condition for the existence of the state is that there be some concentration of authority or power in a society, that there be some division of political labour. Engels, for example, writes that 'The state presupposes a special public authority separated from the totality of those concerned in each case'.[21] Similarly, Kropotkin suggests that 'The state not only includes the existence of a power placed above society, but also a territorial concentration and a concentration of many or even all the functions of the life of society in the hands of a few.'[22] And similar claims are reiterated by many modern writers.[23] This is also the impression one gets from the anthropological evidence, for in the transition from primitive to modern societies such 'functional differentiation', as it is sometimes called, does indeed take place. Certainly the modern state has a plurality of distinct political roles—legislatures, executives, and adjudicators are often fused in primitive systems and talk of political parties and interest groups has only metaphorical application. Functional differentiation is a consequence, however, of a more basic process of the concentration of various forms of social power. Weber's view that the state is a human association which can successfully claim a *monopoly* over the legitimate use of force in a territory is only the best-known formulation of a line of thought running from Hobbes and Locke to its most recent expression in Robert Nozick's sophisticated argument. According to this view, the most important feature differentiating the state from the stateless society is that in the latter the private use of force

[21] F. Engels, *The Origin of the Family, Private Property, and the State*, in Marx and Engels, *Selected Works* (London: Lawrence and Wishart, 1968), 518.

[22] P. Kropotkin, *The State: Its Historic Role* (London: Freedom Press, 1911), 4.

[23] Cf. M. Taylor, *Community, Anarchy and Liberty* (Cambridge: Cambridge University Press, 1982), 4–8.

is permissible whenever morally warranted (for example, to secure one's rights) whereas in the former it is not. In the state, even morally warranted force must be applied publicly.

This theory finds suggestive support in the historical sociology of the modern state. In the transition from feudal society, through the thirteenth century *Ständestaat*, the absolutist, and finally to the constitutional state of the nineteenth century, we see a general, if not quite monotonic, increase in the concentration of social power, together with a unification of the political system.[24] Of particular importance is control over military force and the ability to raise taxes. At the same time, the outcome of the sixteenth-century religious struggles weakened the idea of a single universal authority and paved the way for the emergence of the nation-state as a focus of both political and religious loyalty. These developments were reinforced ideologically by theories of an absolute duty of obedience.

There are two senses, one of them acceptable, in which this set of historical processes might be described as a monopoly. Some have advanced an ambitious *dynamic* theory of the state's supremacy according to which it emerges through a process of *monopolization* of power, or that the rationale for having a state can best be presented in terms of such a process. Norbert Elias subscribes to the descriptive thesis that this is in fact the right sociological model for the emergence of the state; Robert Nozick offers a similar account as a normative explanation or justification for the existence of a supreme authority.

In Elias's view, the monopoly model is a 'relatively precise formulation of a quite simple social mechanism which, once set in motion, proceeds like clockwork.'[25] When there is a large number of people in one area, he argues, certain opportunities and resources become scarce, scarcity breeds competition in which 'the probability is high that some will be victorious and others vanquished, and that gradually, as a result, fewer and fewer will control more and more opportunities',[26] ultimately tending to accumulate in the hands of a

[24] See G. Poggi, *The Development of the Modern State* (London: Hutchinson, 1978).

[25] N. Elias, *The Civilizing Process*, ii. *State Formation and Civilization*, trans. E. Jephcott (Oxford: Blackwell, 1982), 99.

[26] Ibid. 106.

single power. In the final stage of this 'sociogenesis of the state' the privately controlled monopoly tends to escape private control and become publicly run by functionaries. Nozick's argument has a similar structure, but a more adequate explanatory mechanism. He models the emergence of the state as a process by which private customers of competing private agencies for the protection of their rights would find it rational to subscribe to the largest agency, which would therefore ultimately come to dominate the market.[27] It is a model of the emergence of a monopoly among freely competing firms without force or fraud.

Let us consider the dynamic model in more detail. It is often argued that many—perhaps most—monopolies in modern economies are creatures of the state, supported and sustained only by legal regulation. Not all monopolies are like this, however, and the state obviously cannot be. (Unless one is attracted to the view that it is a sort of regulated industry created by divine law—perhaps this is the logical structure of divine right theories.) The state must be a *natural* monopoly, one emerging without protective regulation and purely as a consequence of certain features of the industry, namely protection, in which it operates. Such a monopoly might emerge, for example, if there were increasing returns to scale and a fairly inelastic demand (so that people continue to consume its product as the industry becomes increasingly concentrated). But if this is to be taken seriously we need to know quite a lot about the circumstances of production. Unfortunately, we cannot in fact be confident that the appropriate conditions hold. Are there really increasing returns to scale in the protection of rights? Why must a large and concentrated state be better at protecting rights than small vigilante groups? Are the costs of ultimately conflicting authorities always greater than the risks of having the only supplier in town ignore your claims? And suppose that a monopoly did form. The model is an individualistic one according to which rights protection as offered by the state does not differ in kind as a commodity from the private enforcement of rights in the state of nature; only its

[27] R. Nozick, *Anarchy, State and Utopia*, pt. I.

organization differs. Now, if there are no changes in the basic demand and cost conditions as the state's monopoly forms, then the price of protection will be a decreasing function of its level of output, and output will be a decreasing function of price.[28] But then it will pay the monopolist to restrict output in order to maximize profit, and hence there will be *less* rights protection under monopolistic provision than there would under competitive provision. Or the state might engage in price discrimination, charging more for its services to those better able to pay. If so, rational agents concerned for their rights and possessed of some foresight might well seek to prevent the emergence of a state.

These rather abstract speculations are meant only to raise some doubts about the view that the state has a monopoly of authority in the dynamic sense, that it is a monopolist. But a view as popular as this is unlikely to be entirely without foundation; it does point us in the correct direction. We may instead interpret the notion of a monopoly in a simpler, *static* sense to mean only that the state claims supremacy for its own authority and defends its claims against those of other persons and groups in the same society. This need not commit us to any particular theory about how the claim to supremacy arises or how it is secured. Note also that a supreme authority need not deny that competitors exist: Guelph and Ghibelline were quite aware of the ambitions of the other. A supreme authority is just one which refuses to recognize them as legitimate or at least refuses to concede that their legitimacy has any independent foundation. It is well known that the state has nothing like a monopoly of coercive power: private security firms, organized criminals, large corporations, and unions are only some of the groups sharing in such power. But the state claims to regulate them and will defend itself against some of their intrusions. The extent to which it succeeds in doing so is obviously an empirical question, though one of the first moment. In this sense, the state's authority claims to be supreme; it purports to pre-empt all other authorities and it recognizes no appeal from its own authority to any other source.

[28] The basic argument may be found in W. Baumol, *Economic Theory and Operations Analysis*, 2nd edn. (Englewood Cliffs: Prentice-Hall, 1965), ch. 14.

One must not confuse the supremacy of political authority with the false thesis that political authority must always be *absolute*. All constitutional regimes in different ways recognize and provide for limits on their own jurisdiction. In some cases these are made through bills of rights, in others they inhere in the ordinary law or in political conventions. But the mere fact that political authority is normally limited—and the moral claim that it is vital that it have such limits—does not show in the least that it is not supreme. The extent to which such considerations are operative is a matter of law. Even the power of non-legal reasons for acting, such as the rights of freedom of conscience or the power of prosecutorial discretion, are limited and regulated by law.[29] Like the classical theory of sovereignty, the view of the state as monopolist is misleading in detail, but does point to two truths about the modern state: its claims authority and, even in a pluralistic society, it comes to predominate in this.

6. SCOPE

Another feature of the state's authority is its wide scope: it claims the ability to regulate the *vital interests* of *everyone* within its territory. While its claim to supremacy might be thought of as a formal attribute of political authority, the scope of this claim is a material one.

The question of scope is bound up with the idea of the territory of a state. All modern states are territorial and the regulation of territory forms an important part of international law. Furthermore, unlike morality which seems in principle universal, domestic legal systems are recognized to have only local validity. But their boundaries are rarely purely geophysical or ethnic, and even when they are they must receive legal recognition to become the boundaries of the state. It is sometimes said that the territoriality of the state has even deeper foundations. Hegel thought that ethical life requires concrete expression in a community, that it requires situation in public space.[30] Similarly, Hannah Arendt argued that public

[29] J. Raz, *The Authority of Law*, 30–1.

[30] C. Taylor, *Hegel and Modern Society* (Cambridge: Cambridge University Press, 1979), 84–95.

space has to be spatially instantiated, expressed in a politically appropriated territory where it can live, grow, and find its identity.[31] For present purposes, however, we must distinguish between territory as mere spatial extension and territory as appropriated and contiguous extension. Since the state is an aspect of society it follows trivially that it must be territorially extended in the first sense, since societies are. But need it also be territorial in the second sense? Surely nomadic tribes can interact in the required public ways and sustain political society in the absence of appropriative territorialism. And modern communications technology makes possible in principle a set of overlapping, co-territorial (or non-territorial) global villages. It is possible to conceive of circumstances in which such organizations develop political orderings reasonably close to that of the modern state, and thus the second notion of territoriality drops out.

The real question of scope is thus not about territory at all, but about membership. Liability to the state's authority tends to be non-optional. All those living within a certain area, or all fulfilling certain conditions, are deemed to be bound. Some states allow freedom of entry and exit, and this may seem to render membership optional. We should keep in mind, however, that the state itself regulates these matters as well, through its laws of citizenship and through the extra-territorial effect of certain civil and criminal laws. Although other social authorities, like schools and churches, may also define and control their own membership criteria, none actively enforces such broad claims or has as much success in doing so as the modern state.

7. SIZE

The last special characteristic of the state's authority is related to the previous one. The state is a large entity, composed of many officials who claim authority over a vast society. We are not directly interested in the nature and foundations of authority in families, small groups, the work-place, or in face-to-face communities. It may be that size is an important factor

[31] H. Arendt, *The Human Condition* (Chicago: University of Chicago Press, 1958), ch. 2.

in determining whether or not authority is needed as a technique of social control, whether it will be stable, and how it is to be justified. Perhaps in small groups it is less needed and less desirable. But the problems of the modern state are in part problems of size; however beautiful one finds smallness, it is no part of the aesthetic of the state. The importance of scale is simple. In such large groups, the influence of a single individual is generally nugatory, and this makes the requirements of the regime seem to be relatively external to his or her will, for they are liable only to collective control which requires organization, time, and money. Even in the most open of liberal democracies, the political influence of a single individual is tiny.

I am not suggesting that size is part of the concept of the state. On the contrary, there is no conceptual reason for limiting its application to large scale societies. And it is a consideration which introduces an element of vagueness: just how large is large? Perhaps it is best simply to adopt John Austin's criterion when he says that besides having a sovereign, an independent political society must be 'not inconsiderable' in size.[32] His justification for this restriction is that even families and tribes may have a sovereign, that is, someone who does not habitually obey the commands of others but who is habitually obeyed by the rest. Austin thus incorporates size into the very concept of the state; but that does not seem right and he is driven to it only in order to salvage his sovereignty-based conception of politics. In contrast, my stipulation only flows from the belief that the circumstances of social action differ in morally significant ways as between large and small societies. Where the preferences and actions of a single individual have a noticeable impact on social outcomes individuals tend to reason and act differently than they will in those circumstances where they do not. In any group 'not inconsiderable' in size—say in the order of a hundred thousand or more—individual influence is slight. The modern state is, in this sense, external to the individual and thus takes on an aspect of objectivity which the family normally does not. These are the circumstances of

[32] J. Austin, *The Province of Jurisprudence Determined*, 210.

authority which pose the problems in which we are most interested, and this is the justification for restricting our attention to large societies and their states.

8. SHARING THE SELF-IMAGE OF THE STATE

These then are several distinctive features of the authority which the state claims: it is supreme, of a wide scope, and applies to many people. These features fall far short of providing existence conditions for the state, and they leave unresolved many interesting questions such as the precise role of efficacy in understanding the state's authority, or cases where there are multiple claimants to supreme authority, and so forth. However, these features come fairly close to being necessary to the standard or normal case with which we are all familiar. And none of them is very startling; they merely reflect our common view of political life in modern societies. But, in conjunction with the results of the previous chapter, these rather banal empirical obervations impose some powerful constraints on arguments about legitimacy.

To justify the authority of the modern state is to justify a particular social relation: one in which officials seek to guide the behaviour of others by supplying them with content-independent, binding reasons to act in circumstances in which this authority is supreme, comprehensive, and wide in scope. It is obvious that this will be more demanding than producing reasons why we should generally do what the officials say or finding justifications for the use of coercive power. Yet the relation we are seeking to justify is neither foreign nor mysterious; it is just what is usually understood as the state's power to obligate us to obey, to impose duties on its citizens. The problem of political authority can thus properly be seen as the issue of whether, or to what extent, the citizen should share what we might call the self-image of the state, of whether they should accept its claim to be a duty-imposer. This way of understanding the problem is metaphorical, but helps keep in mind what is really at issue and serves to remind us of the important distinction between a theory of political order—an account of why so many do, and whether they should, comply at all—and an account of particular social relations. Our central issue is not whether people should obey the state, still less to what extent they can be expected to. As the anarchists have seen, the pressing moral problem is whether they should ever obey for the reason that their obedience is required. We may comply out of habit, self-interest, fear, or the conviction that what the state requires of us is, on independent grounds, what is morally best. Moreover, the state could regulate our behaviour without claiming to create duties for us. It can and does also coerce, bribe, and persuade us to comply. We may treat the existence of the state parametrically in our moral calculations, taking note of its claims and assessing them on their merits. Those who comply for such reasons do what is required, but not as required, for they reject the state's self-image as an authority. In this they are like a new recruit in the army who keeps his boots polished out of fastidiousness of character rather than in response to the orders of his sergeant. This may be enough to avoid sanctions, but it is not acceptance of authority. In the political context, I will call such attitudes the strategy of *peaceful compliance* with the state. This is not the relation at issue here. Mere compliance is not a pressing practical or theoretical issue: most people comply, most of the time. The problem of political authority is about the possibility of a particular ground of compliance—the belief that the state has moral authority, that it can create duties for us.

David Hume approaches the problem of political obedience in a way that depreciates the importance of this distinction. He argues that compliance is necessary to promote 'public utility' and then says that this is unattainable unless exact obedience is paid to the command of the magistrate.[33] It is but a short step from this view to conclude that the best security of exact obedience is a willingness to take the magistrate as authoritative. Hume puts this forth as an empirical claim, certified by common sense. Yet common sense seems to point in the other direction, for public utility, however conceived, requires only general, not perfect compliance, and is satisfied by any motivation that produces it. What Hume has to show is that unless a certain kind of attitude is taken to the

[33] D. Hume, 'Of the Original Contract', in *Essays: Moral, Political, and Literary*, ed. E. F. Miller (Indianapolis: Liberty Classics, 1985), 480.

magistrate's commands, they cannot have the beneficial consequences which we agree are wanted. This would establish that a certain kind of social order—a mutually beneficial one—can only or best be sustained through authority relations. If successful, that would provide the basis for one sound, indirect argument for the validity of political authority. Whether such a strategy can succeed is the subject of the next two chapters.

4

AUTHORITY AND CONVENTION

To justify the authority of the state we require an argument which establishes that an institution claiming supreme and wide-ranging authority over many people should be treated as having the power to create binding, content-independent reasons for them to act. In Chapter 2, it was shown that instrumental arguments to the effect that such institutions are particularly valuable must be indirect in nature. On particular occasions, authoritative directives may require acting against the balance of reasons. But it is often thought that this will indirectly serve important values. In this chapter and the next, I examine two popular and influential versions of that thesis.

I. THE CONCEPT OF CONVENTION

There is, no doubt, some sense in which the authority of the state is conventional. Carole Pateman, for example, says that 'Liberal theory . . . was born in conflict with divine right and patriarchal theorists who insisted that relationships of subordination and authority were God-given or natural. It is absolutely basic to liberal theory that political theory is conventional.'[1] This is indeed basic to liberalism, and to many other sorts of political theory as well. But even if true, it only commits us to voluntarism and humanism: authority is to be justified by appeal to human will and interests. It no more supports a justificatory thesis than does the ancient issue of whether social order is *physis* or *nomos*. Humanly created order can be perfectly miserable. We are only interested in whether authority is conventional in some sense which counts as an argument in its favour.

One such notion is that of a valuable, stable regularity of

[1] C. Pateman, *The Problem of Political Obligation* (New York: Wiley, 1979), 6.

behaviour which is somehow arbitrary, though not in the sense of being pointless. If founded on pointless convention (like some outmoded rules of etiquette) the state's authority would be descriptively, but not normatively, conventional. The class of valuable conventions is not empty, as many traffic regulations illustrate. Commonly shared preferences for rapid travel and avoiding injury establish the value of a regularity of driving on the same side as everyone else. Since this could be the left or the right, either convention would be arbitrary. Since there would be little temptation to drive on the opposite side from the others it would also be stable. It is such conventions which figure in the arguments examined in this chapter. I shall attempt to make the notion more precise, but first I wish to present two non-technical versions of it which are liable to an analysis along the general lines just presented.

In his famous attack on the contractarian view that government must be founded on a promise to obey the state, Hume defends a vigorous and subtle form of conventionalism. He is a normative conventionalist in both morals and politics and his account of political authority is consistent with this general stance. Hume argues that promises are no more naturally intelligible as means of binding ourselves than is the duty to obey the government itself, so they cannot ground or explain it. 'The obligation to allegiance being of like force and authority with the obligation to fidelity, we gain nothing by resolving the one into another. The general interests of society are sufficient to establish both.' His theory of justice follows a similar line. While rejecting the view that justice arose through conventions in the sense that it was agreed upon by a group of convenors or contractors, Hume writes, 'But if by convention be meant a sense of common interest; which sense each man feels in his own breast, which he remarks in his fellows, and carries him, in concurrence with others, into a general plan or system of actions, which tends to public utility; it must be owned, that, in this sense, justice arises from human conventions.'[2]

Thus, the conventions which justify and explain political allegiance and other 'artificial virtues' are general rules,

[2] D. Hume, *Enquiry Concerning the Principles of Morals*, ed. L. A. Selby-Bigge, rev. P. H. Nidditch (Oxford: Clarendon Press, 1975), 306.

beneficial (at least in the long run) to each and ultimately sustained only by this shared interest and the well-founded mutual expectation of their observance. 'When this common sense of interest is mutually expressed, and known to both', says Hume, 'it produces a suitable resolution and behaviour.'[3] Such conventions emerge, acquire prescriptive force, and, being followed once, increase the likelihood that they will be followed again the next time. Their normative force is independent of their content, for that is arbitrary; it derives from the way such conventions secure the benefits of public utility. This arbitrariness is especially clear, on Hume's view, in the case of our loyalty to governments. ''Tis interest which gives the general instinct, but 'tis custom which gives the particular direction.'[4] And hence, as he says in one of those wryly sceptical moments which temper his conservatism, 'No maxim is more conformable, both to prudence and morals, than to submit quietly to the government, which we find establish'd in the country where we happen to live, without enquiring too curiously into its origin and first establishment.'[5]

A similar argument was put by one of the early behaviouralists in political science. For G. E. G. Catlin, authority is a form of social control distinguished from force or domination by the fact that it operates by making the conduct of those controlled calculable, that is, regular, foreseeable, and thus alterable.[6] Collective control is sometimes needed to support valuable forms of social organization. Its success depends on the perception of a common interest formulated in convention. This convention, however, is no general will, no *conscience collective*, it is merely a behavioural regularity which has an 'advantage sufficiently apparent to them to influence their actions'.[7] Nor need it be conceptualized as a convention; it need only be seen as the thing to do based upon perceived

[3] D. Hume, *A Treatise of Human Nature*, ed. L. A. Selby-Bigge, rev. P. H. Nidditch (Oxford: Clarendon Press, 1978), 490.

[4] D. Hume, *A Treatise of Human Nature*, 556. [5] Ibid. 558.

[6] G. E. G. Catlin, *A Study of the Principles of Politics* (London: George Allen and Unwin, 1930) 161.

[7] Ibid. 162. This is obviously a necessary condition. Cf. Hume: 'in order to form society, 'tis requisite not only that it be advantageous, but also that men be sensible of its advantages': *A Treatise of Human Nature*, 486.

common interests. It is not necessarily true, however, that all those whom political authority claims to regulate will in fact benefit from it, so the grounds for compliance may differ as between the beneficiaries and the non-beneficiaries. The former appreciate its value in attaining their common interest, while the latter are only involuntarily obedient. This, Catlin claims, places an inherent limit on authority claims: the strength of the beneficiaries must outweigh that of the non-beneficiaries. The normative force of the conventional standards depends only on their stability and existence and not on their moral content. Those in authority, he says, may be right or wrong in their individual views, 'but right or wrong, they represent in their public action the system of order actually constituted'.[8] In summary, Catlin writes:

> Authority is a power exercised in accordance with a convention, whether between two people, one of whom is under a conventional obligation to the other, or over a group of people by those whose function is to enforce the convention of the group. Authority, *as distinct from mere power*, implies a claim to recognition owing to the existence of a convention of wills by which the authority is set up; although, save by habit of acquiescence, this claim is only effective against those who benefit by the convention and whose interest it subserves. Conventions are for members authoritative because with these conventions their wills, thanks to a balance of advantage, concur, and on their wills the conventions are founded. For outsiders, conventions are a power which receives their acquiescence or which they obey by constraints.[9]

Note that for both Catlin and Hume, there is a common core in the idea of conventions as valuable, stable, and arbitrary regularities of behaviour, somehow founded on common interest. Yet each of them rejects any view that the conventions were the product of an explicit act of agreement or consent. For this reason we should draw the contours of conventionalism a little more carefully.

2. CONVENTIONS, CONTRACTS, AND CONSENT

In the eighteenth century, political theorists drew no consistent

[8] G. E. G. Catlin, *A Study of the Principles of Politics*, 165. Cf. 179.
[9] Ibid. 164–5.

distinction between 'convention' and 'contract', and, though to a lesser extent, this usage even persists today. Moreover, both terms have etymological affinities in the notion of a 'coming together'. It is thus for theoretical rather than historical reasons that I wish to stipulate a sharp distinction between them. The basic difference is that, although conventions and contracts are both ways of creating social order, they differ in motivational structure. Conventions, in the sense intended here, seek to remedy what are essentially problems of information among parties sharing a common interest; contracts seek to remedy problems of motivation among parties with partly common and partly conflicting interests.

While conventional standards serve mutual interests, they need not do so optimally since some persons might be better off and none worse off under some other conventional standard. Nor need they maximize utility. But they must be stable so that it pays no single individual to forge off on his own. Thus, such standards need not be *enforced* in order to be *in force*. This isolates conventions from a large class of regularities which provide mutual benefit but with the additional temptation for each to be a lone defector or a free rider; it limits the class of conventions to those situations of co-ordination where each prefers matching his own behaviour with that of the others to not matching at all, and is not so attracted to any particular way of matching that he is ever tempted to go it alone. This means that problems of collective action and public goods are not the correct baseline or state of nature with respect to which conventional norms are to be analysed. Instead, they provide the logical model for contractarian arguments, the subject of Chapter 5. Perhaps there is a little linguistic support for this distinction as well, for we would not normally call rules which inherently depend on enforcement for their existence 'conventional', although we might describe them as 'mandatory' or 'obligatory'; but nothing important turns on this. It is clear that there are two distinct classes of rules, and I will restrict the idea of conventions to those falling in the class described above. They are of special interest, not only because they have in fact figured prominently in certain arguments about political authority, but because they are the simplest avenue along which we might seek an indirect justification. Unlike social contracts, they lack the problem of enforcement, and are in that sense practically simpler as well.

We should also distinguish conventionalism in this sense from those consent-based theories according to which the requirements of the state bind its citizens only if they have consented to be so bound. Such theories must explain both how consent is given, and why it binds. Since Hume, it has been widely thought that any concept of consent strong enough generally to bind citizens to the state is far too strong for the evidence—few if any give such consent. We will return to these issues in Chapter 6. Conventions in the present sense, however, are immune to such objections; they need no convenors and no agreements, just regular, rational behaviour in the context of certain background conditions. Hence, even if 'tacit consent' is not possible, tacit conventions are.

A second difference between conventionalism and consent is that the former theories are always instrumental in character. Conventions are means of promoting an independently existing common interest and are justified to the extent that they do so. As we shall see in Chapter 6, however, this is not necessarily the case with consent theories, for one may consent to obey authority not as a means to securing further goods, but as an expression constitutive of a certain relationship. In this respect consent theory differs from both conventionalism and contractarianism, for the latter are fundamentally theories of social order while the former is not; it is a theory of social relations. To justify the authority relation, the conventionalists and contractarians both attempt to argue that it is importantly connected with the maintenance of a valued form of order.

In political argument, conventionalism, contractarianism, and consent theory are often interrelated and invoked simultaneously. In view of their very different characters, this is rarely an advance. In any case we can only understand and evaluate the independent force of each by testing them on their own. A relatively pure form of conventionalism is therefore the one examined here.

3. CO-ORDINATION PROBLEMS AND NORMS

The logical structure of conventionalist theories can, I think, best be understood by relying on the theory of co-ordination games as developed by Thomas Schelling, David Lewis, and others.[10] This is a specialized notion of convention, but it is one developed in the light of Hume's arguments, and one relied on explicitly or tacitly by most of those writers I am about to discuss.

A group of agents have a *co-ordination problem* (CP) where each must choose between exclusively alternative courses of action, the directly consequential returns of which to each depend on both his own choices and those of the others. Each can completely, transitively, and reflexively order the outcomes in what may be called a preference ranking, and each seeks to do the best he can with respect to his ranking. While the outcomes are thus ranked unconditionally, the strategic choices of each are always conditional on his expectations of the choices of others, and all share this knowledge. The problematic element in the situation arises from the existence of at least two proper co-ordination equilibria, that is, at least two sets of choices for all such that, having so chosen, at least one of them would do worse if any one agent had chosen differently.

In any CP, whatever helps agents settle on a particular co-ordination equilibrium is a *solution*. In a CP situation which recurs over time, certain regularities may emerge in the behaviour of the agents. When these regularities are (parts of) solutions they are co-ordination norms. Adapting Lewis's definition, we can say:

A regularity R in the behaviour of members of population P in a recurring situation S is a *convention*, if and only if, in any instance of S:

(1) everyone conforms to R because

(2) everyone expects everyone else to conform to R; and

[10] T. Schelling, *The Strategy of Conflict* (New York: Oxford University Press, 1963); D. Lewis, *Convention: A Philosophical Study* (Cambridge, Mass.: Harvard University Press, 1969); E. Ullmann-Margalit, *The Emergence of Norms* (Oxford: Clarendon Press, 1977). My account draws heavily on Lewis, ch. 1, and Ullmann-Margalit, 77–93.

(3) everyone prefers that anyone conform to *R* on the condition that everyone conform to *R*; because *S* is a CP and general conformity to *R* is a solution to the problem.

As formulated, this is unnecessarily demanding. We would probably also regard a regularity as conventional if it satisfied the above definition with the universal quantifiers 'any' and 'every' replaced by 'almost any' and 'almost every', or perhaps even just 'most'. Moreover, it is unlikely in any actual case that (2) and (3) will offer complete explanations of the conformity referred to in (1); it will probably do if they are both necessary and important preconditions of the conformity. There are a few other wrinkles too, but we can ignore them for present purposes.

CPs of the above sort can occur in nested structures. A CP which can be defined without reference to any conventions is a first-order co-ordination problem and conventions which solve it are first-order ones. An *n*th order CP is one posed by the existence of an $n-1$th order convention. For example, some conventions might need to be codified. If settling on a code is a CP then codifying them yields a second-order CP. If those codified norms need a consistent interpretation, and if settling on an interpretation is a CP, then interpreting them yields a third-order CP. And so on.

Valuable conventions offer the prospect of an individualistic and instrumental justification of authority based on the need to co-ordinate action. When a convention of the above sort is needed, there is no guarantee that one will emerge. For that to happen each needs to form a correct expectation as to what the others are likely to do. No such clue is offered by the formalities of the problem alone; it depends on there being some further, non-formal, feature which renders one alternative *salient*. Complex CPs which involve many people or which must be solved quickly might lack such a feature. However, if a person could provide a cue by producing some communication which gave reason to choose one alternative and exclude the others, then obedience to his decree would have value.

Let us return to our earlier example to see how the process works. It does not matter (let us suppose) whether we all drive on the left of the road or on the right. But each must drive somewhere and, given the usual preference for rapid travel and avoiding injury, each does best only if all drive on the same side. But how can they co-ordinate their activity and settle on one alternative? If each knew and expected the others to know (and they expected him to expect . . .) that one alternative was legally required, then in the absence of anything else this knowledge would make that alternative more salient in the sense that there would be reason to choose it which does not alter the preference rankings.[11] Thus each would do best by choosing to drive on the required side and none could do better (and some would do worse) by driving what is now the wrong way. Note that it is not necessary that the returns are the *same* for each, but only that, given the others' choices, they are *best* for each. Each might do better had all chosen differently, so the outcome may not be optimal. For instance, there is no reason for visiting Americans and Europeans to drive on the right while in England, even though to do so would reinforce good driving habits back home. While they do prefer all-driving-right to all-driving-left, given general observance of English rules of the road, they also prefer all-driving-left to themselves-driving-right-and-the-rest-driving-left. We might say that each has a common interest in doing what the others do. The degree of sharing of interests, however, lies along a continuum, as we can show by elaborating the example. Assume that, other things being equal, right-handed people like to drive on the right, and left-handed ones on the left. Then consider Fig. 2. In matrix (*a*), Row Chooser and Column Chooser have completely coincident interests; they are ambidextrous and therefore completely indifferent between both driving left (LL) and both driving right (RR). In matrix (*b*) there is a little conflict of interest

[11] It is important that solutions to such games leave the structure intact—as salience does. To change the structure is to change the game and thus avoid the problem. This may offer a practical exit, but it does not solve the problem. Perhaps some problems cannot be solved, but only avoided. In CPs, however, avoidance and solution should be kept distinct in order to be clear about the nature of the resolution. That is why game theorists insist that salience indicators are 'symbolic details' or 'suggestions and connotations' (T. Schelling, *The Strategy of Conflict*, 98, 106) and thus are distinct from the structure of pay-offs. In some cases, the bare formal structure may itself yield a salient outcome, though for informal reasons (e.g., a set of prime-numbered pay-offs might be the 'obvious' solution to mathematicians, though not to moralists).

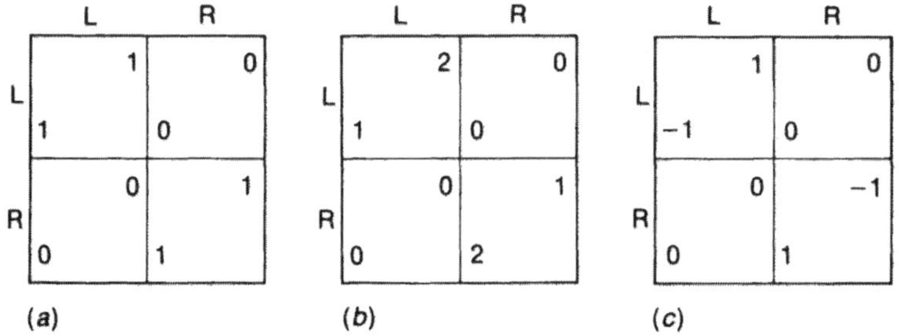

(*a*)

	L	R
L	1 1	0 0
R	0 0	1 1

(*b*)

	L	R
L	2 1	0 0
R	0 0	1 2

(*c*)

	L	R
L	1 −1	0 0
R	0 0	−1 1

The numbers represent cardinal utilities. The lower left pay-offs go to Row Chooser, the upper right to Column Chooser.

FIG. 2

since LL favours Column, who is now left-handed, and RR favours right-handed Row. In matrix (*c*), there is a pure conflict of interest, for Row and Column have each placed side-bets of one unit on the different outcomes; if they both end up driving on the left, Row pays Column one, and vice versa for the right. If matrix (*c*) were the normal CP situation then conventionalism would not get off the ground as a justificatory theory, since instabilities would be too great. Although conventionalism can accommodate conflicts of interest, there must still be a predominance of coincident interests as in matrix (*a*) or (*b*).

We can now see in precisely what sense conventions are an unproblematic form of social order. Once established, they need no external motivation to secure conformity; there is no problem of enforcement, no tendency to anarchy. This does not mean, however, that there are no problems in *establishing* conventions. It might be thought that if the common interest is sufficiently compelling then the solution to a co-ordination problem will be trivial and automatic, and hence that there will be no important role for conventions. Some game theorists have argued, for example, that 'if both players have the same preference pattern over outcomes, then everything is trivial since both players prefer the same outcome above all others.'[12] However, as matrix (*a*) illustrates, this is not always

[12] R. D. Luce and H. Raiffa, *Games and Decisions* (New York: Wiley, 1957), 59.

so. The only sense in which that choice situation is trivial is that it matters not which action the choosers meet on. It does very much matter, however, *that* they meet rather than miss, and their ability to do so depends on their ability to co-ordinate their actions. Hence, the strategic context of inter-dependent choice ensures that the problem does not dissolve into one of the indifferent choice facing Buridan's ass which, the story goes, starved dithering between two equally preferable bales of hay. A single agent in a non-strategic context could properly see indifferent choice as trivial by relying on the practical principle that whichever he chooses he does no wrong in choosing it. To dither over which of two identical postage stamps to place on a letter is a neurotic symptom and not a problem in decision theory.[13] But to be uncertain as between driving on the left and driving on the right *because* one is uncertain what the others are likely to do is not. Indifference does not therefore always produce triviality.

Finally, consider the case of strong but symmetrical preferences among the agents, as in the matrix in Fig. 3. By the above definition, this is a co-ordination problem. Is it also a trivial one? While Row and Column both prefer (AA or BB) to (AB or BA), they are not at all indifferent between their meeting places. AA is very much preferred to BB; indeed, the preference is so strong that it is hard to imagine rational agents ending up anywhere else, and therefore hard to imagine B ever emerging as a conventional solution to this problem. Does this mean that AA lacks the requisite arbitrariness and is therefore not conventional?

	A	B
A	100 (upper right); 100 (lower left)	0 (upper right); 0 (lower left)
B	0 (upper right); 0 (lower left)	1 (upper right); 1 (lower left)

Fig. 3

[13] See E. Ullmann-Margalit and S. Morgenbesser, 'Picking and Choosing', *Social Research* 44 (1977), 757–85.

It is true that AA is not a *dominant* choice in the technical sense, since it is not unconditionally best for each. It is best only on the condition that the other also chooses it. It is, however, very much the best co-ordinated solution and might, for that reason, be salient. Could BB ever emerge as a solution? It might in certain limited circumstances. If BB was a solution to a previous co-ordination problem, similar in all other relevant respects, but in which the pay-offs in the AA cell were (0,0) and if there was great uncertainty about changing the meeting place, BB might remain the norm even when circumstances change so that AA becomes more valuable to each of the parties. Their old habits and uncertainties keep them in a rut, even when another solution would be better for each. Still, it is hard to believe that there is not some value of A such that it becomes worth taking the risk of missing in order to gain the benefits of meeting on a better solution. On this point, more could be said[14] but it would not, I think, importantly affect the argument of this chapter. In calling conventional orders unproblematic, I mean only to assert that the existence of a common interest is sufficient to guarantee the stability of a co-ordinated solution, *once attained.* I make no claim about the ease of attaining it, nor about the comparative value of unattained, yet possible, solutions. These latter points do, however, bear on the role conventions play in justificatory arguments.

4. THE COMMON INTEREST

Conventionalist justifications for authority are instrumental. They depict authority as a necessary or valuable means to securing solutions to CPs, as a way of creating co-ordination norms. The ultimate values served are the common interests of the parties involved.

Few political theories are without some conception of the common good or common interest. Hume's theory of justice, for example, stands or falls with the claim that diligent observance of actual rights to private property is in the long-run interests of each or, as he sometimes says, in the interests

[14] Cf. M. Gilbert, 'Game Theory and *Convention*', *Synthese* 46 (1981), 41–93.

of 'public utility'.[15] Other traditions, descending from Aristotle and Aquinas, conceive of the domain of politics as the common good in a teleological sense: the internal end of a truly human life. It is this conception, and not Hume's, which lies behind T. H. Green's claim that 'an interest in the common good is the ground of political society, in the sense that without it no body of people would recognize any authority as having a claim on their common obedience.'[16] It is Hume's view, however, which has come to dominate in the modern world which has largely lost the sense of a functionally ordered nature. It is a spartan conception—individualistic, empiricist, and instrumentalist. The only trouble lies is making it believable.

The first difficulty is in giving some account of the existence of a common good in our conflict-ridden societies. Without even considering the possible modes of self-deception and false consciousness, there is just too much observable conflict for us to be satisfied with any pieties about the general interest or platitudes about the long run. First, there is zero-sum conflict between individuals and classes over power, status, and other 'positional goods',[17] in which there simply are no jointly realizable benefits and where the gain of one is the loss of another. Secondly, there are wide areas of partly conflicting interests over such 'public goods' as clean air, where incentives to be a free rider mean that attainment of common interests is inherently unstable. Subtracting both sorts of conflict leaves little room for common interests which motivate us to co-ordinate our actions.

[15] That is why Hume's theory, though consequentialist, individualistic, and desire-based, is none the less not a version of utilitarianism, contrary to common opinion. As John Rawls says, 'all Hume seems to mean by utility is the general interests and necessities of society. The principles of fidelity and allegiance derive from utility in the sense that the maintenance of the social order is impossible unless these principles are generally respected. But then Hume assumes that each man stands to gain, as judged by his long-term advantage, when law and government conform to the precepts founded on utility. No mention is made of the gains of some outweighing the disadvantages of others. For Hume, then, utility seems to be identical with some form of the common good; institutions satisfy its demands when they are to everyone's interest, at least in the long run.' *A Theory of Justice*, 32–3.

[16] T. H. Green, *Lectures on the Principles of Political Obligation* (London: Longmans, Green, and Co., 1950), 109.

[17] The term is due to F. Hirsch, *Social Limits to Growth* (Cambridge, Mass.: Harvard University Press, 1976).

Perhaps these are just surface appearances, however. Is there none the less a common good shared at a deeper level? This line is taken by John Finnis in his important reworking of the theory of natural law. Although he would reject the description, his theory is a version of conventionalism which argues that the authority of law is justified by its unique capacity to co-ordinate a broad range of human activity for the common good.[18] In Finnis's usage, 'co-ordination' takes on a broad meaning, including the central case of this chapter, but also the mutuality of restraints discussed in the next.[19]

Conceptions of the common good may differ on at least two counts—on an evaluative dimension (what is *good*) and on a structural dimension (in what sense the good is *common*). Finnis's conception is both individualistic and non-aggregative. This much it shares with the common interests of the CP model. It is individualistic because there exist basic values which are objectively good for each person[20] and it is non-aggregative because these values are not fully commensurable.

[18] Finnis's argument has considerable affinities with the more traditional Thomist account in Y. R. Simon, *A General Theory of Authority* (Notre Dame: University of Notre Dame Press, 1962), especially ch. 2. Although Simon is innocent of the rhetoric of modern game theory, it is clear that the nerve of his argument is also a conventionalist one: in large communities where the common good can be attained in several different ways, authority is needed to unite people in a common way of acting. This may reduce the air of paradox in calling Finnis a conventionalist even though he believes in objective values. The oddity vanishes if we remember that the conventionalism being considered here is a normative thesis only, i.e., a thesis about how we justify certain rules of action, and not a claim about what is ultimately valuable. For Finnis and Simon alike, the latter cannot be a matter of convention, but the former is. In this respect, there is a large difference between normative conventionalism and, e.g., Hobbes's view.

[19] J. Finnis, *Natural Law and Natural Rights* (Oxford: Clarendon Press, 1980). Finnis thinks that this broad usage exempts his theory from some of the criticisms advanced here, and in my, 'Law, Co-ordination, and the Common Good', *Oxford Journal of Legal Studies* 3 (1983), 299–324. He clarifies his position in 'The Authority of Law in the Predicament of Contemporary Social Theory', *Notre Dame Journal of Law, Ethics and Public Policy* 1 (1984), 115–37. The introduction of some conflict of interest, however, does nothing to extricate Finnis from the conventionalist predicament, and the inclusion of mutuality of restraints is just a version of the contractarian argument considered and rejected in the next chapter. But Finnis now makes clear that he rejects the instrumental conception of rationality. That raises the question of the extent to which he is entitled to talk of co-ordination problems at all or to invoke them in an instrumental argument for authority. I shall not discuss these interesting issues here.

[20] Finnis says, 'the common good is fundamentally the good of individuals (an aspect of whose good is friendship in community)': *Natural Law and Natural Rights*, 168.

According to Finnis, aggregative conceptions of the common good, such as utilitarian ones, are literally meaningless, senseless.

In what sense then is the plural, objective good for persons a common good? Finnis holds that it is common because there is both instrumental and inherent value in the structures of interdependence among persons which make co-ordinated action necessary. The basic values are not such that a unique way of ordering our affairs is prescribed by reason. Even within the demands of fairness and reasonableness, choice remains, and this must be settled authoritatively. The appearance of pure conflict is, therefore, just that. To take an impartial view and give full account to the legitimacy of the diversity of basic values will dispel the illusion:

> For a legislator or judge, considering the problems of social order generically, the pure conflict situation cannot be conceded to exist as between the members of a community: A and B may be in a pure conflict situation here and now; but A might have been in B's position, and vice versa; so, in advance or generically (i.e. for the purposes of selecting rules and conventions), people of A's and B's sorts have a convergent interest in containing, modulating, and conditioning the possible loss (and gain).[21]

It is this claim which lends plausibility to Finnis's extension of the term 'co-ordination' beyond the standard usage to include cases of mutuality of restraints, for example, where individuals' immediate interests are in real conflict: each does best if he alone is exempt from the restraints, so that the ideal for each is to be a renegade in a law-abiding society.

Let us examine the argument more closely. What are the relevant sorts of people into which A or B fall? If I am a politically powerful polluter, under which description am I to be considered the equal of powerless, disorganized consumers? Why should we believe that a common good exists between these two? The assumption seems to be that no one can be so sure of regularly dominating in a conflictual situation that he would not want some mechanism for regulating gains and losses. Now, it may be true that there is no one sufficiently powerful to wish to risk unregulated action in all cases, but

[21] Ibid. 255.

there may be some who need not fear at least certain others and with whom the conflict is therefore real. Does it make any difference that, as Finnis says, the basic values are good for any and every person?[22] This is too weak, for the fact that certain things are potentially good for each person only ensures that the goods are primary or basic. But primary goods could be radically competitive in structure, such as power or wealth. These are good for 'any and every person' but pose no first-order co-ordination problem; there may be primary goods without a common good in this sense. Perhaps some work is done by the claim that 'each of these [basic] values is itself a "common good" inasmuch as it can be participated in by an inexhaustible number of persons in an inexhaustible variety of ways or on an inexhaustible variety of occasions.'[23] While this might imply that the basic goods are never fully realized, it can also be taken to mean that there is no scarcity or competition in them. How plausible is this? It may be true for some of them, but is more dubious in the case of others. Certainly over the elements of what Finnis calls the 'framework conditions' for a reasonable social order—such as a system of education, management of natural resources, a scheme of justiciable rights, and so on—scarcity and competition seem endemic. At this point we must return to his view that in the long run pursuit of basic goods there is a sharing of aim among persons, and that any radical competition is finally illusory. In the last analysis, we are all in it together.

In distinction to the Humean idea of common interest as updated in the CP model's notion of mutual gain, Finnis offers an updating of the Aristotelian and Thomist picture of a deeply shared common fate, grounded in a plurality of objective common values. Neither is quite acceptable as it stands: the former is too cavalier about observable conflict, and the latter has difficulties in sustaining the structural claims. This problem is a deep one, but as our concern in this chapter is normative theory rather than value theory I shall say little more about the possibility of a common good.[24] To give some backbone to the arguments which follow, however,

[22] Ibid. 155; cf. 168.

[23] Ibid. 155.

[24] For further remarks, see my 'Law, Co-ordination, and the Common Good'.

we may assume that it lies either in such narrow-gauge concerns as uniform traffic regulations, money, and weights and measures, or in very broad ones like a joint interest in some fair framework of legal rights and duties whose content is none the less underdetermined by reason alone. Obviously, one who finds the former too limited or the latter too vague to ground the authority of the state will in that measure find conventionalism less plausible.

5. UNANIMITY OR AUTHORITY

If a common good exists, then we may justify authority instrumentally if we can show that social relations with its distinctive features are necessary to attaining that end. Steven Lukes accurately describes the conventionalist conception of authority thus: 'Here authority is the solution to a predicament: a collectivity of individuals wish to engage in some common activity or activities but cannot agree on what is to be done. Co-ordinated action is necessary but unachievable if everyone follows his own judgement.'[25] Why should we believe, however, that the surrender of judgement—part of the very concept of authority—*is* needed to co-ordinate action?

Perhaps there are no other alternatives. Yet this is not so in general. It is quite normal for customs and conventions to emerge in CP situations and most real CPs (fashions, etiquette, finding lost friends, and so on) are in fact solved without authority. Why does the same not hold for those instances of co-ordination needed in political life? Finnis has offered an argument to the point. He says that, 'There are, in the final analysis, only two ways of making a choice between alternative ways of co-ordinating action to the common purpose or common good of any group. There must be either unanimity, or authority. There are no other possibilities.'[26] The contractarian alternative of securing co-ordination by explicit agreement is ruled out since the exchange of promises presupposes unanimity (at the very least on the rule that promises should be kept) and a unilateral promise is said not

[25] S. Lukes, 'Power and Authority', in T. Bottomore and R. Nisbet, eds., *A History of Sociological Analysis* (London: Heinemann, 1979), 642.

[26] J. Finnis, *Natural Law and Natural Rights*, 232.

to be binding unless accepted by the promisee. The next step is to discredit unanimity in any open-ended political community, especially one incorporating some autonomy for particular groups and individuals, where people are fallible in practical reasoning, and where there is legitimate diversity of interests and life plans.

The argument takes this form:

(1) to solve a CP one needs some way to choose between admissible equilibria;
(2) there are only two ways to choose: (a) unanimity or (b) authority;
(3) unanimity is impractical (and therefore unreasonable) in politics;
(4) so, authority is needed.

I have already said in Chapter 2 that, as a method of social choice, the unanimity rule has grave disadvantages: it imposes huge transaction costs on the parties, for the agreement of all is sometimes impossible and always difficult to attain. This is particularly true in the case contemplated, so premiss (3) seems secure. Let us now consider the dilemma to which that result is applied, namely, the claim that authority is the only alternative to unanimity. One might suppose that there are many other methods of social choice worth considering. Take, for example, simple majority rule. Is that not an alternative between unanimity and authority? Here, Finnis's argument holds good. It cannot be; for how would we effectively establish majority rule? Either it would have to be the product of a prior unanimous social choice yielding that rule or it would have to be authoritatively imposed. Clearly, this analysis applies to other social choice mechanisms as well, thus making (2) seem quite plausible. But will it, more particularly, apply also to customary or conventional regulation? The extension is tempting. Strictly speaking, of course, to settle on an alternative by convention does not require unanimity, but only a substantial convergence of opinion. But let that pass. There is a more important objection to the relevance of the dilemma posed in (2). The true-sounding first premiss actually conceals an ambiguity which infects the whole line of argument. From which point of view is it true that 'one needs' a way to choose between possible solutions? Whose need is this? It might be, in conformity with the previous remarks, the community which needs such a way as a matter of social choice. If so, then the rest follows. On the other hand, (1) may not refer to a social choice problem at all, but rather to a problem of individual choice: each agent needs some ground on which to choose. So understood, however the dilemma does not arise. Each chooses only for himself, although he succeeds only if most others choose as he does. The problem of individual choice is one of choosing as others do. While it might be true, nothing in the above argument shows that we need *any* sort of social choice mechanism to do this, for there may be some feature, clear to all, which renders one alternative salient. Finnis, in contrast, does see (1) as stating a problem of social choice, for he tries to establish the existence of a common good by taking the point of view of 'a legislator or judge, considering the problems of social order generically'.[27] The reason for taking that standpoint is to block the sceptical suggestion that social conflict is ultimate and thus there is no common good. Now, it is true that a legislator or judge must secure the agreement of all or act authoritatively. But to understand the problem in this way, as a matter for someone adjudicating or legislating an alternative for a whole community, is just to see it from the point of view of an authority. No individual in the CP, however, need take this point of view. Each tries to co-ordinate his own behaviour with that of others on the basis of what expectations he predicts will be generally shared. Each decides whether *he* will wear a lounge suit or dinner jacket, drive on the right or left, say 'isn't' or 'ain't', require two or three witnesses to a will, and so on. He does not ask the generic question of which alternative would be best, of what the universal norm should be, unless that helps answer the individual question of what he ought to do. Where all the choices are linked through expectations, there is no need for someone to speak authoritatively, or to take the point of view of an authority. Customary regulation is thus a third alternative between authoritative imposition and unanimity. Unlike the latter, it should not be understood as a

[27] Ibid. 255.

mode of social choice at all. Co-ordination is a problem of individual choice in a strategic context. To take the alternative view, and interpret (1) as a thesis about social choice, is already to see the solution to the CP as something to be agreed upon, enforced, adjudicated, or imposed rather than as something evolving or emerging from the nesting of shared expectations. It is to assume rather than show that authority is needed. The argument thus fails. To show that authority is needed one must establish, not merely that unanimity is an unacceptable method of social choice, but also that non-authoritative means of establishing conventional solutions are unlikely to succeed.

6. AUTHORITY AND THE CREATION OF CONVENTIONS

Let us be clear about the aim of conventionalism. It is not supposed to offer an analysis of what authority *is*, but a justification for why it is needed. The nature of authority is explained as in Chapter 2. The nature of conventions has been explained in this chapter. What we now require is a way to show that authority is needed to establish conventions which serve the common good.

Joseph Raz has offered an argument of the correct form. There are, he says, at least two ways of justifying authority: by the special knowledge of those whose utterances are to be regarded as authoritative, or by 'the requirements of social cooperation'.[28] When we cannot check the soundness of advice or opinion we must either disregard it or follow it without checking. The latter is justified 'if we are certain of the adviser's motives and if we trust his knowledge and judgement better than our own.'[29] Note that this is only a partial surrender of judgement; while we cannot evaluate the advice we can and should evaluate the other reasons relevant to treating it as authoritative. Raz concludes that, 'in many cases we must either forgo the advantages of relying on the knowledge and judgment of others or regard their views as exclusionary reasons.' Having already said in Chapter 2 that political authority is primarily practical rather than theoretical

[28] J. Raz, *Practical Reason and Norms*, 63.
[29] Ibid.

I will not pursue this line further. It is, however, closely related in structure to another argument for authority. 'A similar line of reasoning', Raz says, 'will apply to authority based on the need to co-ordinate the action of several people. *All political authority rests on this foundation* (though not only on it).'[30] He writes:

> Our purpose is to show that if authority is to be justified by the requirements of co-ordination we must regard authoritative utterances as exclusionary reasons. The proof is contained in the classical analysis of authority. Authority can secure co-ordination only if the individuals concerned defer to its judgement and do not act on the balance of reasons, but on the authority's instructions. This guarantees that all will participate in one plan of action, that action will be co-ordinated. But it requires that people should regard authoritative utterances as exclusionary reasons, as reasons for not acting on the balance of reasons as they see it, even when they are right. To accept authority on these grounds is not to act irrationally or arbitrarily. The need for authority may well be founded in reason. But the reasons are of a special kind. They establish the need to regard authoritative utterances as exclusionary reasons.[31]

To establish fully that this concept of co-ordination is the same as ours, we need to show that it excludes situations in which valuable conventions are unstable and inherently in need of enforcement by sanctions. This is consistent with Raz's claim that 'Even a society of angels may have a need for legislative authorities to ensure co-ordination.'[32] Furthermore, he says (and rightly) that sanctions provide only first-order, and not exclusionary, reasons to obey the law. If law depended on coercion and sanctions to guide behaviour, then it would not be authoritative, for authority is a method of co-ordinating behaviour *without* resort to either advice or coercion. This, however, is simply entailed by both theories; it does not establish their equivalence. There is stronger evidence in his endorsement of the conventionalist thesis when arguing against the recognitional account of authority, namely, the conception of authority as giving reasons for *believing that* there are certain reasons for acting. This merely reduces practical to theoretical authority. Moreover, 'It is . . . unable

[30] Ibid. 64 (emphasis added).

[31] Ibid. [32] Ibid. 159.

to account for the role of authority in the solution of coordination problems. Those are problems where the interests of members of the group coincide in that, among a set of options, the members prefer that which will be followed by the bulk of the members of the group above all else.'[33] The crucial argument then follows:

> There are many such problems of great importance to the orderly conduct of any society. A wise man can tell me which options belong to that set, but he cannot tell me which of the set to choose before it is known what the others will do. Sometimes that can be known on the basis of existing facts. Many people are likely to believe that many will choose a particular option and therefore they will choose it themselves: hence, one has reason to follow them and choose it as well. Sometimes, however, there is no option in the designated set that will be the obvious choice. In such cases, what one needs is something that will make a particular option the one to follow. This is something practical authorities often do (or attempt to do). They designate one of the options as the one to be chosen and, if their action is regarded as a reason to adopt that course of action, then a successful resolution of the problem is found.[34]

One could scarcely hope for a clearer statement of the conventionalist justification than this. It is instructive to compare it with a line of argument suggested by Finnis. Raz has in mind actual co-ordination problems, whereas Finnis applies similar reasoning to explain the social function of law in solving a counterfactual, deep, or generic problem of establishing some fair framework within which to pursue our reasonable plans of life where a variety of frameworks would do. On such foundations, Finnis argues that, 'The ultimate basis of a ruler's authority is the fact that he has the opportunity, and thus the responsibility, of furthering the common good by stipulating solutions to a community's co-ordination problems.'[35] Furthermore the ruler's stipulations are claimed to be binding:

> In any event, authority is useless for the common good unless the stipulations of those in authority (or which emerge through the formation of authoritative customary rules) are treated as exclusionary

[33] J. Raz, 'Authority and Consent', *Virginia Law Review* 67 (1981), 108.
[34] Ibid. 108–9. Cf. J. Raz, *The Morality of Freedom*, ch. 3.
[35] J. Finnis, *Natural Law and Natural Rights*, 351.

reasons, i.e. as sufficient reason for acting notwithstanding that the subject would not himself have made the same stipulation and indeed considers the actual stipulation to be in some respect(s) unreasonable, not fully appropriate for the common good.[36]

At least on the issue of law's co-ordinative function and its role in the justification of political authority, Raz the positivist and Finnis the natural lawyer seem to be in broad agreement.

7. THE NECESSITY FOR AUTHORITY

Let us distinguish two theses about the value of authority for the purposes of establishing conventions for co-ordination. Authority might be a necessary condition of co-ordination, or it might be a sufficient condition. If it were necessary then it would be of value as a necessary means to a valued end. If, on the other hand, authority were only sufficient, then its value would depend on whatever it is that makes authority preferred to other sufficient conditions for solving the problem. Both Raz and Finnis accept the stronger thesis: an authority can solve a CP only if his requirements have exclusionary force. Finnis says that otherwise they would be 'useless'; Raz says that 'Authority can secure co-ordination *only if* the individuals concerned defer'. Let us begin with this claim.

For authority to be a necessary condition for a solution it would have to be the case that (1) there is a CP, (2) authority is capable of solving it, and (3) it is not possible to solve it otherwise. Are these requirements met? The truth of (1) has already been supposed for the sake of argument by assuming the existence of a common good. Condition (2) is obviously sound: if an authority's utterance does make one of the options the one that each expects all to follow (i.e., if it makes that option *salient*) then the problem is indeed solved. (However, where there are *n* permissible options, the authority must be able to exclude $n-1$, and that is perhaps expecting a lot. Often, he may just narrow it down to two or three, and then each follows the one he thinks best on balance.) The important assumption, however, is (3). Is there any way to show that authority is a unique solution to certain problems?

36 Ibid. 351–2.

Raz says that there are cases where one alternative cannot be singled out on the basis of 'existing facts'. That would seem to be one case where authority is needed to create salience. But what sort of things should we include in the class of existing facts? We cannot say, 'any fact not dependent upon authoritative utterances', for that makes authority uniquely able to solve such problems, but only by definition. 'Existing facts' might mean 'facts not dependent upon actions intended to solve the problem'. For example, the fact that most people are *right*-handed might be enough to start a convention of driving on the right. But the complement class (of non-existing facts) is quite heterogeneous, for exercise of authority is not the only action which might be intended to solve the problem. In particular, people might agree or promise to follow a particular alternative. Quite apart from the presence of any other reasons for keeping promises, the bare *fact* that they promised now makes that alternative salient, even where there was no reason to promise to follow it. This cannot be considered an existing fact, for it came about only with action aimed at solving the problem. Perhaps Raz is thinking only of cases where there are no existing facts, however trivial, and no practical possibility of fact-creating actions apart from authoritative utterances. This might be the case if, for example, the problem has to be solved too quickly to permit deliberation and agreement, and if there are no other cues prominent enough to yield reliable and shared expectations. It is not easy, however, to find examples with these characteristics. A good one, if a bit contrived, is due to Edna Ullmann-Margalit:

There is a large crowded hall, and there is a large crowd of people gathered outside it. There are four doors, one at each corner of the hall. Due to some emergency, all the people inside are to be replaced by all the people waiting outside in a hurry, say within five minutes. A general scramble is of course to be anticipated, tramplings and disorder; it is also quite likely that the crowd exchange will not be achieved within the specified time. However, the situation could be resolved if someone managed to take the initiative and scream loud and clear 'North and South doors—EXITS, East and West doors—ENTRANCE.' As soon as this pronouncement is made, and provided that everyone expects the others to have heard it, each person has a good reason to obey: even if the closest door to me, an insider, is the eastern one it is still in my own interest to try to move towards either north or south. Everyone is interested in a state of general compliance with this pronouncement; moreover, given that there *is* general compliance with it no one can benefit by individually behaving differently.[37]

Suppose the pronouncement would have solved the problem. Would it have done so authoritatively? In so doing would the person who uttered it have become an authority? According to the arguments of Raz and Finnis, he would. But that means that the utterance provides content-independent and exclusionary reason to choose North and South as exits, and East and West as entrances. That it would be content-independent is easily seen, for the convention established would be arbitrary: under a suitable description, the utterance is a reason for choosing an alternative without regard to the nature of the alternative chosen. Does it also provide a reason for choosing the specified door and a reason for not acting on the reasons for choosing any other door? In this example there are at least six possible, useful, stable, and arbitrary rules; six conventions would have done. That means that the utterance must exclude reasons for acting on the other five. Now, while it may have had this effect, it need not have. And, most importantly, without having any exclusionary or binding force, the utterance would still have solved the problem. The reasoning is as follows.

By shouting the command, the person in the example made one of the alternatives salient, that is, brought it about that there was a shared expectation, perhaps at several levels, that it was the one that would be chosen by most or all. Certainly some such cue was needed, for there were no existing facts in the example, nor any time for promises or agreements. However, by issuing the command, the person *altered* what it would be reasonable to do on balance. Given a generally shared expectation that one alternative will be followed, there is no longer any appeal whatsoever in going to the wrong door, for in doing so one would be swimming against the tide

[37] E. Ullmann-Margalit, 'Is Law a Co-ordinative Authority?', *Israel Law Review* 16 (1981), 350–1. She writes in reply to C. Gans, 'The Normativity of Law and its Co-ordinative Function', *Israel Law Review* 16 (1981), 333–49.

which, by hypothesis, one has no interest in doing. But note: these non-options (i.e., those which are not salient) leave no practical trace—one does not hanker after them, and they exert no residual attraction from any point of view; they are simply outweighed. To achieve an equilibrium by appealing to or creating a conventional norm, one need only act on the balance of first-order reasons. Even in the absence of existing facts, one can solve CP just by providing ordinary reasons in favour of one of the alternatives. One could suggest, advise, persuade, or threaten the others to follow it. Each would act rationally in weighing the likelihood of the rest following that option, O_1, as opposed to any of $O_2, \ldots O_n$. Where there is no existing reason to choose any of them over the others, and a first-order reason is then given to choose O_1, it follows that there is some reason to choose O_1 and no reason to choose $O_2 \ldots O_n$. If all other options are outweighed, then O_1 will enjoy general compliance. Hence, equilibrium can be secured without authority.

Someone might object as follows: viewing the proposed solution as binding to the exclusion of the others would increase the reliability of the others following it (since they would regard themselves as bound to), so authoritative norms and utterances would have an evolutionary advantage over non-binding conventional norms. Being more likely to succeed on any given occasion they are more likely, by force of precedent and salience, to be followed the next time and will thus come to predominate as a mode of guiding behaviour in situations like the one described. Two replies may be offered: (1) It is true that doubts about differential weighting of the options by all other parties would vanish with the emergence of an authority. But doubts about differential scope restrictions (i.e., about the kinds of reasons to be excluded) would arise. Problems of vagueness and the interpretation of rules would therefore mean that expectations about others' behaviour will still be less than certain. There is no a priori reason to think that doubts about weight are more serious than doubts about the scope of rules. (2) Recall that authority is needed, according to this view, because there are no *other* salient clues to follow (i.e., no pre-existing facts and no way to create new ones non-authoritatively). But in that case, exactly what is supposed to be excluded? Not anything that would validly have counted as a first-order reason, for by hypothesis there are none. The point of binding commitments in general is to insulate our practical reasoning against valid considerations on which there is reason not to act. If there are no such reasons, then the resort to commitments of that kind is unnecessary. Thus, there is no reason to think that authoritative norms will enjoy an evolutionary advantage over other types, because there is no environmental characteristic which favours them.

A conventionalist might, however, further object that while the existence of a CP always provides some reason for conformity it may not provide an overriding reason. Each may still have preferences among the possible outcomes such that authoritative requirements are needed to single out a particular one. But this plays fast and loose with the description of the problem. If contrary preferences are strong enough to outweigh preferences for conformity, then there is no common interest strong enough to create a CP and the problem will instead be one of bargaining or arbitration, the outcome of which depends on threat advantage or considerations of fairness. Neither of these provides a conventionalist justification for authority. If, on the other hand, conflict of interest is less than the interest in conformity, the problem remains one of co-ordination, but the above arguments against the necessity of authority hold. Either way, the introduction of conflicting interests does not help.

8. THE SUFFICIENCY OF AUTHORITY

Perhaps the conventionalist thesis is being assessed too stringently here. Even if authority is not necessary to solve CPs, it might be sufficient. And even if its solution is not dominant (best no matter what) it might be reasonable or permissible. To rely on authority in such circumstances does not violate the plausible principle of practical reasoning that one ought never to act for a reason which is defeated (i.e., outweighed or excluded).[38] However, that principle is purely

[38] For this principle and its defence see J. Raz, *Practical Reason and Norms*, ch. 1.

formal and not sufficient to ensure that it is reasonable to rely on authority, since the error in overcommitment is not one of acting for defeated reasons, but of being more tightly bound to a person or standard than is warranted by the point of commitment. In a CP, the point is individualistic and instrumental. Each aims at his best (and that may include anything from self-interest to the value of co-ordination for its own sake), subject to his expectations about the actions of others. But I have already argued that each can attain his best without being committed, since authority is not a necessary condition of achieving co-ordination. Is the overcommitment thus involved in treating conventional standards as authoritative, or treating as authorities those with the power to create them, a serious error in practical reasoning, or merely an excess of caution? Perhaps in a one-off case (like Ullmann-Margalit's example) overcommitment would have few adverse effects—though it might mean that, say, an optimal solution was bypassed. However, in any regularly repeated situation, where precedent and convention do give cues for solution, authority's potential for harm is greater. To be committed to conventional solutions as a result of someone's utterances, is to be bound to them, and in CP situations this will introduce unattractive and pointless rigidities. As environmental conditions change, an ordinary convention can be expected to change too; it has dynamic and evolutionary potential. A country which drives on the left may begin to drive on the right when its neighbours do and if there is increased traffic between them. Or consider the rules governing property holdings. If these are conventional regularities (a dubious assumption, perhaps) they could be expected to change as the dominant modes of production do. The set of property rules governing land could be expected to differ from the salient set of rules governing copyright or joint stock companies. To treat these rules as authoritatively binding will make them less responsive to exogenous change. It is true that they cannot be up for renegotiation at every moment, or they will not serve their purpose. But if they really are conventions in the interests of each, then the stability of the social environment will generate all the stability to which they are entitled (assuming that their point is to moderate conflicts of interest under scarcity, or to provide a stock of value, or to create a means of exchange, and not to be a brake on social change; if the latter is the case, they are almost certainly not conventional).

To think that convention could be a source of authority is to mistake the special characteristics of each. Indeed, it is a major function of authority in political systems not to solve first-order CPs, but to *prevent* them from being solved, or to *impose* non-conventional solutions. Laws against cartels, trusts, and other forms of price-fixing may be justified as attempts to destabilize conventional solutions to the fixers' CPs. Other laws seek to replace conventional solutions with authoritative ones preferred on grounds of efficiency or justice—one might think of Sweden's switch to driving on the right, or Canada's shift from imperial to metric measurements, or legislation permitting children to receive their mother's surname. Of course, many conventionalists argue that it is not such first-order CPs, but rather more general ones, which ground the theory. Not only the content of law, but to a certain extent even its form is underdetermined by reason alone, and thus some conventional element is always present. For instance, the final power to resolve social disputes must reside somewhere and its location is partly arbitrary—with us the courts, with others the priests. But this harmless truism does not carry us very far, for the location of final authority is only *partly* arbitrary and that is the least interesting and least important part of the explanation of why we allocate it to the law courts. The important part is that we accept the complex cluster of values associated with the rule of law. If the arguments I have adduced are sound, then the observation that law is something less than wholly rational does little to sustain conventionalism about its authority.

9. THE NORMATIVITY OF LAW

This argument has a further consequence. A major task of legal theory is to explain the 'normativity' of law—how is it that law can (claim to) be an action-guiding institution? But if this is among our aims, the arguments of this chapter suggest that one would do well to steer clear of a conventionalist analysis of it. Law always claims authority, and conventional rules are not validly authoritative. This is surely a disappointment, for in other respects the co-ordination theory of convention seems to have great promise in uniting two features of law that have been uneasy companions in other theories: laws purport to guide action but they are, in some sense, matters of social fact; they are both normative and positive. The appeal of conventionalism, as Gerald Postema, one of its most careful defenders, puts it, is that 'this notion of convention, when properly understood, successfully bridges the gap between social fact and genuine obligation—reconciling the two theses—because a convention is both a social fact *and* a framework of reasons for action.'[39] This is true, but it is not sufficient. This version of conventionalism suffers the same problem as do sanction-based theories of legal duty: it explains how the law guides action, but it explains it the wrong way.[40] Sanctions provide only ordinary reasons to act, in other words, reasons which must be weighed in the balance along with other competing claims. Sanctions are needed precisely to motivate those who *reject* the exclusionary force of legal reasons, that is, they are needed to outweigh considerations (such as self-interest) which those people will not exclude. But conventions are in no better position for, as I argued above, they too provide only ordinary reasons for compliance. This has an important upshot. If law were only a matter of social convention, then its claims to authority would be fraudulent. And, if the co-ordination theory of convention is taken to be the appropriate account of the existence of social rules, then it follows that no legitimate legal system is simply a system of social rules.

Conventionalism also fails to account for the judicial obligation to identify and apply those rules which meet the legal system's ultimate criterion of validity. In H. L. A. Hart's theory, this criterion is the rule of recognition—a customary norm of the officials that directs them to treat only certain things as sources of law. A grossly over-simple example would

[39] G. Postema, 'Coordination and Convention at the Foundations of Law', *Journal of Legal Studies* 11 (1982), 165–203. See also C. Gans, 'The Normativity of Law and its Co-ordinative Function'.

[40] J. Raz, *Practical Reason and Norms*, 161–2.

be the rule that whatever the Queen in Parliament enacts is law. The existence of such a rule is a matter of social fact, but when it exists it functions as a normative standard for judicial behaviour. It justifies the application of legal rules but if it is challenged itself, Hart suggests, legal justifications come to an end, for the judges can only point to the brute, inert fact of their professional habit.[41] As many critics have seen, however, this threatens the normativity of law and appears *ad hoc*. If the answer 'this is just how we do things' is sufficient reply to serious questions of constitutional legitimacy, then why not also to doubts about all other rules? Why ever appeal to the rule of recognition?

Postema sees Hart's theory as requiring a somewhat different answer: 'At bottom, his claim is that the authority of criteria of validity ultimately rests not on the justice, correctness, or truth of the criteria as a matter of critical morality, but rather on convention.'[42] And the theory of co-ordination problems, he argues, explains just how these social conventions come to have normative force, for in that strategic context, mere predictive expectations of others' behaviour become deontic expectations when backed up by obligations based on principles of fairness or detrimental reliance. Judicial duty is explained by this strategic context. Law is a public, rule-based, and reason-giving means of helping citizens solve their co-ordination problems. But for the rules to be understood and followed, there must be shared interpretations between the officials and subjects, and this also depends on co-ordination. Postema further claims that the need for coherence among officials presents another CP of settling on common criteria for identifying and applying law. Moreover, citizens are entitled to expect this kind of coherence from an institution which claims authority over them and induces expectations about its own behaviour, and a correlate of their entitlement is the judicial duty to apply the law to the case at bar. The rule of recognition is not therefore simply a static fact about judicial behaviour, but a dynamic response to a continuing and complex problem of general co-ordination, and one which imposes genuine obligations on its subjects.

[41] H. L. A. Hart, *The Concept of Law*, 102–5.

[42] G. Postema, 'Coordination and Convention at the Foundations of Law', 171.

There are two reasons for thinking that this ingenious argument is inadequate as a theory of judicial duty. In the first place, for the reasons already given, the demands of co-ordination neither necessitate nor warrant treating derived conventions as authoritative. This is not to deny that in such strategic contexts there is reason to follow the rule of recognition. But that was never a mystery anyway. Given the facts of professional ethics, self-interest, and the fear of sanctions, it would be surprising if judges and citizens were not motivated by the law. The point is that neither this nor its ability to co-ordinate activity justifies treating law as authoritatively binding. Does it help to introduce the notion of detrimental reliance, that citizens rely on judges behaving in regular ways and thus judges are duty-bound to continue so to behave? This would indeed create obligations of the right form. But here the difficulty is that the existence of the convention is nothing more than one explanation of why such an expectation takes root and citizens come to rely on judicial behaviour. The validity and nature of the judicial duty is not accounted for by the convention, but by the principle of detrimental reliance. The convention helps us locate the duty, to discover which judicial practices it applies to, but not to explain it. Secondly, it is an immediate consequence of Postema's theory that judicial duty to follow the rule of recognition depends wholly on the inability to change it, and this inability means lack of brute causal power, not want of normative capacity. An opinion leader who can change conventions is not bound by them, in fact or in principle. (That is why high class people who dress outlandishly are thought to be *avant garde*, while low class ones are merely ridiculous.) This would not matter if legal rules, including the rule of recognition, were impervious to the behaviour of individual judges, but they are not. The legal system is quite unlike the perfectly competitive market in which prices must be taken by each agent as given. Rather, differences in causal power are built into the legal system, increasing as one moves up the hierarchy of courts, and varying with judicial personality and prestige. But the duty to apply and interpret the law is not correlated with any of these attributes. It does not bear more lightly on higher courts than on lower, or more lightly on clever and popular judges than on dim and obscure ones.

I should, in conclusion, make clear that none of this is to deny the *descriptive* adequacy of the conventionalist thesis. It is quite plausible that the state does as a matter of fact play an important role in co-ordinating behaviour in the way that these writers and many others have argued. But the view that this capacity warrants subjects or officials granting it the authority it claims cannot be accepted. In essence, the reason is simple. Conventionalism presupposes that conformity with convention is always conditional: each should conform if and only if he expects the others to do the same. When he does expect this, he has no reason to do anything else. It is part of the concept of authority, however, that it is binding. One who is bound to a standard of behaviour conforms to it unconditionally (though perhaps within limits). Common to all forms of practical commitment is their capacity to insulate agents from conditional, calculating allegiances. If the only value of the state's authority were that attributable to useful conventions, then it could never validly claim allegiance of this form.

Doubtless there is some sense in which conventionalism about the foundations of authority is true, for political life, as part of human thought and practice, is neither divinely guaranteed, naturally imposed, nor transcendentally presupposed. This conventionalist thesis is a flabby one; it merely reaffirms a sort of humanism while exhibiting a lack of sentimentality about authority. These may be healthy attitudes, at least in our societies, but they do not stake out an interesting justificatory thesis. About that we can be more definite. Citizens who treat the law as authoritative cannot validly view it as merely conventional; those who treat it as conventional are wrong to view it as authoritative. In this central sense, its authority cannot be founded on convention.

5

THE SOCIAL CONTRACT

In the last chapter, we saw that one account of the role of authority in promoting common interests could not be sustained. But the conventionalist view is not the only way of specifying the general idea that authority relations are needed to serve social co-operation, and the appeal and familiarity of that idea in the history of political thought encourages us to look for some other way of rendering the fundamental intuition. The present chapter investigates another alternative: the notion that authority is something that rational people would agree to in order to solve certain problems of collective action associated with the production of beneficial public goods.

1. WHAT IS CONTRACTARIANISM?

The image of the social contract has enjoyed wider historical and political appeal than have the assumptions underlying contractarianism as a distinctive philosophical position. Rousseau's *Social Contract*, for instance, rests on an argument which is neither instrumental nor individualistic enough to merit the title. Locke's political theory comes closer to the ideal type, although it is better seen as a version of the more general theory of consent. Kant, in explicitly detaching the notion of the social contract from the doctrine of actual consent, and Hobbes, in rendering the notion of rationality in a particularly thin form, are nearer what I have in mind. In any event, the goal here is not to retrace the history of contractarian ideas, but to examine them in one influential contemporary form.

A contractarian argument attempts to show that authority would be agreed to by rational persons in the initial position of the state of nature. This initial position has certain affinities to the context of a co-ordination problem, but should be sharply distinguished from it. Like the CP, this is a situation in which common action could yield mutual benefits to the parties; unlike it, such action is not self-sustaining but rather is inherently fragile and unstable. It is not an equilibrium strategy in the sense of Chapter 4. A contractarian seeks to justify the authority of the state as a means to, or perhaps a substitute for, equilibrium. Whereas the problem of co-ordination is largely one of information, of providing or establishing a signal which renders one alternative salient, the problem of the social contract is one of motivation: the parties know which actions will be mutually beneficial and which mutually harmful, but are not adequately motivated to perform them. One major weakness of the conventionalist position is thus overcome. Recall that the notion of the common good seems obscure on conventionalist reasoning: at the ordinary empirical level there is too much apparent conflict and it is difficult to find a convincing argument for deeper commonalities of interest. This problem is grist to the contractarian's mill, for precisely what he expects to find is conflicting interests of a particular sort.

David Gauthier prefers to characterize contractarians in a broader way,[1] counting as members all those whose arguments for social institutions appeal to mutual advantage. Whereas a utilitarian would argue, for example, that a desirable system of property maximizes the *sum* of advantages for all relevant persons, the contractarian test would be whether it benefits *each* person; the thrust is distributive rather than aggregative. This is, however, only a necessary condition of contractarian thinking. Although it adequately distinguishes between utilitarianism and contractarianism, it does not distinguish between the latter and conventionalism, nor even between contractarianism and certain rights-based theories which also address their appeal to individual interests rather than to sums but which understand 'advantage' in a different way. Moreover, Gauthier's suggestion would count as contractarian all who appeal to the Pareto criterion, for it too is a principle of mutual advantage. Perhaps it is not wrong to prescribe such a usage, but it is not as sensitive as the present one. It also has some counter-intuitive consequences, such as rendering Hume a contractarian, and this only invites confusion.

[1] D. Gauthier, 'David Hume, Contractarian', *Philosophical Review* 88 (1979), 3–38.

Thus, I will take contractarianism to be the view that the initial position is the unstable one described above, and that in that context we should frame political arguments to appeal to mutual advantage in accordance with an instrumental theory of reason and a subjective conception of value. On this view, contractarianism is a social theory, committed to certain theses about the nature of the social world as well as to certain theses about practical reason: it supposes that the 'state of nature' is a collective action problem and that agents are rational and self-interested in the sense described in Chapter 4. Since, however, the nature of their motivation is central to this argument, it may now be useful to consider it in a little more detail.

A general problem with theories of rationality which are grounded in self-interest is knowing exactly what interpretation to give the latter. Since all interests are the interests of some self, there is a trivial sense in which any action can be said to be in self-interest. Typically, however, social scientists have sought to give the idea some explanatory power by giving the notion some content. Often they assume that people generally seek to increase their personal wealth, prestige, and power. It is surprising—dispiriting in fact—to see just how well such an unappealing model often works. But it cannot claim full generality as an explanatory theory and has little or no appeal as the foundation for a normative theory. As one of the early marginalists realized, it is not such personal egoism but rather 'non-tuism' which characterizes even economic behaviour. Since people may desire even wealth for altruistic reasons, it is to a particular kind of relationship, not a particular set of aims, that we should look: 'If you and I are conducting a transaction which on my side is purely economic, I am furthering your purposes, partly or wholly perhaps for my own sake, perhaps entirely for the sake of others, but certainly not for your sake. What makes it an economic transaction is that I am not considering you except as a link in the chain, or considering your desires except as the means by which I may gratify those of someone else—not necessarily myself.'[2] Thus the egoistic motive in which I consider myself

[2] P. H. Wicksteed, *The Common Sense of Political Economy*, ed. L. Robbins (London: Routledge, 1933), I. 174.

alone should be distinguished from the economic relationship in which I may consider the interests of anyone but you.

But an even thinner version of rationality is available without quite lapsing into vacuity. For even if I take satisfaction of your desires as my end, we can still appraise my pursuit of them in terms of efficiency and consistency. Accordingly, we can call behaviour rational irrespective of the content of its aims. Each individual is conceived to have subjective goals whose satisfaction he desires efficiently to achieve, but these goals may have any content. It is this notion which the modern theory of utility seeks to describe and measure. It begins with the bare concept of *preferring* one alternative to another.[3] Consistency conditions strong enough to yield a weak ordering among all alternatives are then imposed, and this ordering is cardinalized by relying on further assumptions about choices between lotteries (i.e., probability distributions over pairs of alternatives). The result is a function associating the ordered set of outcomes with real numbers. That scale we may call a *utility function.* Note that *whatever* is preferred is assigned a higher utility number; one alternative is not preferred to another because it has a higher utility. And since value is exhausted by utility there is reason to pursue one alternative rather than another only if it has higher utility, that is, if it is more preferred.

To this conception of value we add the idea of reason as maximization. To act rationally is to maximize one's utility, subject perhaps to certain quantitative constraints.[4] The rational actor prefers more to less. When outcomes are certain he pursues the one with the higher utility; when they are risky he pursues the one with the highest expected utility, that is, the highest utility after discounting by the probability of receiving it. When a course of action leads to several exclusively alternative outcomes, its expected utility is the sum of the expected utilities of those outcomes.

What then is mutual interest? In general terms, it is a state of affairs which benefits everyone. A utilitarian will approve a situation in which the total benefits outweigh the total losses.

[3] For a useful introduction, see R. D. Luce and H. Raiffa, *Games and Decisions*, ch. 2.

[4] That is, constraints such as budget lines, and not normative prohibitions such as Robert Nozick's 'side constraints'.

In contrast, appealing to the regulative idea that a rational person would not agree to any policy which made her worse off, the contractarian holds that we should approve a situation if and only if each person is made better off. More weakly, if we suppose that rational persons are not motivated by envy, we can say that they will veto a situation only if it makes them worse off. Hence, we can regard some state of affairs as *optimal* if and only if departure from it will make at least one person worse off. (If there is more than one such state of affairs, then they cannot be compared with respect to optimality.) This reflects the intuitive contractarian idea that each person is to be regarded as having a veto over social policy.

Among theories satisfying these criteria we may draw a further distinction. *Unrestricted contractarians* hold that all social and political relationships are to be analysed and justified along contractarian lines and that human nature is entirely given pre-socially. Hobbes and certain neo-classical economists are the best examples here. In contrast, *restricted contractarians*, such as Locke and John Rawls, typically limit the scope of their arguments to political relationships and only some moral notions while allowing that other aspects of human nature and moral life are not accounted for by the rationality of hypothetical agreement. It is a nice question whether restricted contractarianism can be made coherent. Here, however, I avoid that issue by considering only unrestricted versions of the theory, free from the complicating influences of natural law or intuitions about intrinsically fair original positions. That would be a risky strategy if our main interest were in the theory of justice, but bearing in mind that we are only assessing the justifiability of authority in reasonably just states, we can simplify the discussion somewhat.

Finally, I want to set aside the vexed question of whether a theory resembling the one just sketched can give an adequate analysis of our central moral concepts and judgements.[5] That task would require showing that all moral principles serve the mutual advantage of rational persons and showing how morality differs from sophisticated forms of prudence or, if it does not, why we do not believe that it does not. Those who

[5] Interested readers should consult D. Gauthier, *Morals by Agreement* (Oxford: Clarendon Press, 1986).

accept contractarianism as a kind of moral theory will regard the arguments assessed here as moral arguments; those who do not will see them as having some other function, perhaps as general and abstract economic arguments in favour of authority. This is a matter of indifference for present purposes. However we understand the character of contractarianism, our agenda is whether it can justify the kind of authority which the modern state claims. But I must forestall one possible objection to this view. It is of the nature of authority that it purports to impose binding, content-independent reasons for action on its subjects. This fact is usually and properly described as the power of authorities to obligate their subjects. In political contexts it is evident in the claim that the enactment of a statute creates duties for citizens and officials to behave in certain ways. But if authority creates obligations, how can we entertain a form of justification which might not be moral? Are obligations not moral concepts? Or are we to suppose that 'obligation' in these contexts has some different, technical sense from when it is used in the ordinary moral argument? No such supposition is necessary. In the first place, there may well be prudential justifications for certain moral practices, even if this is not true of all. Secondly, even if one were willing to regard these obligations as having some special meaning, they would share with moral obligations certain formal features, including their binding and content-independent force. It is an important question whether contractarian arguments can account for these structural features of authority relations. I shall argue that they cannot, so that the further question of whether contractarianism can account for the peculiarly moral nature of the obligations will not arise.

2. PUBLIC GOODS AND PRISONER'S DILEMMAS

It is an interesting fact about contractarian reasoning that the general economic conception of rationality of which it is a part has had its greatest success in explaining why authority is *unnecessary* in order to attain desirable social states. While one might naïvely think that the individual pursuit of self-interest would lead to the escalation of conflict and the missing of chances to attain common interests, the great achievement of modern welfare economics has been to identify an important set of conditions under which this is not so. In particular, the competitive free market can be shown to tend towards an equilibrium, and every competitive equilibrium is an optimal point.[6] That is, acting independently and without authoritative direction, rational individuals will behave in socially optimal ways, in ways that produce outcomes to which they would all agree. This result is now so familiar that it takes a moment's reflection to remember just how extraordinary it is, and how powerful is common-sense resistance to the conclusion.

This resistance is not, however, merely the product of ignorance or ideology. For observation does suggest that purely self-interested behaviour often fails to yield harmonious outcomes in the common good. How can this be? The free market model is an idealization of reality; the mathematics is unimpeachable, but its empirical relevance questionable. A necessary condition of the optimality of free competition is that all economic effects are internal to the exchange relation, so that the price of goods fully reflects the costs of production. But there are many cases in which this is not so. Factories produce cars but in doing so also produce pollution which is a cost borne even by those who do not buy the automobiles. Cars are therefore cheaper than they ought to be. This example illustrates a negative external effect, but there are many positive ones as well. National defence benefits even those who refuse on conscientious grounds to do their share of providing it; technical innovations can improve productivity even in firms which spend little on research and development. These spill-overs, or externalities, are imposed by *public goods* which have the unusual characteristic that, in their pure form, they are *non-rival* (the quantity of them consumed by any one does not perceptibly limit the consumption by others) and *inexcludable* (if the good is provided for some it is available for others and none may feasibly be excluded from enjoying it).[7]

There are many such goods in any society: national defence, a clean environment, public health, technical innovation,

[6] See, e.g., J. Quirk and R. Saposnik, *Introduction to General Equilibrium Theory and Welfare Economics* (New York: McGraw-Hill, 1968), ch. 4.

[7] M. Peston, *Public Goods and the Public Sector* (London: Macmillan, 1972), 9–14.

saving for the future, and countless others all have significant aspects of publicity. The degree to which goods are public is variable, as are the reasons for their publicity. Many goods are only *technically* public in the sense that owing to contingent features of their production or consumption they create externalities. A loud stereo system is a public good (or bad) in an apartment with thin walls, but not in a soundproof room. It may become feasible or worthwhile to exclude people from a certain previously public good thus privatizing it. We think of clean air as a nearly pure case, but in densely populated cities gas masks and home air filtration systems would be a way of allocating it only to those who pay. And private property can itself be understood as a way of enclosing the previously public good of common property. There are other goods, however, which are necessarily constituted by their external effects and are thus *essentially* public. Aspects of friendship, or benevolence, or life in a free society are partly excludable goods which are non-rival in consumption. But to think of altering them in some way so that they could be bought and sold on the market would not only be to privatize them, but to change their natures. Friendship is just not friendship when it must be purchased.

The importance of public goods is that the general theorem stated above does not hold in their case: competitive equilibria are no longer necessarily optimal. This can be seen by considering Fig. 4, which illustrates the well-known game of Prisoner's Dilemma (PD). In the matrix, each seeks to maximize his utility by choosing whether to Co-operate (C) with the other, or to Defect (D) from co-operation. (Perhaps

	C	D
C	5 / 5	0 / 6
D	6 / 0	3 / 3

FIG. 4

they are deciding whether or not to carry a gun, or to co-operate in a scheme of voluntary petrol rationing, or whatever.) Yet each can decide only for himself and cannot influence the decision of the other, except by signalling his own move. In particular, binding agreements between the parties are not possible. In such circumstances, each does his best when the other co-operates and he defects, second best if both co-operate, third best if both defect, and worst of all if, like a sucker, he co-operates while the other defects. Both are symmetrically placed and have full knowledge of the situation. Hence, if she thinks that he will defect then she should defect in order not to be taken for a sucker; if she thinks he will co-operate, then she should defect and take a free ride. The result of each aiming at his or her best is thus that all attain their second worst. The DD outcome dominates all others since no one has any reason to choose C, no matter what the others choose. Yet notice that the CC outcome is optimal, for no departure from it could make someone better off without making another worse off. This is the dilemma.

The matrix in Fig. 4 shows a schematic two-person PD, but the forms in which we encounter such problems usually involve many people. It has been shown that public goods problems can be modelled by the many-person PD.[8] Characteristically, a certain level of co-operation is needed in order to produce the good, but the fact that it is not feasible to exclude anyone from it means that each has reason to defect, no matter what the others do. The optimal level of contribution is thus unlikely to be attained. These are examples of cases in which, as economists say, the market tends to fail. They are also cases in which authoritative provision by the state has been thought to be justified on the ground that authority relations can do what exchange relations cannot.

3. THE PRISONER'S DILEMMA DILEMMA

Before proceeding further we should make a few observations

[8] R. Hardin, 'Collective Action as an Agreeable n-Prisoners' Dilemma', *Behavioural Science* 16 (1971), 472–81; T. C. Schelling, 'Hockey Helmets, Daylight Saving, and other Binary Choices', in his *Micromotives and Macrobehavior* (New York: W. W. Norton, 1978), 213–43.

about the PD as an analytic tool. The dilemma, as I said above, is that if each agent aims at his best, all attain their second-worst. Yet this is the best that each can guarantee for himself, since whatever the others do it is always best for each to defect and thus defection dominates co-operation. But the other horn of the dilemma is that the co-operative outcome is optimal. We therefore have a forced and unpleasant choice between dominance and optimality, between individual security and mutual interests.

It is important to note three features of such situations:

(1) In the strict sense of the term, the PD has a solution: universal defection is a stable equilibrium point. When we talk about 'solving' PDs we mean attaining optimality.

(2) The PD does not always pose a problem from the point of view of social theory. That is, we do not always want to see the optimal outcome obtained. We do not want perfectly competitive firms to be successful in solving the *n*-person PD of price-fixing.

(3) The dilemma is not in a straightforward sense a paradox. Whether there is anything paradoxical about it depends on showing that both optimality and dominance are principles required by a single conception of rationality. It is possible that they are, but that requires complex argument of a kind which does not concern us here.

Now notice that, as an uninterpreted problem in the theory of games, there is not much one can say about the PD. Each does best by choosing D. Each would do better in terms of his preferences if he could choose outcomes (i.e., sets of choices for all agents) instead of alternatives, but by definition he controls only the latter. An ambiguity may emerge, however, in switching from the formal PD to an interpreted version with its prisoners, public goods consumers, law abiders, and so on. If the PD is only meant to model *one aspect* of their choice situation, then it may make sense to say new things like, 'If the optimal outcome could be enforced then each would do better', or 'Each would do better if he could trust the other', and so forth. In the formal context, however, we suppose that whatever is true of the agents and relevant to their choice is revealed in their preferences, and that the dilemma must be resolved, if it can be at all, internally by explaining how the choosers change their own situation. If we relied on a purely external dodge, such as an enforcer coming from nowhere, or a trust norm emerging without explanation, then it would simply show that the outcomes or orderings are not as the PD model supposes.

In the modest interpreted version, in contrast, it is always possible that something is true of the agents which is not true solely in virtue of the formalities of the decision problem. Consider a norm of trustworthiness. Each might reckon that optimality could be attained at a known cost in trust, and in certain circumstances such a norm might emerge and be reinforced. Yet if it is, it cannot be incorporated in the formal model, for it is never up to the agents to *choose* such a norm (or enforcers, or meta-rationality, or second-order preferences, or anything else), since that would then have to come under the theory of choice and its outcomes would have to figure in the pay-offs. If we are told to regard agents as in a PD situation, but also that defection violates a trust norm, we must decide whether such a violation changes the preference rankings or not. In the formal PD, it must count in the rankings if it is to count at all for nothing is true of the agents which is not there revealed. In an interpreted PD, on the other hand, norm-violation may be added as an incentive, provided that it is not to be encompassed by the choice theory. (Otherwise it is no help: each does best if everyone except himself is trustworthy, and a second-order PD is produced.) But, if it is not so encompassed, then the choice theory neither prescribes nor predicts the outcome, which will depend on exogenous factors.

The prisoner's dilemma poses a harsh choice between security and mutual interests; the *prisoner's dilemma dilemma* poses a choice between treating the decision theory as exhaustive of the situation or not. Either interpretation is in some circumstances useful, but one must take great care not to waver between the two and thus play fast and loose with the preference orderings. In using the tools of game theory we therefore face a dilemma regarding their use: either treat them as a comprehensive formal apparatus of known properties, or as an interpreted theory of human action subject to overriding of various sorts. An unrestricted contractarian will prefer the first horn on the ground that it gives maximal scope to his theory. He will not admit the existence of overriding motivation of a different sort; the *deus ex machina* holds no attraction for him. The contractarian view of reason and value is meant to be sufficient to the task at hand. It would plainly not do for an unrestricted contractarian to argue that authority provides an *irrational* solution to the problem of public goods.

This point is relevant to an important argument due to Amartya Sen.[9] The reason the matrix in Fig. 4 appears as a dilemma is that, from our point of view, we can see that it would be better if both Row and Column chooser had preferences other than the ones they have. That is, we would prefer that their preferences were different. Why would this point of view not be equally accessible to them? Would they not see that this matrix is an irrational game and therefore prefer to play another? It seems that a richer structure is needed even to represent the dilemma as they see it: the thought that each would do better if he had other preferences seems to suggest that he has reason to prefer other ones. In particular, compare the matrix in Fig. 4, the PD, with that in Fig. 5, which is an Assurance Game. In the latter, there are two equilibria instead of one and CC can be achieved without need for enforcement if each is assured that the other will co-operate. Sen claims that if each acted *as if* he had AG-preferences each would do better in terms of his actual PD-preferences. Hence, AG-orderings are preferred to PD-

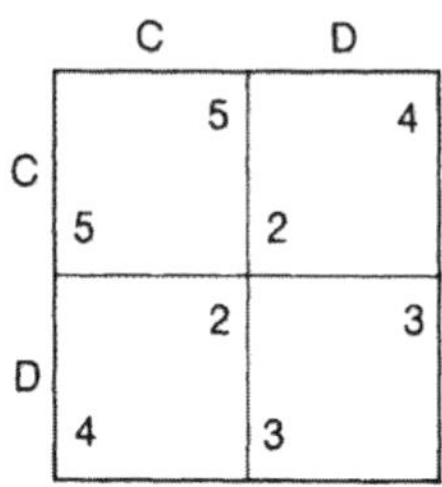

FIG. 5

[9] A. K. Sen, 'Choice, Orderings and Morality', in S. Korner, ed., *Practical Reason* (Oxford: Blackwell, 1974), 54–67.

orderings. Even the economically rational, he argues, should be able to order their preference profiles such that if X is the set of all possible outcomes and π the set of all possible orderings of the elements of X, then they should be able to take a 'moral view', defined as a quasi-ordering Q of the elements of π. Moreover, they will in this case be unanimous in their Q-orderings since each prefers AG-preferences to PD-preferences.

We must tread carefully here. The temptation to work entirely within the uninterpreted calculus of second-order preferences is strong and potentially misleading. How should relation Q be interpreted? Sen himself suggests that it means that one alternative is morally preferred to the other, or that it is more deserving of praise. It is unclear, however, just how these interpretations should themselves be cashed in the coin of preference satisfaction. Consider the alcoholic who wishes to change his preferences: he prefers whisky to water but prefers to prefer water to whisky. But what gives his second-order desires normative force? If he need only act *as if* he had such second-order desires, then what moves him? In a PD, this problem runs deep. We may reinterpret Fig. 4 by letting C now stand for 'choosing AG-preferences' and D stand for 'choosing PD-preferences'. This gives a second-order PD of the same form as the original (and still higher-order dilemmas are possible if we can rank our Q-orderings). To speak of morality as a Q-ordering here does not seem to help, unless it can explain how it motivates in spite of actual preferences. Here, we confront the Prisoner's Dilemma Dilemma. The notion of meta-rankings does provide a logical apparatus capable of representing the notion of a second-order reason. To provide the formal structure, however, does not *solve* the PD, nor does it show why we should, in the initial position, recognize the force of second-order reasons. That argument remains to be made.

4. THE AUTHORITATIVE PROVISION OF PUBLIC GOODS

A rigorous statement of unrestricted contractarianism can be found in the writings of those who devote their attention to the economic analysis of political institutions, often called 'public-choice' theory. While it would be wrong to suggest that there is a tight credo among these writers, many of them would accept that, 'Social order, as such, implies something that resembles a social contract, or quasi-contract . . .' and that 'a contractarian approach carries its own defence once individual values are accepted as the base materials'.[10] From this perspective the justification for the authority of the state takes the form of arguments for the existence of a public sector of authoritative allocations of goods as opposed to the market allocations of the private sector.

Authoritative action, such as a system of taxation to supply valuable public goods, is often said to be a necessary means to secure co-operative action for mutual interests. Suppose the individually rational do need a system of taxation to supply national defence. What is their reason for regarding the tax laws as binding? Would they not be rational to cheat on their tax returns if doing so were worth more than the expected penalty? It seems then that we must rely on sanctions in order to change their preferences by penalizing undesired behaviours. Would they agree to this and would their agreement be sufficient to secure it? Each would agree to it only if it made him better off in comparison with where he began, and that raises the question of what we should regard as an appropriate initial baseline. It is obvious that the unanimity criterion when applied to *de facto* initial holdings will be excessively conservative and will simply entrench existing bargaining power. But let us set that aside, together with the equally deep question of how they will come to divide up the gains of mutual co-operation among themselves. Suppose that either threat advantage or a system of fair division would secure unanimous agreement. Would this provide a satisfactory justification for political authority? To make that case we need to show that the special characteristics of authority as a mode of guiding behaviour have an indispensable or valuable role to play in solving their problem.

The argument turns out to be more complex than one might initially suppose. It goes like this:

(1) There is a significant number of valuable public goods.

[10] J. Buchanan, *The Limits of Liberty* (Chicago: University of Chicago Press, 1975), pp. ix, x.

(2) The market will fail to provide many of these, or fail to provide them in optimal quantity.
(3) An authority system, including for example taxes and subsidies, would be either a necessary or a particularly good way of providing them.
(4) Such an authority system would be sufficient to provide them.
(5) So, rational people in the initial position would agree to the existence of an authority system.

Let us begin with the first two claims. We may safely concede the first premiss, keeping in mind that some public goods (such as mutual trust among members of a cartel) are undesirable. The market failure argument, however, is in fact narrower than is sometimes realized. Though sound, it shows that the general connection between exchange and optimality does not hold, that is to say, it does not hold in general. The argument removes the *guarantee* that competition will serve mutual interests, but leaves open the possibility that in some cases it will.

That there can be no simple connection between market failure and authority can easily be seen. First of all, it is not necessary that there should be market failure in order to warrant authoritative action. When markets succeed they produce efficient outcomes, but that criterion is distribution-free. A state of affairs in which I own all the property and one in which you own it all are each optimal since departure from either could make one person better off only at the expense of the owner. Yet we are only very rarely indifferent about the distributive question of *who* should hold property and, if all property were to be in the hands of a single person, we would regard the distributive question as of the greatest importance. In ordinary circumstances, many forms of state action are thought to be justified on grounds of justice rather than efficiency, even when market failure is not in question.

Secondly, market failures are not sufficient to warrant authoritative intervention. Externalities in consumption may not upset the marginal conditions for optimality, or they may do so in a degree or manner which does not warrant a collective response. All sorts of meddlesome preferences about how others should behave, what they should value, and how they should lead their lives create externalities. Suppose that you decide to dress in a way that the rest of us find tasteless to the point of offensive and that your sartorial display is neither excludable nor rival; it is a public good (or bad). It would surely be permissible for us to attempt to persuade or bribe you not to dress as you would otherwise prefer but, should the market fail, few would think that we should have the authority to impose obligations on you to behave as we wish. Yet the logic of the situation is no different from the standard externalities argument; what distinguishes this case is that the competing value of liberty is also in play. Even supposing that there is no general right to liberty, the rights to specific liberties, such as freedom of expression or association, will be implicated often enough in social choice for the simple market-failure argument to be blocked.

Thirdly, consider a favourable case in which authoritative action really is needed to supply some public good and no independent values are put in jeopardy by this response. Even here, we must remember that the reliance on authority itself has further effects which, when counted in the decision, may change the calculations. Parallel to market failure there are cases of what we might call 'government failure' in which the mechanisms of authoritative decision fail to produce the sorts of outcome which are held to justify their existence. To take only one particularly worrisome instance, to aim for the optimal supply of some public good by a system of obligatory taxation, the government will need some index of demand for that good. Consider national defence. Since the benefits of general security are non-rival and non-excludable, people will be under-motivated to pay for them. Suppose, however, we try to gauge how much they value it by a series of votes, or by a survey questionnaire which elicits their willingness to pay. Clearly there will often be incentives to misrepresent their real level of demand, or to vote strategically. The technical literature on this problem suggests that it may well be insoluble.[11] And on top of this there are all the usual sorts of

[11] See A. Gibbard, 'Manipulation of Voting Schemes: A General Result', *Econometrica* 41 (1973), 587–601; M. A. Satterthwaite, 'Strategy-Proofness and Arrow's Conditions', *Journal of Economic Theory* 10 (1975), 187–217.

risks and transaction costs attendant on regulation of an activity by centralized government.

5. ANARCHIC PROVISION

These considerations limit the scope for contractarian argument in one direction, for they suggest that authority is less than universally successful in solving the problems. Further considerations limit it from the other end, by showing that in some cases non-authoritative solutions are also possible. If this is so, then authority is not always necessary to solve public goods problems.

5.1 *Pure jointness of supply*

In some cases, complete participation is needed for public goods to be provided: the defection of a single individual brings the whole system crashing down. Clean air in a train compartment depends on each refraining from smoking. So long as the marginal individual benefit is worth the marginal individual cost, we can be sure that such goods will be provided. Although analytically interesting, few public goods of political importance have this feature. A single individual's failure to pay taxes has no perceptible effect on the level of provision of social welfare.

5.2 *Sympathy*

Thus far we have assumed that people take into account no one's welfare but their own in deciding what to do. But there is nothing in the logic of the underlying value theory which commits us to this position. It is possible to widen the affective horizons of economic man to include what Hutcheson, Hume, Butler, and Smith called 'natural sympathy' or the 'moral sentiments'. This will remain compatible with the theory of rationality so long as sympathetic preferences are capable of entering the agents' utility functions in the normal ways. The idea here is that one is less likely to take a free ride if he considers the interests of others. It may be, for example, that the satisfaction of each, V_i, depends not only on his own desires but also on the desires of others, that is, on their consumption vectors:

$$(1)\ V_i = u_i(x_i, x_j);\ i \neq j$$

One treatment of interdependencies in economic welfare takes just such an approach by making i's welfare dependent on both his own and on j's *incomes*.[12] This, however, extracts j's preferences from the picture entirely. It has the consequence that i prefers j being at a higher level of income, even if j is an ascetic whose welfare would thereby be reduced. This does not seem to be an appropriate model for sympathy which should at least require that interdependent preferences are not meddlesome. This condition is satisfied by functions of the form:

$$(2)\ V_i = [u_i(x_i),\ u_j(x_j)];\ i \neq j$$

In this case, i's welfare depends both on the satisfaction of his own desires and on j having his wants (as given by his own preferences) satisfied as well. While some general results can be proved using such a model,[13] much depends on the exact functional form of the interdependence. A common assumption is that it will be a linear combination of the pay-offs of all individuals, say of the form:

$$(3)\ V_i = [(1 - w)u_i + (w)u_j];\ i \neq j,\ 0 < w < 1$$

where w is the weight which i gives to j's welfare. The restrictions on w prohibit pure selflessness. If all I want is that your desires be satisfied and all you want is that my desires be satisfied, then, depending on how one looks at it, we have either no problem of social conflict at all, or an irresoluble one. Even if we fix first-order desires so that there is after all something to satisfy, and allow each to be selflessly benevolent, then the two will just trade interest identities and pursue each other's interests as vigorously as their own. Where desires conflict it does nothing to let someone else attend to their satisfaction.

[12] H. M. Hochman and J. D. Rodgers, 'Pareto-Optimal Redistribution', *American Economic Review* 59 (1969), 542–57.

[13] M. Kurz, 'Altruistic Equilibrium', in B. Bellassa and R. Nelson, eds., *Economic Progress, Private Values and Public Policy* (Amsterdam: North-Holland, 1977), 177–200; A. D. Danielson, 'A Theory of Exchange, Philanthropy and Appropriation', *Public Choice* 24 (1975), 13–26; G. Daly and J. F. Giertz, 'Benevolence, Malevolence, and Economic Theory', *Public Choice* 13 (1972), 1–19.

Outside such extreme cases, however, variations in w may avoid the problem by changing the structure of the game. For example, there is some weight w* beyond which a Prisoner's Dilemma becomes an Assurance Game, where each will co-operate if and only if he is assured that the other will. For the numerical example of Fig. 4, w* is 1/6. If the agents value each other's welfare at a higher rate, the dilemma will vanish. If each valued his own pay-offs in Fig. 4 at a rate of 2/3 and the other's pay-offs at 1/3, then that game would be transformed into the one shown in Fig. 5 in which each will co-operate if he is assured that the other will. In that case, both joint co-operation and joint defection are stable equilibria, so there is no temptation to take a free ride. And at still higher values of w even assurance is not needed to secure co-operation.

Note that Fig. 5 is a version of the co-ordination problems discussed in Chapter 4. To transform a PD into a CP is to resolve one kind of problem by replacing it with another. Although often more tractable in that it lacks the deep instability of a PD, the CP does not establish any special need for authority, as we have already shown in our discussion of conventionalism. In any case, the general idea here is that the moral sentiments may motivate voluntary co-operation in the absence of a state or other authoritative institution. The vicarious affects put society back in by circumventing the need for a central authority to guarantee the provision of public goods. It may be that the state is needed in such a picture to sustain the moral sentiments at an appropriate level, and to channel them to appropriate objects, but in that respect the state does not act authoritatively but merely persuasively, like any other form of moral order.

5.3 *By-products and entrepreneurs*

In other cases, valuable public goods can be supplied as by-products to certain forms of private activity, or by the action of individuals acting on private incentives. The cases of so-called 'selective incentives' are essentially by-products.[14] Under the usual legislative arrangements, all workers in a unionized industry benefit from the collective bargaining over

[14] M. Olson, *The Logic of Collective Action* (Cambridge, Mass.: Harvard University Press, 1971), 51, 133–4.

wages and working conditions. These may be inexcludable and thus create certain incentives for other shops not to unionize but to ride freely on the higher wage rates in the industry in general. But by supplying various excludable goods such as credit unions, travel agencies, housing loans, and group insurance plans, the private incentives to union membership can be made to support the public goods benefits. Entrepreneurs may take similar advantage of private incentives. A politician in search of personal wealth, prestige, and power, which are all themselves private goods, can be motivated to supply public goods to the population. This case, however, involves the prior existence of some kinds of authoritative mechanism of legislation, through which politicians act, so it cannot provide a fundamental solution to the problem at hand.

5.4 *Learning to co-operate*

Our examples thus far have been in one respect quite artificial. Most actual decisions about whether or not to contribute to the provision of public goods are not in fact made simultaneously, with pay-offs received immediately, and devoid of future consequences of the decision taken. We are not normally confronted with single, isolated decisions of whether to respect others' personal security, or pay our taxes, or keep the environment clean. Rather, social life is a continuing series of similar and interdependent situations. We know from experience that people do behave differently in isolated, anomic interactions than they do in the context of ongoing and regular ones, in part because the stakes are higher in the latter case. One has a persisting reputation to consider, and others' reactions are determined by their memory of earlier interactions as well as the structure of current ones. Among the first to notice this was Adam Smith:

> When a person makes perhaps twenty contracts in a day, he cannot gain so much by endeavouring to impose on his neighbours as the very appearance of a cheat would make him lose. Where people seldom deal with one another, we find that they are somewhat disposed to cheat, because they can gain more by a smart trick than they can lose by the injury which it does their character.[15]

[15] A. Smith, *Lectures on Jurisprudence*, ed. R. L. Meek, D. D. Raphael, and P.G. Stein (Oxford: Clarendon Press, 1978), 538–9.

In such circumstances, theories about others' behaviour admit of tests, and the behaviour itself may be modified by the communication of information. We might expect, therefore, that in a repeated series of public goods problems agents will use this information to their mutual advantage and learn, albeit in a conditional and groping way, to co-operate for mutual gain.

This intuitition is in fact correct, though only under some fairly restrictive assumptions, as Michael Taylor and others have demonstrated.[16] In repeated iterations of such games conditional strategies are available to the players in which they attempt to link their future behaviour to their opponents' present behaviour. For example, I might defect to begin with, but then co-operate if you do and continue to co-operate until you defect. Or I might co-operate at the outset and continue to do so until you defect, whereupon I punish you (and myself) by defecting for a certain number of turns before beginning to co-operate again. In a large number of plays, the number of possible strategies is astronomical, but not all of them are plausible or interesting, and rational agents might find ways to choose among them. If some of the preferred strategies are both co-operative and in equilibrium, the agents might learn over time to provide certain public goods.

It is true, however, that only a subset of all desirable public goods could be so provided. Consider the effects of the duration of play. In a finite series of games, there is no reason to co-operate on the last play since the whole idea of super-game strategies is to trade present costs (the risk of being taken for a co-operative sucker) for future benefits (the chance of learning to provide mutual gains). But if there is no future there are only costs involved, so the last game should be treated as an isolated one and all should defect. But then the conundrum of negative induction looms, leaving in sequence the second-last, third-last . . . and finally the first game as the end of the series in which co-operation is rational. It seems to follow that in any finite series of plays defection is always

[16] See M. Taylor, *Anarchy and Cooperation* (London: Wiley, 1976); R. Axelrod, *The Evolution of Cooperation* (New York: Basic Books, 1984). For some criticism of this general line see M. Laver, *The Politics of Private Desires* (Harmondsworth: Penguin, 1981), 50–9, on which I have also drawn.

required. Whatever the best formal resolution of the seeming paradox, two features of social interaction give us a practical escape from it: the number of plays is large and its termination date unknown. And future benefits are discounted back to present value. This provides that conditional co-operation is rational under certain conditions: if defection is orderly (so that co-operative behaviour does not decay too quickly for learning to take place), if defection is easily monitored (so that it will not go undetected and unpunished), if the rates of discount for future benefits are not too high (so that present benefits are not more valuable than the threatened loss of any future ones), and if discount rates are not too divergent among players (so that there is some strategy which best teaches a lesson to all other learners, fast and slow).

These conditions sound restrictive, and they are. In the first place, it is likely that co-operation on a very large scale will be ruled out, for defections will be too hard to detect and less worth punishing. And some very distant benefits, such as those accruing mainly to future generations, will be too heavily discounted to reward present co-operation. If this is so, then many of the actual public goods by which the authority of states is commonly justified will either not be produced or will be produced only in smaller quantities than desired. That conclusion may lead in one of two directions. It might be taken as an argument in favour of small, stateless societies. Those public goods which remain beyond the reach of such groups would then count among the costs of anarchy and would need to be balanced against the gains of other sorts to be had from small-scale, communal living. On the other hand, we might regard the conclusion as demonstrating the irrelevance of theories of anarchic provision to political theory, for our concern is not with families and small communal groups, but with large and impersonal ones like the state.

This broad, though far from exhaustive, account of possible modes of anarchic provision does cast some further doubt on the general contractarian argument. For it shows that there are some valuable public goods for which, even if the market fails, non-authoritative provision may succeed. Perhaps, with some ingenuity, these methods could be shown to apply to many public goods; nevertheless, they are unlikely to apply to all. The following argument is even more damaging to the contractarian case.

6. AUTHORITY AS A PUBLIC GOOD

The contractarian theory of the state begins with actual public goods which need to be provided: the management of natural resources, security of the person, national defence, and so on. Suppose conditions favourable to the theory such that these goods will be inoptimally provided in circumstances of anarchic provision. Authoritative directives, through tax and subsidy schemes, and supporting legislation and institutions, could, let us further suppose, do the job. But how do we produce authority on the contractarian theory? By mutual agreement. The provision of authority must be internal to the community and not imposed externally from above, a 'third power' as Engels calls it. It is indeed the *result* of the successful creation of authoritative mechanisms that they appear relatively external to their subjects, but that externality is a consequence only of the social circumstances of the modern state and the nature of authority.

Now in the postulated conditions, the existence of an authority system has certain features which make its internal provision unlikely. It has been noted that the existence of a legal system is *itself* a public good and that adherence to its requirements is a capital investment.[17] Thus the following second-order dilemma arises: the provision of certain public goods requires authoritative norms, but the provision of authoritative norms is a public good. Each prefers that only he breaks the law, and in a large society disobedience can only be imperfectly monitored. For this reason sanctions are needed. But applying sanctions is a public good, and so on. So long as enforcement is internal and the agents rational, the attempt to establish authority will generate a string of higher-order PDs. (It will also generate higher-order co-ordination problems in the interpretation and administration of authoritative directives.)

[17] J. Buchanan, *The Limits of Liberty*, 15.

The essential difficulty here is one familiar to many sorts of contractarian reasoning. The notion of a binding agreement itself presupposes the possibility of securing certain commitments, otherwise there is nothing to stop each pressing for the ideal contract in which everyone but himself agrees to restraints. That would obviously never secure unanimous agreement. Buchanan supposes that in some circumstances, 'Each person will recognize that unilateral defection cannot succeed and that any attempt to accomplish this would plunge the system back into a position that is less desirable for everyone than that which is attained upon adherence to contract.'[18] But at least in the modern state the factual premisses of that argument are false: unilateral defections on a scale sufficient to upset optimality do not bring the system crashing down. In the post-constitutional contract (where it has been decided that some public provision is to take place and rules governing the production of particular public goods are to be established) Buchanan tries to side-step the problem by readjusting the initial assignment of rights so that 'membership in a community is defined so as to compel participation in the genuine postconstitutional contracting for public goods, provided that an effective rule of unanimity is insured.'[19] But that sleight of hand is too obvious to convince: it is as if we could maximize welfare by defining only the best-off as persons. What one needs at this point is an argument to show that defection is *unfair*. Whether that judgement could itself be grounded in contractarian reasoning is a famous problem which I will not discuss here.[20]

Gauthier offers an interesting suggestion which seeks to accommodate the notion of binding commitments to contractarian theory. He proposes that we modify the economic view of rationality as maximization. That view is quite well adapted to certain environments, for instance, those in which agents are radically independent or in which the only games

[18] Ibid. 65. [19] Ibid. 40.

[20] It is perhaps significant that its most noted proponent, John Rawls, rejects unrestricted contractarianism and interprets his argument in ways that seem increasingly distant from the classical contractarian tradition. See his 'Kantian Constructivism and Moral Theory', *Journal of Philosophy* 77 (1980), 515–72; and 'Justice as Fairness: Political not Metaphysical', *Philosophy and Public Affairs* 14 (1985), 223–51.

they play are against 'Nature'. In circumstances of interdependence such as those of public goods, however, it fares less well. Indeed, here it may be said to be self-defeating, for the more perfect its observance, the less likely are agents to fulfil their aims according to that very theory. This suggests that we might ask which conception of rationality it would be rational to choose in the circumstances. Gauthier argues that it would not be economically rational to choose the economic conception of rationality. Instead, we should prefer what he calls 'constrained maximization':

> A person acting interdependently acts rationally only if the expected outcome of his action affords each person with whom his action is interdependent a utility such that there is no combination of possible actions, one for each person acting interdependently, with an expected outcome which affords each person other than himself at least as great a utility, and himself a greater utility.[21]

On this view, each should do the best he can, not given the *actions* of the others, but given their *preferences*. By allowing him to participate in agreements like social contracts, it does in fact maximize his overall utility. (It is not quite this simple; it also presupposes some criterion of fair division.) The advantages are obvious: unlike the straightforward maximizer, the constrained maximizer can undertake and carry out agreements which permit each to satisfy his preferences better than would be possible through independent action alone.

The theory of constrained maximization thus aims to make co-operation not only best, but stable. This, however, depends on others also accepting constrained maximization. This psychological state, however, may not be easily verifiable and, if it is not, it would be rational to hang on to one's old conception of rationality just in case. Indeed, if one were certain that others would change their conceptions of rationality, you should also hang on to your old one and take a free ride. Now it might be supposed that it is not rational to make an agreement which it is not rational to keep. That, however, is true only if conceptions of rationality are not up for choice. When they are, a new strategic dimension is introduced. If

[21] D. Gauthier, 'Reason and Maximization', *Canadian Journal of Philosophy* 4 (1975), 427.

one knows that others will transform their conceptions of rationality to make and keep optimal agreements, then one will do better by seeming to transform one's own conception and then making but not keeping the agreement. It might be objected that the transformation is ratchet-like, and that once effected precludes shifting back to straightforward maximization, thus making it impossible only to seem like a constrained maximizer. But that is not so, for constrained maximization contains straightforward maximization as a limiting case. When the number of persons acting interdependently is *one* they are equivalent. Hence, a constrained maximizer will still know how to maximize in a straightforward way and will do so whenever he acts independently. It will therefore be both possible and rational to make agreements, and then, by acting as if the situation were one of independent decision, fail to keep them. Gauthier says that 'the prudent man considers it rational to *become* moral';[22] but he would do even better by pretending to become moral.

To get around the difficulties of higher-order public goods problems, the contractarian argument needs a two-stage structure: (1) the provision of political authority, (2) the authoritative provision of other public goods. But only if the solution to (1) is independent of the solution to (2) will it be satisfactory. Let me explain. Suppose that we could show that authority systems, themselves public goods, can be provided without the need for a higher-level enforcement mechanism, say through one of the methods of anarchic provision discussed above. That would appear to offer an adequate solution to (1) which we could then turn against (2). But why would the method of anarchic provision not work *directly* on (2), without recourse to (1) at all? After all, if we could convince rational agents to obey laws requiring that they pay taxes, then could we not use a similar argument to show them the rationality of paying taxes, laws or no? It might be said that we could indeed, but the state, through its regulatory and executive agencies, would still be needed to measure demand and co-ordinate payment. That may be so, but those functions will be essentially co-ordinative ones, and thus not authorita-

[22] Ibid. 432.

tive. A successful contractarian argument therefore requires *different* solutions to (1) and (2). It needs to explain how the public good of authority comes to be provided in some way consistent with recognizing the need for authority to provide public goods.

This would be possible if authority systems are public goods susceptible to anarchic provision while first-order public goods are not. Can such an argument be made out? Recall that authority exists only when people treat certain practical requirements as commitments which bind independently of their content: they exclude certain reasons for acting. In the contractarian story, the reasons to be excluded are obviously those which tempt free-riding. The principle of dominance is to be excluded in favour of the principles of optimality and fair division, within the scope of collective action problems. But political authority has further features which follow from the supremacy and scope of the state's claims together with the size of the population they regulate.

(1) Its requirements are of general application. The laws claim to bind everyone and hence in a large society they claim to bind many people. This is not to be mistaken for the false view that laws are always general in the sense that they cannot regulate properly named individuals.[23] They can and do. The content of law remains open. It is just that even individualized directives claim general validity; they are part of the legal system.

(2) Authority systems are not public goods of pure joint supply. Indeed, they are relatively impervious to individual action in two ways: their requirements are not easily altered by any single individual who is bound by them, and their existence can withstand some, though not widespread, disregard. Both are common-sense features of law. One citizen's voice does little to change it, and his disobedience little to upset it.

(3) Recognition of authoritative requirements, and even compliance without acceptance of law's authority, generates a pure external economy from which few can feasibly be excluded. Hence, as a result of (2) each knows that excluding self-interest in favour of mutual interest is not needed to

[23] F. A. Hayek, *The Constitution of Liberty*, 153–4.

produce the benefits which make the system possible and that the marginal increase to him in benefits due directly to his own participation is negligible. His compliance is therefore a cost to him and a benefit to others, nothing more.

(4) The modern state is large and anonymous so that close personal relations between citizens are few and it is difficult to feel that one has a stake in the common good.

(5) There may be widely differing tastes for public goods (including authority) or at least widespread uncertainty about the extent to which such tastes differ. Even in reasonably just societies, the demand for a system of civil liberties, a clean environment, or the preservation of historic buildings varies among people. In less just societies, these effects are exacerbated. Blacks may want less national security if their combat risks are greater, young people may want less restraint if their salaries have been reduced in order to fight inflation, women may want less stability of the home environment if it is supported by their unpaid household labour.

The cumulative effect of these five points does indeed distinguish the authority of the state from other public goods. It shows that authority is a relatively pure public good whose value is a matter of dispute, which does not exhibit pure jointness of supply and is unlikely to have the features favourable to anarchic provision. Indeed, authority is much *less* likely to be produced than are many of the first-order public goods whose production is supposed to justify it in the first place. Some of them may be privatized through sophisticated pricing mechanisms or readjustments of property rights, others are purely joint in production, some emerge anarchically among solidary subgroups who learn to co-operate with each other over time. Because it is among the purest of public goods, the authority of the state is among the most vulnerable to the calculus of self-interest. It cannot, therefore, be the self-supporting foundation of a two-stage contractarian argument of the type suggested.

7. THE NEED FOR COERCION

It is often argued that the insolubility of the collective action problem points to a general and persisting need for coercion in human society.[24] Indeed, many public choice contractarians have, I think correctly, seen that this is the real upshot of their argument: it is in some circumstances rational for all to agree to a mutual coercion scheme which forces them to co-operate by rendering defection too expensive and thus altering their preferences. 'The essence of democratic government', writes William Baumol, 'may then be the voluntary acceptance of a central agency of intimidation designed for the attainment of the desires of the public.'[25] Moreover, they feel that so far from offending against the values of voluntarism and consumer sovereignty which underpin the theory, a system of mutual terror serves them:

> In this event the *absence* of coercion may be construed to result in a vitiation of consumer sovereignty, since the individual consumer is by himself in no position to obtain the object he desires. (. . .) it may well pay every member of the community to subject himself to a coercive arrangement whereby his own and everyone else's contribution is enforced.[26]

As we have seen, however, the coercion must be external in origin, for the parties to a mutual coercion agreement would seek to extort others for their own benefit, thus replicating the original problem at a higher level.

In some respects, such an external coercer resembles Hobbes's sovereign. His solution to the problem of providing the public good of social peace and ending the war of all against all is based on agreement, or covenant, but 'Covenants, without the Sword, are but Words, and of no strength to secure a man at all', Hobbes says, 'and therefore it is no wonder if there be somewhat else required (besides Covenant) to make their Agreement constant and lasting; which is a Common Power, to keep them in awe, and to direct their actions to the Common Benefit.'[27] In the need for coercion

[24] For example, J. H. Sobel, 'The Need for Coercion', in J. R. Pennock and J. W. Chapman, eds., *Coercion: Nomos XIV* (Chicago: Aldine, Atherton, 1972), 148–77.

[25] W. Baumol, *Welfare Economics and the Theory of the State*, 2nd edn. (London: LSE-Bell, 1965), 57.

[26] Ibid. 133.

[27] T. Hobbes, *Leviathan*, ed. C. B. Macpherson (Harmondsworth: Penguin, 1968), 223, 226.

and its justification both Hobbes and his modern-day followers are agreed. But there is a fundamental difference between their theories.

Although coercion is a familiar feature of states, we saw in Chapter 3 that it is not a distinctive one, and that coercion and authority are quite different ways of guiding action. The state does coerce, but only its comprehensive claim to legitimate authority distinguishes it as a form of social order. If we left the story with the appearance of the 'sword', as Hobbes puts it, we would have justified a coercive apparatus, but not a state, for the latter claims the power to obligate its citizens and not merely threaten them or alter the environment in ways so as to make recalcitrance more costly. Why is this not enough? It certainly is an achievement of social theory to explain and justify the need for coercion. But it is an achievement of the wrong sort, owing to the nature of coercive threats as reasons for action.

The state cannot, for reasons discussed in Chapter 3, hope to coerce everybody, though there may be circumstances in which standing threats of coercion would be enough to motivate valuable forms of social co-operation. Could such threats be authoritative reasons? The argument of Chapter 2 was that authoritative reasons to act are binding and content-independent. Now, threats are content-independent reasons: if my reason for obeying your orders is that I am threatened with prison otherwise, then the mere fact that you have threatened me gives me grounds for fearing my safety, provided that you are sufficiently credible. One of the features of authoritative reasons is therefore shared by threats. But the second is not. Threats work because their undesirable consequences outweigh the profit of ignoring them. If a threat of five years' imprisonment is insufficient to motivate my compliance, it can be adjusted upwards to six years, seven, and so on, until we reach a point where the rational person will think that the discounted risk is worse than compliance. But the economics of threats do not therefore model the binding force of authority: they do not generate exclusionary reasons. The function of threats is not to set aside or replace the agent's reasoning about the merits of the case, but to change his assessment of those merits. Threats can therefore never be more than secondary motivation for compliance with authority, calculated to secure the compliance of those who will not recognize its binding force. For this reason a justification of coercion is not a justification of authority.

Few modern Hobbesians, particular those writing in the public choice tradition, have given enough thought to this crucial issue. But the confusion of coercion and authority is not, however, a mistake which they inherit from their master. Hobbes's own argument does not end with the appearance of 'the sword' to enforce contracts; it immediately goes on to explain how authority is created. Bearing in mind that for Hobbes authority is the right of doing any action, he says:

> The only way to erect such a Common Power . . . is to conferre all their power and strength upon one Man, or upon one Assembly of men, that may reduce all their Wills, by plurality of voices, unto one Will . . . and therein to submit their Wills, every one to his Will, and their Judgements, to his Judgment. This is more than Consent, or Concord; it is a reall Unitie of them all, in one and the same Person, made by Covenant of every man with every man, in such manner, as if every man should say to every man, *I Authorise and give up my right of Governing my selfe, to this Man, or to this Assembly of men, on this condition, that thou give up thy Right to him, and Authorise all his Actions in like manner.* (original emphasis)[28]

Thus, for Hobbes, the essential step in the creation of authority is not the fact that the capacity for coercion appears on the scene, but rather that this capacity is created by an individual submission of judgement and will. It is in this that the requirements of the sovereign become binding. The transfer of right is the authorizing step, but its content, that is to say, authorising a *sovereign*, depends not just on the power to coerce, but centrally on the submission of individual judgement. Where Hobbes fails is in trying to show that it is rational to surrender oneself to an omnipotent and self-interested sovereign who would be tempted to be an extortionist or who could be bribed by others to extort. Nor does he explain why rational agents would try to create authority as opposed to a device for mutual coercion.

Finally, even if one can show coercion to be in some cases

[28] Ibid. 22–7.

desirable or optimal, one has not provided a contractarian argument for it until one has accounted for its provision. It does not adequately mesh with the contractarian theory of reason and value to conclude that public goods problems show that each *needs to be coerced* for this is a state of affairs, an outcome, and agents in the initial position are not able to choose outcomes but only strategies. There is no such strategy as 'being coerced', for this is not a way of acting but a way of being acted upon. Indeed, the very notion of rationality is a form of appraisal suited to the active rather than the passive voice; we evaluate actions and not happenings as rational. As Gauthier puts it, 'There is no way of being acted on which is as such either rational or irrational; there is no *rational patient* corresponding to the *rational agent*.'[29] But the need for coercion is passive in this way: it is nothing more than the need to be coerced. It is unsurprising that there is such a need, for it is merely a redescription of the very problem we have been examining: individually maximizing behaviour may sometimes lead to inoptimal situations which, by definition, it would be better not to be in. A contractarian theory of authority cannot be satisfied with such a bland restatement of the facts. It must attempt to explain why rational agents would agree to an authority system; it must identify a strategy which fits this description and is open to the agents. 'Being coerced' is not a strategy, and 'authorizing a sovereign' is not open to them.

8. EXPLAINING SOCIAL ORDER

It is useful to consider the largely sceptical results of this chapter and the previous one in order to draw out some common themes and set the stage for another form of argument. Both conventionalists and contractarians share an individualistic and instrumental view of practical reason and seek to justify authority in such terms. In that framework, however, it is difficult to find a justification for regarding the requirements of the state as authoritative, although there may be other attitudes which it is appropriate to take, for example,

[29] D. Gauthier, 'Reason and Maximization', 424.

to see them as useful threats or wise counsel. The authority which the state claims is unjustified on either account. Given purely individualistic goals and an instrumental conception of rationality, it follows that to treat the state's requirements as binding is to be overcommitted to them, to be bound to them in a way that their point cannot justify. This is a normative thesis. It does not, however, follow that the state cannot be conventionalist or contractarian in a descriptive sense, since it is possible that its subjects wrongly believe that the power to create valuable but arbitrary regularities, or a system of reciprocal restraints, warrants treating the derived standards as of binding force. Could it therefore be that conventionalism or contractarianism are explanatorily adequate theories of the state?

The explanatory structure of these theories is a demanding one. They model the behaviour of rational agents of a pure moral psychology who choose and act consistently and for their own benefit. They may therefore seem one-dimensional as moral beings, but it is this very feature which makes the theories so powerful and elegant. It creates, so to speak, a pre-established harmony in their souls. Having only one type of motivation, albeit manifest in various forms, there is no possibility of deep inner conflict, no pluralism of the personality, no repression. Duty and desire are merely the shorthand and longhand descriptions of one phenomenon. While this simplicity and rigour give the model its strength, they also render it unable to tolerate pluralism in explanatory structures. This in turn explains why the descriptive version of this thesis is no more acceptable than the normative one. For the state can only be descriptively contractarian or conventional if its rational subjects *miscalculate* and accord instrumentally valuable standards more compelling practical force than they are entitled to have. To treat such standards as mandatory or categorical rules when they can be no more than prudential or technical ones is to err in practical reason. But explanations based on hypotheses of rational behaviour leave no room for such errors: rational agents do not miscalculate in such fundamental ways. It may seem then that we must leave even the descriptive treatment of authority to what some political theorists have called the 'mysterious and inexplicable world of the irrational'.[30] What is certain is that any insight into that world cannot come through the existing model. Irrationality would have to be grafted onto that structure giving just the kind of pluralistic theory that individualistic, maximizing, instrumentalists cannot tolerate.

How would it look? Perhaps economic rationality would work up to the level of rule formation where a personality disposition towards authoritarianism takes over to yield the mistaken thought that these rules are binding. Or perhaps the mistake itself is useful; perhaps it is an evolutionarily stable strategy. We might then invoke a Humean argument, basing rule-formation on public utility and then allowing the irrational adherence of praise and blame to form accretions around these rules to make them more stable and to explain their apparent binding force. The common trouble of all such theories is that the mechanism which explains the *existence* of rules is at war with the mechanism which explains their *bindingness*. If public utility accounts for all the rationality there is in rules, then there would be no reason to attach praise and blame to them in the suggested way; rather, we should encourage a systematic demystification of the rules by admitting that they are not binding at all and that no real blame can attach to their infringement. Since disobedience provides its own punishment and obedience its own reward (at least in the long run), various deterrent devices such as coercion and social pressure should provide all the extra stability needed. It would only add insult to injury to further blame them for their failures.

This argument raises an important background issue. What do indirect consequentialist arguments have to explain? Often it has been thought that the agenda is to explain the existence and utility of social rules. In the case at hand, this amounts to the view that they are to explain the existence and utility of political order. Indeed, many have argued that because they can do neither these theories are at fault. And because the argument has been set out this way, proponents of indirect theories have been satisfied when they have been able to show

[30] W. H. Riker and P. C. Ordeshook, *An Introduction to Positive Political Theory* (Englewood Cliffs: Prentice-Hall, 1973), 62. This is to prejudge, however, the important arguments of Marx, Freud, and Pareto.

that useful social rules may exist and that social order can thus be explained. This way of setting the problem has encouraged many philosophers, decision theorists, and others to argue that social order can indeed be so explained, that utilitarians would evolve a norm of truth-telling or promise-keeping, that they would learn to co-operate with each other, that some public goods would be provided in a community of rationally self-interested agents, that such agents could learn a form of altruism, and so on. It is a demanding and technically difficult task to state necessary and sufficient conditions for any of the above forms of order, let alone to prove existence theorems for social order generally. This research will continue under its internal imperatives and we will learn much from it. Equally, however, there are things we cannot learn from it, for certain important issues lie beyond the constraints of that research programme. Among these are the normative differences between certain forms of social order—such as the difference between authority and its alternatives.

Contractarianism, like conventionalism, is unable to justify the authority which the state claims. Both are able to explain and justify some forms of social order, but not that sort which the state is. They are thus philosophically anarchistic theories for although each may permit and sometimes require allegiance to the state, it does so for the wrong reasons. The arguments of Chapters 4 and 5 suggest that it is wrong to think that the rigours of an individualistic and instrumental consequentialism justify political authority. It may show the utility of custom or coercion, but not the acceptance of binding and content-independent commitments. That is true of direct forms and any indirect forms built on conventionalist or contractarian models. For Hobbes, of course, the practical problem of securing obedience was not solved. Where mere compliance is in doubt it is easy to believe that social order is a general problem and to expect an appropriately general solution. This expectation persists even today, and even in relatively self-conscious works of modern social theory. But for all that it is an error. Not all forms of social order are problematic and even among those that are, the differences between forms of order are more important than the gross distinction between order and chaos. As a form of social order the state is distinctive in claiming supreme and wide authority over the lives of many people. So far from requiring such a form of order, a rigorous, instrumental, and one-dimensional individualism prohibits it.

6

THE CONSENT OF THE GOVERNED

THAT political authority is properly founded on the consent of the governed has, at least since the seventeenth century, seemed almost truistic. We turn naturally to consent, not only because of its centrality in the democratic tradition, but also because consenting is a common and normal way of binding ourselves. The power to do so is one which we might legitimately want to have; to justify it is to explain why. The problem of political authority is whether there are any valid reasons for wanting to be able to bind ourselves to the state. The structure of consent-based arguments for authority is thus radically different from that of contractarian or conventionalist ones which attempt to show that authority is necessary or particularly useful in establishing and securing valuable forms of social order. They fail because the link is very much weaker than their proponents hold. In contrast, consent theory posits a more direct connection based on the appealing view that the free and informed consent of rational persons binds them to obey. This is not to base social relations on the requirements of social order, but to base one kind of social relation on another.

1. CONSENT AND CONSENSUS

The notion of consent as a form of binding commitment does not, of course, exhaust the ordinary meaning of the word, nor does it capture all shades of the term as used by modern philosophers and social scientists. This divergence seems especially wide in the persistent habit of political scientists, sociologists, and journalists of speaking of the need for governments to 'manufacture', 'mobilize', or 'engineer' consent to their activities and policies. To the social philosopher, this will conjure up the same horrors as the suggestion that states can 'legitimate' their rule through coercion, manipulation, and propaganda: it drains the term of its normative force. If consent were a product which governments find it useful to create through the usual combinations of threats and offers, then it would be hard to see what role it could possibly play in the justification of authority or anything else. Government by consent would be something to be avoided. How then does this deviant usage arise? Note that it is not simply a result of the social scientist taking an external point of view. It is not a descriptive or uncommitted version of the participants' concept of consent; it is an inversion or perversion of that concept. It is because consent is a way of binding *oneself*, of creating a self-assumed commitment, that it seems a plausible foundation for political authority in the first place. When consent is something engineered by the state and thus flowing from top to bottom, any notion of government founded on consent becomes nonsensical; if anything the relationship would run the other way—consent would be founded on government. We might expect such a move from absolutists or cynics, but hardly from those enthusiasts of liberal democracy who so often utter it. What motivates them?

The answer lies partly in a confusion of consent with the related but different notion of consensus. A government enjoys a consensus of opinion when most people are agreed about its status and value. This notion is often what writers actually have in mind. P. H. Partridge, for example, gives a list of 'examples of political and social conforming behaviour which may plausibly be said to be connected with the idea of consent'[1] which include: acquiescence resulting from duress, threats, manipulation, apathy, habit, custom or tradition, from socialization and the internalization of norms, and finally, as a result of permission given deliberately in advance, with or without subsequent approval of the permitted action. Partridge recognizes that many political theorists would only count the final items as authentic instances of consent, but refuses to join them, maintaining that it is unfruitful to ask which of these conforming behaviours really counts as consent when they flow into each other naturally and without a clear conceptual or phenomenological break. Moreover, he says,

[1] P. H. Partridge, *Consent and Consensus* (London: Macmillan, 1971), 31.

'the structure of any more or less stable system of political authority depends heavily upon most of the relationships present in our continuum.'[2]

That may be so. But we should not use 'consent' as a conceptual waste-basket for all the various causes of conformity and stability any more than we should equate 'authority' with stability itself. In Chapter 1, I argued against the latter view in showing that a theory of political authority and a theory of stable government answer different questions and that the connection between their answers is at best a contingent one. The identification of consent with consensus fails to respect that distinction. Consensus is a state of mind or public opinion which does tend to generate stability and order in society. It may be active or passive, more or less well informed, and have as its causes all of those listed above. But it cannot justify authority. Consent is a possible candidate in that role only because it is active and performative and demands a certain level of information. It is not mere acquiescence or even approval. I do not deny that consent is commonly accompanied by such positive attitudes, only that it can be identified with them. The primary functions of the concepts of consent and consensus in social and political theory are, in fact, dramatically different. Consent has always been a standard of critical assessment capable of being brought to bear on various forms of stable social order, including highly consensual ones. To ask of a society in which there is widespread acquiescence to the rulers whether the subjects have consented to such control, whether it is a consequence of their agreement, is to raise the stakes in political argument from a mere concern for stability to a concern about its sources. Thus, the distinction between a government which enjoys the consent of its citizens and one which thrives in an atmosphere of consensus—however secure and profound—is one of principle. The doctrine of consent is a way of protecting individuals against the weight of consensus; it is a bulwark against unreasoned and mechanical attachments to social institutions.

[2] Ibid. 45. Cf. also 50–1.

2. CONSENT-BASED THEORIES

Here, I wish to examine not all theories according to which individual consent in the stronger, performative sense is *relevant* to the existence of a duty to obey, but only those theories in which it is at least in part the *ground* of that duty, that is to say, where the fact that an individual has consented is a sufficient if defeasible reason for holding him to be under the duty. This excludes cases where consent is merely a limiting condition of authority. If God commands us to obey all those who rule for the common good, and if the test of the latter is whether we consent to their rule, then we are never obligated without our consent. But it is not our consent itself which generates this obligation; God's will does and consent is merely among the necessary applicative conditions. This is not a consent-based theory in the sense which interests us here.

Equally, I do not consider theories according to which consent need not actually be given at all, although a test of hypothetical consent is relevant to ascertaining the existence of an obligation. There is an important difference between regarding someone's actual agreement as a reason for later holding him to be bound by it and regarding an unmade agreement which it *would have been* rational to make as such a reason.[3] Kant is a prominent exponent of the hypothetical consent test in political morality, and he makes it quite clear that this test has nothing to do with actual consent and is in fact perfectly compatible with explicit dissent.[4] But to establish that it would be rational to agree to some policy only proves that there is some reason to follow it, not that the reason is dependent on our agreement. Hypothetical consent theories are best understood as versions of contractarianism, whose merits have already been considered in Chapter 5. In contrast, a consent-based theory offers a reason for compliance

[3] See R. Dworkin, *Taking Rights Seriously* (Cambridge, Mass.: Harvard University Press, 1978), 151–3.

[4] He writes, 'if it is at least *possible* that a people could agree to it, it is our duty to consider the law as just, even if the people is at present in such a position or attitude of mind that it would probably refuse its consent if it were consulted': 'Theory and Practice', in H. Reiss, ed., *Kant's Political Writings* (Cambridge: Cambridge University Press, 1970), 79.

which is dependent on the fact of agreement itself. This obviously differs from the contractarian test for the reason that one may have a binding obligation consequent on an agreement which it was irrational to make. A consent-based theory is thus a theory of self-assumed commitment according to which actual individual consent itself justifies holding citizens to be under a certain duty.

Political authority is justified by consent at least when consenting is a way of undertaking an obligation. This is not to claim that 'undertaking an obligation' is an adequate definition of consent. Consenting may have other normative consequences, such as waiving or transferring rights; and it may have non-normative consequences, such as expressing trust or affection. For our limited purposes, however, we may regard the characteristic result of consent to the state's authority as the acquisition of an obligation on the part of the consenter. This is not an essential feature of consent in general. Sometimes it may create no duties for the consentor: a parent may consent to a teacher's exercise of authority over his or her child without also becoming liable to that authority. And sometimes consent does not create any duties at all: an offer to buy a house creates in the offeree a power to accept the offer and, correlatively, a liability in the offeror, but no duties until the contract is accepted and binding. In the political realm, however, one does not have the option of consenting to the state's authority over others only and to give one's consent is to recognize its right to command and one's own duty to obey.

A satisfactory understanding of consent, however, must be more than an account of consent's characteristic consequences; it must also include the means through which they are brought about. Consider the following normative change: I acquire an obligation to pay you $100. Now, this might have come about in various ways. For instance, I might have promised to make you a present of $100. Or I might have contracted to give you $100 in exchange for a book. Or, having assaulted you and broken a tooth, I may owe you $100 in compensation. The normative consequences of each of these stories is the same, and yet there are morally significant differences in the tales. Only the first two are consensual.

Hence, although consent does have characteristic normative consequences, one cannot identify it with such consequences. That is why we cannot accept the initially appealing claim of John Plamenatz: '[T]o consent . . . is always to do or to take part in doing something which the doer knows, or is presumed to know, creates in another a right he would not otherwise have.'[5] It is unproven and unlikely that a given normative change which resulted from consent could not have occurred otherwise. Moreover, to accept Plamenatz's definition in the present context would be to accept, as part of the *concept* of consent, that nothing else provides a valid ground for the state's right to obedience correlative to the citizen's obligation to obey. This is unhelpful. We want to assess the force of consent-based theories in comparison to others, so there is no point in starting out with the assumption that consent creates a right that the state could not otherwise have.

Excessive attention to the purported normative consequences of consenting clouds the issue at hand. What is needed is a modal rather than a consequential definition, one which identifies consent as a peculiar means of acquiring obligations, not as a peculiar set of obligations. John Simmons suggests that a necessary element in such a definition would be that consent is an act which brings about a normative change 'through a suitable expression of the consenter's intention to enter such a transaction and involves the assuming of a special obligation not to interfere with the exercise of the right accorded.'[6] Although such intentional undertakings are at the core of the concept of consent, it is sometimes also held to extend to actions of a different sort. If I sit down in a restaurant and order a meal, I consent to pay the listed price. This is so whether or not I give an explicit promise to do so, and even if my intention is to leave before paying. When one boards an aeroplane, one consents to being searched, and signs sometimes point out that no one need submit to a search if he chooses not to board. The structure of these examples is the following: I freely perform an action, knowing that it is understood to entail some duty, and I am therefore bound by

[5] J. P. Plamenatz, *Consent, Freedom and Political Obligation*, 167.

[6] A. J. Simmons, *Moral Principles and Political Obligations* (Princeton: Princeton University Press, 1979), 77.

that duty. It hs been suggested that these examples show that Simmons and others who identify consent with acts intended to assume obligations are wrong because in the above cases that intent is absent, and that having the obligation is even compatible with having the intention to avoid it. Thus, it is said that consent is given by any act done in the belief that it will create duties, because it is generally known to be done with such beliefs.[7]

Even if for some purposes these practices might be classified as acts of consent, the main justification for recognizing them as duty-creating is quite different from that in cases where consent is the voluntary assumption of an obligation. In the restaurant or airline cases, the underlying principle is one of estoppel, justified as a means of protecting the interests of the parties who might be harmed if the agent later rejected the duty on the ground that he had no intention to assume it. If one's behaviour in a restaurant gives others reasonable grounds for relying on the belief that one will pay, and if they do so rely, then one is bound to pay. The estoppel principle does indeed yield obligations. For our purposes, however, the important question is not whether as a matter of linguistic practice or moral theory that principle should therefore be counted as a species of consent, but whether it could equally count in the justification for a duty to obey the state.

If we are to be regarded as consenting simply by performing some action in the knowledge that a duty will follow, this cannot be justified by reference to the harm denial would cause to the interests of the *state* or its authorities. It is a major normative assumption of democratic theory that the state has no legitimate interests of its own; it must serve the interests of its citizens. Properly understood, this assumption is neutral between consent theorists and their critics. It should be distinguished from McTaggart's colourful claim that, like a sewage-pipe, the state is only of instrumental value.[8] Political

[7] J. Raz, *The Morality of Freedom*, 80–8.

[8] 'Whatever activity it is desirable for the State to have, it will only be desirable as a means, and . . . the activity, and the State itself, can have no value but as a means. And a religion which fastens itself on a means has not risen above fetish-worship. Compared with worship of the State, zoolatry is rational and dignified. A bull or crocodile may not have great intrinsic value, but it has some, for it is a conscious being. The State has none. It would be as reasonable to worship a sewage pipe, which

life may also have intrinsic value, that is to say, value not simply as a means to some other end; but it may not have any value which is not value for its citizens. Hence, the estoppel argument for implied consent cannot justify holding them to be under a duty.

Perhaps it is intended that citizens should be held under a duty not for the sake of the state, but for the sake of other citizens. In complying peacefully, each so acts in the knowledge that he thereby acquires a duty to obey and can therefore later be held to it. Unlike the restaurant or airline cases, however, this knowledge is not knowledge of a social or institutional rule, but of a political argument. Whether we have a duty to obey is controversial, not something we must accept if we wish other things bundled together in some package of benefits. For that reason, it is unlikely that the appropriate sort of reliance is very widespread. There is, moreover, a more powerful objection to this view. The argument does not show that, when others do rely on my compliance, I should be estopped from denying the duty to obey, that is, from denying the legitimacy of the state's claim to authority. At best, it shows that I ought to comply, not that I ought to accept the state's self-image. My fellow citizens may well be harmed if I fail to do my part by shirking the draft or evading taxes, but what harm do they suffer if, while complying for their sake, I *reject* the state's claim to moral authority? The strategy of peaceful compliance cannot be shown to frustrate the interests of anyone but the officials of the state, and we have assumed that they are not entitled to protect these interests. A consent theory of the correct form, therefore, will be one which assimilates consent to a kind of voluntary obligation to obey, justified by arguments about the value of this mode of acquiring obligations.

Before considering some of the more important criticisms of consent theory, we should be clear about its ambitions. Many arguments against it are really aimed at showing that it cannot 'account for' the authority of the state over all its citizens, since many do not consent and the consent of many

also possesses considerable value as a means.' J. McT. E. McTaggart, 'The Individualism of Value', in his *Philosophical Studies*, ed. E. V. Keeling (London: Edward Arnold, 1934), 109.

more is not valid. But is it true or even plausible that the state enjoys authority over all of us? Is this supposed to be a transcendental argument for the possibility conditions of something about which we all agree? Surely not. Authority is a triadic social relation among the authority, the subject, and the required action. My consent cannot bind others unless I am already authorized to bind them, so whether everyone is bound to obey turns on whether everyone has consented. Some theories, like Locke's, do seem preoccupied with the universality of the duty. In fact, this is a characteristic feature of theories of political obligation, and in Chapter 8 we shall consider some of its implications. Yet this is a strange ambition for a consent theorist, for in stretching the concept in the directions of tacit, implied, or hypothetical consent, one runs contrary to the individualistic and critical spirit of consent theory. These moves attempt to make political obligation an almost automatic consequence of living in a state and, in view of its critical function, that is precisely what it must not be. The source of this confusion is plain enough. The authority of the state is so commonly taken for granted that it appears almost part of the natural order. Political theory thus takes on the guise of an explanatory business, offering more or less correct descriptions of how the state comes to have the authority it claims over everyone within its territory. A good theory is one which shows why this is so, a bad one fails at the same task. This is to reverse the priorities, however. It might be true that citizens are bound to obey only if they consent, and at the same time true that few of them are bound precisely because they have not consented. To put it another way, consent theory may offer a correct conception of what it would be for the authority of states to be justified while at the same time offering an explanation of why it is not. Just as the best conception of free will may support the conclusion that we do not have it, the best conception of legitimate authority may show that it does not exist.

3. SIGNS OF CONSENT

Consenting is thus a way of intentionally altering a background array of rights and duties, through the beliefs and desires of the parties. The vehicle for the communication of these intentions is a conventional one. Perhaps this is clearest in the commonest mode of consent, promising. The conventional elements of promising govern, for a particular society and a particular normative change, which signs will count as promises; whether, for example, one needs to use the words, 'I promise', whether a nod counts as 'I do' in a marriage ceremony, and so on. Note that this is quite different from the claim that promising *is* conventional. We must take care to draw the distinction made in Chapter 2 between the thesis that certain obligations can only be incurred through specific conventional means from the thesis that the normative ground of the obligations is conventional. The latter, we may recall, is true only if the obligation would lose its force if it ceased to be practised among some social group; the former is true whenever members of the group must invoke a convention in order to be bound.[9] The importance of the conventional element is that it makes the question of whether someone is bound by her own consent turn partly on factual questions about the nature of conventions required and whether she invoked them. A large part of Hume's famous attack on consent theory was based on scepticism about these facts. He denied that citizens actually do anything which counts as consenting to the authority of the state. But what counts? Oaths of allegiance? Continuing residence? This particularly difficult question is densely empirical. Political theory can do no more than suggest certain constraints on interpretation.

One unacceptable answer makes the criteria purely normative: ϕ-ing counts as consenting to x if ϕ-ing has the same normative consequences as agreeing to X. This presupposes that one already has in mind certain paradigmatic instances of agreement and that other actions are equivalent if their normative consequences are. This is the structure of one

[9] Stanley Cavell argues against John Rawls that promising could not be a social practice because it could not be optional in any human society. Even if true, this does not show that promising is not conventional in either of the above senses. It is consistent with promising being a necessary human institution that its normative force depends on it actually being practised and that promises are made through conventional means of communication. Cf. J. Rawls, 'Two Concepts of Rules', *Philosophical Review* 64 (1955), 3–32; and S. Cavell, *The Claim of Reason* (New York: Oxford University Press, 1979), 292–312.

version of the 'tacit consent' argument: if continued residence within the territory of a state can be shown to generate the same rights and duties as would undertaking an oath of allegiance, then such residence is a mode of consent. The argument fails because it ignores that consenting is a peculiar *way* of creating such rights and duties and may have a peculiar justification. Although consent always has normative consequences, those consequences can usually be arrived at in other ways, so we cannot reduce the conventional criteria to those consequences.

The opposite extreme makes the criteria purely descriptive, a matter of the existence of a social rule which can be determined in purely value-neutral ways. On this view, the question of whether people are bound to the state by consent cleaves neatly into two distinct questions: the factual question of whether the signs typically counted as consent in this context have been performed, and the normative question of whether such consent, if given, would bind. The nature of the conventional criteria thus appears to be a sociological rather than philosophical matter. Although more plausible, the central problem with this alternative is that there is no such sufficiently settled and accepted rule determining which actions count as consenting to the state's authority because in most societies this is itself a matter for political argument, involving deep and perhaps intractable normative disputes. If we were to believe some philosophers, we might think that in western democracies there is a social rule that voting in free elections binds one to obey the winner, provided that he or she exercises his or her powers constitutionally. Others disagree. To what colourless social facts might we appeal to settle the question? There are no politically innocent actors whose behaviour will count as neutral evidence. The social meaning of voting is hotly disputed, not because some of the facts which might settle it are complex or obscure, but because political argument is all-pervasive. Now, this is not a general feature of conventional social rules; it has nothing to do with the fact that those rules are unwritten or lack an authoritative interpretation. The social meaning of a great many actions is not deeply contested: a slap in the face expresses disapproval. Nor is it even true that the meaning of all consent-giving actions is essentially contested: it is largely settled what is needed to consent to the use of one's organs for transplant purposes after death, or what counts as consent to be married. The point is the narrower one that there is no settled social rule determining what counts as consent to the state's authority. One who does not accept the authority of the state will not accept that peaceful residence in the country commits her to it.

Although the conventional criteria for what counts as consent and the normative conditions governing its validity are analytically distinct, they tend to co-vary strongly. In general, we may suppose that the more rigorous the validity conditions for a particular species of consent (e.g., that it must be voluntary, fully informed, public, etc.) the more demanding will be the conventional signs. And roughly speaking the more central and important the interests which are at stake, the clearer will be the sign of consent that is required to effect them. This idea should be familiar from other contexts. In our legal systems, for example, contracts to sell land must be made in writing; an oral agreement which is valid for many other purposes is not enough here. Now, the state claims comprehensive and supreme authority over many people's vital interests, so we should expect that a very clear sign would be required to count as consent—and such is the position of traditional consent theory.[10] This places a normative constraint on the interpretation of social action in this realm. If the putative sign of consent is something trivial and common, or whose meaning is a matter of deep dispute, then it is unlikely to signify such an important relationship. Mere residence, therefore, is not enough, a public promise to obey the laws is, and between lies a realm of contest. This constraint is, however, just a presumptive one; it can be rebutted by independent evidence of the consenter's beliefs and intentions. She may regard singing the national anthem as a sign of her consent, and others may know and accept this. In this sense the descriptivist is correct: any action might count as consent. In general however, we lack such independent evidence. The interpretative presumption urges us not to

[10] See A. J. Simmons, *Moral Principles and Political Obligations*, 64.

respond to this uncertainty by invoking tacit consent as a fiction, but by denying that consent has occurred. This is a conservative strategy, but one eminently justified by the stakes. For consider the two types of error that are possible here. Our test for consent may report a false positive: holding people bound when they are not; or a false negative: denying that they are bound when they are. We cannot simultaneously minimize the risk of both errors. Which then should we regard as more serious? The risk of a false negative can easily be avoided by the citizens themselves, for they are always at liberty to give an explicit undertaking to obey. A false positive could of course also be negated by an explicit denial; but how will they know in advance which behaviours will be counted as expressing consent? How will they know that denial is called for? It might be said that a blanket, once-and-for-all, denial would suffice. But so long as the ability to create obligations is not waived, it is always possible that later actions of compliance, perhaps even of peacefully travelling the highways, as Locke says, will be counted as a change of heart. Above all, the seriousness of the obligations undertaken suggests that it would be reasonable to regard the false positive as a worse error, and to adopt the conservative strategy in order to avoid it.

Peter Singer, however, has argued for the opposite interpretative assumption. 'It must', he writes, 'be reasonable to assume consent on the part of a person who votes without in any way indicating that his vote is not to be taken as an indication of consent. This must be reasonable, not because people who vote as a matter of fact usually do consent, but because there is a conceptual connection between voting and consenting. What would be the sense of having a vote if no one ever accepted the result of the vote?'[11] Singer supposes that the answer must be, no sense at all. But this question is ill posed, and the answer over-simple. In the first place, they may not take the view that, in refusing consent to the authority of the state, they will *never* accept the result of the vote. They may accept it when they agree with it and in those cases of disagreement when the consequences of resisting are,

[11] P. Singer, *Democracy and Disobedience* (New York: Oxford University Press, 1974), 50.

on balance, bad. As a result, they may comply quite regularly, without ever surrendering their judgement. Secondly, it seems groundless to insist that there is a conceptual connection between voting and consenting if this is merely the claim that it would be wrong to *call* it voting if it did not express consent. There is nothing linguistically improper about describing an anarchist's action in marking her ballot for the least bad candidate as 'voting'. Finally, the conceptual connection argument offers an answer to the wrong question. We are not to ask, 'Why would anyone set up a practice of voting knowing that participating in it will not express consent?' but rather, 'Is it possible to make sense of the individual decision to vote even if that individual does not regard herself as thereby expressing her consent?' The answer to the latter question is decisively in the affirmative: she may vote to minimize her losses.

Singer's most important argument for the authority of the state has little to do with consent at all. He regards voting as a fair compromise among people who would each like to be a dictator but realize that such an arrangement would never command enough support to be instituted. An equal share of voting power they regard as a good second-best solution. In itself, however, this argument is too weak, for it only shows that democratic arrangements have real merits; it does not show that we are bound to obey them. Singer deploys a second argument in support of that conclusion. He appeals to the principle of estoppel:

> In voting, one's voluntary behaviour leads others to the reasonable belief that one consents to the majority decision-procedure. After the event, one cannot say that one never consented—or, to be strictly accurate, even if one says that one never consented, one is still obliged as if one had consented.[12]

The disclaimer states the truth of the matter. Singer realizes that this argument does not show that citizens have actually, though tacitly, consented to obey. In fact, their normative position is only one of what he calls 'quasi-consent'. But quasi-consent is not a consent-based principle. Even if voters are bound to obey because failure to do so will frustrate the

[12] Ibid. 52.

legitimate expectations of others, it is not a consequence of having consented. To believe otherwise is to make the mistake of identifying consent with its normative consequences. The weakness of the estoppel argument itself is twofold. First, the factual premiss is dubious: many vote without relying on the ultimate compliance of everyone else. Secondly, if sound, the argument only justifies compliance with the state, not acceptance of its authority. This point was argued above.

Thus, the estoppel argument fails, and there is generally no independent evidence of the meaning of voting. In the liberal democracies there is no law or settled social practice which makes voting a sign of consent, and the right to vote is not conditional on one's acceptance of the state's authority. If this is so, then the interpretative assumption takes over. Given what governments do and claim authority to do, must we interpret voting as a sign of consent, or are there other explanations of what voters are about? Plainly there are. Whether or not one votes, one will be governed by the preferences of those who do. If one believes that one's vote will make a difference to one's own or others' welfare, then it is instrumentally rational to vote: in view of its low costs it minimizes one's losses. And even if one is not instrumentally efficacious, one may vote in order to express and reinforce sincere preferences over the outcomes. Any of these would explain the social meaning of voting without invoking the improbable hypothesis that voters thereby intend to bind themselves to the state.

It may be said that this argument only applies to voting and not to stronger forms of participation. Radical participation theorists like Pateman follow Rousseau in arguing that only widespread, continuing, democratic, and morally serious participation in political parties, trade unions, juries, and the like counts as consent, but that, when given, this binds participants to obey.[13] It must be conceded that this is a stronger argument, though not for the reasons one might think. Such participation makes it more likely that consent if given is valid, because in these circumstances the cognitive and volitional validity conditions of consent are more likely to

[13] C. Pateman, *The Problem of Political Obligation*.

be fulfilled: it is more likely to be both free and informed. At the same time, these are contexts in which citizens have greater independent reasons to participate. In smaller groups sharing certain goals and interests individuals are likely to have more influence than they do in the large and rather anonymous state and thus to have stronger instrumental reasons for participation. Moreover, participation may work a moral transformation in citizens, giving them further reasons to participate: it is educative, morally uplifting, and may even be required by fairness or a duty to share in the life of the group.

None of this shows that strong participation cannot count as consent; again, it merely provides alternative explanations of its social meaning. Alternative explanations are not necessarily competing ones. If such participation were accompanied by other conventional signs, such as promising to obey, or writing articles supporting such commitments, then it would count as consent. Of course, such signs would be sufficiently clear on their own. The point is not that participation can never count as consent, merely that we cannot so count it without independent evidence of its meaning. Governments sponsor and encourage the stronger interpretation, but this is to be resisted. We rightly require evidence more compelling than either turn-out figures or even the existence of a grass-roots democracy.

4. VALIDITY

Doubts about the signs of consent only go to the question of whether or not consent has been given. No general sceptical arguments can succeed on that score; one would have to show in particular cases that consent has not been given. Yet consent may be given and still be invalid: the conventional act may be performed and still fail to have its purported normative consequences. The most important of these validity conditions are the volitional and cognitive requirements, for a binding promise must be both free and informed. Thus far, I have criticized consent theorists who are too ready to read consent into various social acts. At best this shows that consent is more rarely given than is often assumed. I now consider certain objections that may be raised even when it is not in doubt that the appropriate signs have been performed.

4.1 *Hard Choices*

Some have argued that it is of the nature of the state's authority that consent to it cannot be freely given. Clearly, there are particular circumstances in which consent to political authority will not bind, for example, if it is extorted at gunpoint. Can this argument be made more general? In his essay, 'Of the Original Contract', Hume attempts to do so. He argues that continued residence can not be counted as an expression of consent because the only alternative is so harsh as not to constitute a real alternative at all:

> Can we seriously say, that a poor peasant or artisan has a free choice to leave his country, when he knows no foreign language or manners, and lives from day to day by the small wages which he acquires. We may as well assert that a man, by remaining in a vessel, freely consents to the dominion of the master; though he was carried on board while asleep, and must leap into the ocean and perish the moment he leaves her.[14]

To Hume's suggestion that we are like hostages, some would reply that our condition is more like that of stowaways, seeking the benefits without paying the fare. It is an understatement to say that we do not yet possess an adequate theory of how, if ever, hard choices are coercive or constitute duress.[15] It is clearly not sufficient that they be highly motivated, for that would nullify Hobbes's social contract which, if the argument is sound, all parties strongly prefer to the state of nature. If hard choices are to be characterized as unfree, then they cannot be identified solely by use of the comparative or ordinal judgments of value which any agent must make in order to behave rationally. We need conceptual resources which allow us to say that an offer of your money for

[14] D. Hume, *Essays: Moral, Political, and Literary*, ed. E. F. Miller (Indianapolis: Liberty Classics, 1985), 475.

[15] See, for example, R. Nozick, 'Coercion', in P. Laslett and W. G. Runciman, eds., *Philosophy, Politics and Society*, 4th ser. (Oxford: Blackwell, 1972), 101–35; H. Frankfurt, 'Coercion and Moral Responsibility', in T. Honderich, ed., *Essays on Freedom of Action* (London: Routledge and Kegan Paul, 1973); and D. Zimmerman, 'Coercive Wage Offers', *Philosophy and Public Affairs* 10 (1981), 121–45.

your life is coercive, even though one rationally chooses to secure one's welfare by handing over the money, while also maintaining that not all cases of choosing a lesser evil are coercive ones. The only way of doing this is to admit absolute or cardinal judgements of value, and that is a notoriously difficult business.

But let us suppose that this can be done and that we can identify objectively hard choices such that anyone forced to make one would be subject to a kind of duress which would invalidate their consent. And suppose further that emigration is indeed well below the threshold of objective acceptability. The argument is not yet won, however, for one needs to show that the alternative to which one is driven is that of accepting the authority of the state. Is this so? Perhaps what is at the bottom of Hume's complaint is that in a world of states, one can re-enter the state of nature only with the help of others. If most people are happy to consent while you are not, then it may seem that you have no choice but to submit to the inevitability of some state's authority. But this is not correct. Even if one would perish outside a state or there is no viable exit route, it does not follow that one must accept its authority in order to live inside it. One always has the option of conditional submission without consent, of peaceful compliance. This will normally be enough to avoid sanctions. What of those exceptional times when oaths of allegiance are required and loyalty tests proliferate, when one must either 'love it or leave it'? Such a state would provide sanctions not only for lack of compliance, but also for lack of commitment. In such circumstances, the options of consent or exile would obviously be extortionate; they would signify that the state was so unjust that one's consent could not in any case bind.[16] Hume's way of generalizing the argument from duress will not work, and it is hard to see what other form would. This is at least one objection from which consent-based theories remain secure.

[16] Moreover, no public policy would warrant such irrational measures. First, they would be self-defeating, for doubts about the sincerity of consent would be endemic. Secondly, in any class-divided society, the means to leave would be disproportionately in the hands of the wealthier and better educated citizens, as Hume saw. But then those for whom 'exit' will be an attractive option are just those whose support would be most valuable were they to remain behind. Cf. A. O. Hirschman, *Exit, Voice, and Loyalty* (Cambridge, Mass.: Harvard University Press, 1970), 44–54.

4.2 *Uncertainty*

In order to bind, consent must be not only free, but also informed. Whether the justification for consent lies in the protection it offers the interests of the consenter, or the way it empowers her to express her will, certain kinds of cognitive failure will defeat the point of consenting. One must understand, at least roughly and in general, what one is consenting to. About some things, it is not possible to be clear-minded. For example, one cannot promise to do logically or practically impossible things: ought implies can. Despite the rhetorical excesses of certain anarchists legitimate authority is not, as I argued in Chapter 2, a contradiction in terms: consent to obey is not *logically* impossible. It might, however, presuppose a commitment which is defective on other grounds. Impossible promises do not bind, but neither do some very vague ones. Perhaps the social contract is void because it is, as lawyers say, 'uncertain'.

We should distinguish two kinds of uncertainty or open-endedness which may arise in assuming obligations. One is *vagueness*, as in the extreme case, 'I promise to do something for you'. Here, the act-type is so open as to defeat any point in promising, for it is inherently unclear what would count as keeping the promise. But this is quite different from *content-independence*, as in 'I promise to obey all your commands'. Here, although it is not known in advance which act-tokens will be required, it is known which act-types are, namely, obedience to commands. This sort of open-endedness consists in the fact that the required acts are those which pass a certain test of form, that is to say, that they are commanded. Thus when political theorists object[17] that a promise to obey the state would not bind because it would be a 'blank cheque' or a 'wild card' they might have either sort of open-endedness in mind.

We cannot specify just how much vagueness will defeat a promise. In the common law, the traditional view was that courts would not write a contract for the parties and so vagueness about their main duties under the agreement would void it. There can be no doubt that, in view of the volatility of

[17] J. H. Reiman, *In Defense of Political Philosophy*, 2–4.

democratic politics, some vagueness is inevitable. It is a sound piece of folk wisdom that the platforms of political parties are designed to run on rather than stand on. Moreover, our main political duties are created by law, which is inherently general in form, requires interpretation, and provides for judicial discretion. For those reasons and to that extent, they are vague. However, a reasonably just state will be one committed, through the rule of law, to such clarity as is humanly possible in the determination of political rights and duties. Since consent can only bind to a just state, it can only bind where clarity is not so problematic as to defeat any intention to bind oneself.

That leaves content-independence. This does not defeat voluntary obligations. As I argued in Chapter 2, it is part of their very nature: a promise to ϕ binds not because of the value of ϕ-ing but because of the value of keeping one's promises, whatever their content. This is compatible with there being limits on what we can legitimately promise to do and with promises having only prima-facie force. One must distinguish content-independence not only from vagueness but also from absoluteness of obligation. Godwin asks, 'Why should I promise that I will do everything that a certain power, called the government, shall imagine it convenient, or decide that it is fitting, for me to do? Is there in this either morality, or justice, or common sense?'[18] If his point is that one should not concede authority where it claims to be absolute, then he is right. Although political authority of its nature claims to be supreme or final, it cannot in justice claim to outweigh all other moral considerations. But if instead he challenges the rationality of committing oneself to a standard independently of its content, he is wrong, for all voluntary obligations do that and, as we have seen, the anarchist must rely more heavily on voluntary obligations than must those who favour the state's non-voluntary arrangements for providing certain goods and services. But to rely on voluntary obligations is to rely on commitments which claim to bind in virtue of their form and not their content. Uncertainty is therefore no special obstacle to consent theory.

[18] W. Godwin, *Enquiry Concerning Political Justice*, 229.

4.3 *The Assurance Problem*

There is, however, at least one difficulty which seems particularly problematic here. However the details are worked out, it is clear that consent-based theories are especially demanding when compared to either contractarian or conventionalist ones. It is necessary that citizens have actually done something that amounts to consent in order for them to be bound; however well-ordered the society the authority of the state will remain illegitimate without this further ratification.

The strength of these demands may give rise to certain worries. The public knowledge that a society is justly ordered and its government legitimate is itself a social asset, as John Rawls notes.[19] It provides for stability and reliability of certain expectations which are in turn of great instrumental value. Even people disposed to act justly towards others may not do so when they lack assurance that others will do the same, and the public knowledge that they will is therefore important. But suppose that individual consent were a necessary condition of the state having legitimate authority to make laws, regulate their affairs, and so forth. Given that there is no simple reliable and universal sign of consent—having abandoned the view that mere residence or participation can be so considered—will there not be considerable doubt about the allegiance of the others? Rawls argues, 'citizens might still wonder about one another whether they were bound, or so regarded themselves. The public conviction that all are tied to just arrangements would be less firm, and a greater reliance on the coercive powers of the sovereign might be necessary to achieve stability.'[20] The risks would be too great and could be avoided by agreeing that the foundations of legitimacy should rest, not in principles of obligation which depend for their validity on voluntary acts, but on non-voluntary natural duties which bind all regardless of their own actions or states of mind.

There is indeed some risk of the sort Rawls contemplates, but he has made it seem more serious than it in fact is by over-simplifying the sources of stability that can be expected in a just society. We are not forced to conclude that where consent

[19] J. Rawls, *A Theory of Justice*, 336.

[20] Ibid. 337.

is in doubt, coercion will be needed. Compliance with a just order will have many sources, including prudential considerations, the recognition of natural duty, limited benevolence, and the fact that what the state requires of us is often what we have independent reason to do. The role of consent should not be mistaken. It is not to be evaluated as a stabilizing device for social order, but as a legitimating device.

4.4 *Circularity*

Among Hume's several arguments against consent theory, one is often felt to be particularly persuasive. He contends that it is not necessary to ground the duty of allegiance in a duty to keep promises because both are conventional or artificial virtues which have a common source in the requirements of public utility:

> We are bound to obey our sovereign, it is said; because we have given a tacit promise to that purpose. But why are we bound to observe our promise? It must here be asserted, that the commerce and intercourse of mankind, which are of such mighty advantage, can have no security where men pay no regard to their engagements. In like manner, may it be said, that men could not live at all in society, at least in civilized society, without laws and magistrates and judges, to prevent the encroachments of the strong upon the weak, of the violent upon the just and equitable. The obligation of allegiance being of like force and authority with the obligation to fidelity, we gain nothing by resolving the one into the other. The general interests or necessities of society are sufficient to establish both.[21]

Hume feels that his answer has other merits as well, such as being consistent with common sense and received opinion. (Only a philosopher, he thinks, would believe that consent is necessary to establish authority.) But its most attractive feature is that it avoids what Hume takes to be the circularity of consent-based theories: If you say that we should obey because we should keep our word, 'you find yourself embarrassed, when it is asked, *why are we bound to keep our word?* Nor can you give any answer, but what would, immediately, without any circuit, have accounted for our obligation to allegiance.'[22]

[21] D. Hume, *Essays*, 481.

[22] Ibid.

Hume sees a small truth here, but makes a large error. It is correct that no complete theory of consent can fail to provide some independent account of why consent-giving acts should be thought to bind. It may be of the nature of promises that they bind, but there is always room for an explanation for why we have a practice with such a nature at all. It does not follow, however, that such an explanation renders consent redundant in the justification of authority. To say that consent-based theories are incomplete is not to say that they are circular. That latter would be true only if the explanation for promises were the *same* as the explanation for authority. Hume argues that it is in so far as both fall under the general rubric of public utility or common interest, although he says (most clearly in the *Treatise* Bk. III) that they are founded independently on two different species of such utility. Is it enough to defeat consent theory that neither is more necessary to human society than the other, and thus neither deserves to be given explanatory priority? Hume wants to suggest that both promises and authority have conventional foundations of the same sort. But, as we have already seen in Chapter 4, this argument is weak. Promises and authoritative requirements have in common the fact that they purport to create binding commitments—to obligate—and the conventionalist theory cannot give a satisfactory account of why this should be so. Moreover, one may agree that consent and authority must each have *independent* explanations of their validity, while denying that they have the *same* explanation. Hume is willing to admit that they serve different departments of public utility, and perhaps that large and accommodating notion can cover almost anything; but it may instead be the case that they serve different interests entirely. Moreover, something like that must be true if consent is to be possible as a ground of authority. Hume says that his argument is a modest one: 'My intention here is not to exclude the consent of the people from being one just foundation of government where it has place. It is surely the best and most sacred of any.'[23] The notion that there is something particularly valuable about consent does not sit well with the idea that other sources of the duty to obey

[23] Ibid. 474. The editor, E. F. Miller, notes that this disclaimer was added by Hume in the edition of 1753.

have the same priority and necessity as it does. What Hume's argument establishes then is not that any account of consent which does not justify it by public utility must be circular, but that one is always entitled to enquire further why a particular species of consent is thought to be binding at all. Let us consider the kinds of answer one might give to that question.

5. JUSTIFICATIONS FOR CONSENT

The practice of consenting is sometimes justified by its *instrumental* value in attaining certain ends which are independent of the act of consent. For example, a patient's consent is normally needed before any medical procedure may be performed. Here, the practice has a protective function in securing the patient's well-being either because he is thought to be the best judge of his own welfare, or because of an independent interest in liberty. Political consent, however, involves the assumption of an obligation to obey, so we cannot appeal directly to the protective role. Perhaps promising to obey the law would save time and effort in thinking about what one ought to do, or it would reinforce pre-existing reasons for obedience. Even in a reasonably just state, however, possibilities for miscalculation are rife, and excessive attention to the secondary reasons for obedience tends to distract us from the primary ones. This is particularly true in circumstances of rapid social change. Furthermore, in all such efficiency-based arguments, it is too easy to neglect the broader effects that such wide-ranging commitments might have on moral character. Citizens could become irresponsible, lazy, and sloppy in their habits of thought. A resulting general decline in critical awareness might have adverse effects even in a just state, for injustice can emerge unintentionally as laws become obsolete. Still, it must be admitted that none of these considerations show that it would never be rational to have such an institution. For some citizens the calculations may come out right, and perhaps no stronger conclusion can fairly be expected of such a speculative argument. Or can a stronger case be made out?

Perhaps the instrumental benefits of consent are general and mutual ones. The power to consent might be claimed to enable individuals to enter into a social contract in order to sustain and promote valuable forms of co-operation. Here, however, we run up against the difficulties described in Chapter 5: collective action problems do not in general require authoritative solutions, and the creation of authority itself poses a prior collective action problem. It does not help to suppose that consenting to a system of mutual restraint or shared obligations would be fair, since we ought anyway to do what is required by fairness, and the most that consent could add to its requirements are the reinforcing instrumental benefits discussed above. Are we to suppose that each might stand to gain enough by his unilateral consent for that to validate it? It is possible to imagine such circumstances in special cases: a convicted criminal, for instance, might be offered his liberty in exchange for a promise to obey the law. Most would value their freedom at a sufficiently high rate to make this worthwhile, and for some criminals anyway it would not be a harsh bargain. Indeed, the least we could expect of those who intentionally violate just laws and thereby show themselves to be insufficiently motivated by the demands of justice is that they undertake a public commitment to those laws. It is not difficult to imagine a biography and a social history which would make the bargain of liberty for obedience seem fair. However, the whole idea that such a deal might legitimately be struck already presupposes the existence of an authoritative apparatus of adjudication and enforcement in order to determine who has become liable to such an offer. We are surely not all to be treated as criminals.

These considerations suggest that a general instrumental justification for consent in the political context is unlikely to be found. That leaves open the possibility of a *non-instrumental* justification. Promising in general may have expressive as well as instrumental functions, for it may provide a means of expressing the agent's commitment to certain values and projects. Can this idea be extended to the political context? Joseph Raz has argued that it can, at least to some degree, for consent to be bound by the law may be an appropriate expression of a valuable attitude towards one's society, 'an attitude of belonging and of sharing in its collective life'.[24]

[24] J. Raz, The Morality of Freedom, 91.

Rousseau's fairly complete identification of the citizen with the state might seem unappealing, but there is no reason not to suppose that more moderate attachments might not be of value. The role of consent in such a framework is parallel to the role that voluntary obligations play in private morality. An important part of moral life is its creative aspect, through which we structure our moral worlds by assuming commitments to certain projects and particular people, especially through the creation of valuable human relationships like friendship or marriage. It is true that consent has an instrumental role to play here, for the reason that it makes obligation dependent on the agent's will and he or she is presumptively the best judge of his or her own interests. But beyond this it may play a constitutive role in creating these relationships. The consensual element in marriage, for example, is not merely a device to secure optimal partners, but is an essential aspect of the relation. How far can such reasoning be extended to political life?

Suppose that identification with a justly ordered community is of inherent value; how does this bear on the authority of the state? In any society, the primary locus of such ties is not likely to be the state, but rather the competing and narrower loyalties of religious and ethnic groups. In many states, ethnic nationalism provides for stronger bonds of identity than does political authority and when it is not accompanied by intolerance is a legitimate source of value, however dubious its historical foundations or narrow its outlook. Such sources of obligations compete with the state for the loyalties of their members. The state claims supremacy, however, and actively enforces its claims: it decides which groups will be officially recognized and protected—whether any group of worshippers is a church, any band of partisans a political party, any collection of workers a trade union. What in the theory of expressive consent could underwrite such pretensions?

It might be thought that it is provided for by the fact that it is consent to be bound by *law* which expresses the valued social union and that in any society it is the nature of legal institutions to be predominant and unique. But the valued relationship is not 'union under law'—that would trivialize the theory. Rather, consent is said to express 'an attitude not to the law but to the society whose law it is. It expresses an attitude to the law as an aspect of that society (which it can be only if the law is felt to express social conventions and outlook)'.[25] In a just society, this attitude has expressive and non-instrumental value. Raz thinks it is a matter of fact that in our society consent to obey expresses such identification. It is not, of course, the only way in which it is or may be expressed. In a state with an official religion, or perhaps even a national sport, consent to the authority of the regime may not be the clearest or most appropriate statement of one's loyalties. Nor does he think that this is the only complete expression of loyalty. His point is simply that respect for the law, which includes the acceptance of an obligation to obey it, may be justified as an expression of identification with the community whose law it is.

How is it that respect for law can express attachment to the community? One is tempted to say, because it is the community's law. Now, it is true that a legal system exists only in a particular society, but that is not enough to establish the proper sort of relationship between the two. Rather, the argument depends on law being an *aspect* of that society. Yet the existence of law does not presuppose any such correspondence between its requirements and social convention and outlook. Many laws lag behind, and others stride in advance of, shared outlooks and do so without being unjust. In those cases law claims authority which cannot be justified by expressive consent, for it is not an 'aspect of society' except in the trivial sense that it is that society's law. And since law is always a mixed bag in terms of its relation to social convention, attachment to the latter would be better expressed by selective adherence and support.

Expressive theories can thus have no more than a subordinate role in the justification of authority. Like expressive theories of punishment, they get the order of explanation backwards. Punishment cannot be justified as an expression of society's indignation at a crime; it is the fact that punishment is warranted on independent grounds that justifies such an expression of indignation. Likewise, consent is not justified

[25] Ibid.

because it is the expression of a valued relationship; it is the value of the relationship that justifies its expression in consent. To validate the sort of organic relationship between individuals and their states contemplated by the idealists and other political romantics, one therefore needs an argument for the value of political relationships which are constituted, not merely by relations of belonging, but by relations of commitment. If such an argument can be made out then it might extend the scope of consent-based arguments. We will return to that problem in the next chapter.

6. THE VALUE OF CONSENT

Consent does much better in justifying the authority of the state than do the other theories. In favoured circumstances it can be valid and thus it is a genuine source of legitimacy. The justifications for the validity of consent do suggest, however, that there are probably no strong reasons for citizens of the modern state to want the power to bind themselves to obey. Consent given for inadequate reasons does bind, but a theory of the state should be embarrassed to take refuge in the maxim that 'Chancery mends no man's bargain'. While consent is thus an important justification for political authority, the fact that there seems to be no compulsive account of its validity also means that it is not a general justification. There are citizens of just states who not only do not consent, but whose consent, if given, would not bind. The range of application of consent is therefore narrower than is sometimes thought; many fewer consent to the state's authority than the democratic tradition has been inclined to suppose. It may therefore seem puzzling that democratic political theory has been unanimous in praising government by consent. Can so many have been taken in by an error? Another explanation is available. We must not infer from the truth that consent-based theories of authority have only limited validity the falsehood that a state which governs with the consent of its citizens is no better than one which does not. We can more clearly understand the value of consent if we do not regard it merely as a potential ground of authority. Consent has other functions as well. When John Plamenatz came to have second thoughts about this issue, he wrote, 'The important question is not, To what extent does the duty of obedience arise from consent? It is much rather, Under what conditions is government by consent more to be desired than other forms of government?'[26] These conditions depend on consent having functions other than its characteristic one of authorizing action. For example, although approval is neither a necessary nor sufficient condition of consent, it very often does accompany it, and consent is therefore normally good evidence of the citizens' approval. Approval itself is only a secondary value, but in a reasonably just society it is better that the state act with it than without. A government should respond to the wants of its citizens as far as justice permits and, because they often have the best information about their own wants, consenting provides a means of communicating it. Moreover, the practice of consent is non-instrumentally good for citizens because it requires deliberation about matters of public concern and the exercise and development of cognitive skills and moral sensibility. Cynicism about the educative value of democratic government is often a product of excessive expectations. It would be foolish to pretend that political activity is the unique or paramount forum of practical education, but it is for all that an important one.

Both the educative and communicative functions of consent are secondary in the sense that they are parasitic on consent as a means of creating relations of commitment between ourselves and others. Taken by themselves, they could not explain the value of consent, for approval may be expressed and education fostered in other ways. Yet their role in accounting for the common view that government by consent is a particularly desirable way of running a constitutional regime is an important one. If one considered only the core normative function of consent, it would be hard to explain the appeal of this view. If all consent did was authorize officials to act in certain ways then a government enjoying greater consent would be one which is more highly authorized, nothing more. But that is not itself a value-contributing characteristic. We do not think a police chief more worthy than a constable just

[26] J. P. Plamenatz, *Consent, Freedom and Political Obligation*, 172–3.

because her authority is greater or more secure, nor do we regard the decisions of a final court of appeal as more just or even more legally sound than those of lower courts solely for the reason that they are more binding. Likewise, we must look to the ancillary functions of consent to explain its full role in political theory. Its primary functions show why democratic theorists are correct to regard consent as a justification for authority; but only its ancillary functions show why government by consent is to be prized.

7

COMMITMENT AND COMMUNITY

To this point, we have rejected two and given qualified acceptance to one of the popular justifications for political authority. Neither the power of government to create conventions serving the common good, nor its capacity to solve certain problems of collective action warrants citizens taking its directives as binding. These are, indeed, among the important functions of government and they do contribute to its value. But they do not justify its authority. To do that we must find principles which recommend regarding the state as a duty-imposer, as having the power to create binding, content-independent reasons to act. The traditional theory of consent succeeds here. But it is equally true that its scope is limited: not many of us have, in fact, consented. It follows then that the state has legitimate authority only over some of its citizens.

Some may feel that the modesty of our conclusions to this point is a consequence of a particular philosophical perspective which underlies the three families of theories we have been considering. To be sure, there are profound differences among them: the two instrumental theories of social order offer very different pictures of the ills which authority is alleged to cure—different pictures of the state of nature. And consent theory is unlike each of these in offering an argument which does not represent authority as a necessary or desirable means of securing a valued form of social order, but rather as a product of another form of social relation. Yet despite these differences all three share one important feature. They are in a perfectly obvious sense *individualistic* theories, for central to their fundamental explanatory and justificatory apparatus are individual human beings and their interests.

Is it perhaps this individualism which puts political authority beyond their reach? That was suggested at the conclusion of Chapter 5. The contrary view is, however, a popular one. Only Leviathan, it is claimed, can tame Hobbes's warriors: the more demanding the id, the more repressive the superego. Perhaps for this reason radicals of many persuasions (including Rousseau and Marx) have felt that it is only through self-transformation and the rejection of individualism that the problem of domination can be solved. But it is a consequence of the argument thus far that a social theory can accommodate a very large measure of individualism without conceding the authority of the state. So far from providing the ground for authority, individualism militates against it. Would it perhaps follow that, in relaxing individualism, we would provide a context in which authority is more justifiable? This chapter investigates one such way of enlarging the scope of legitimate authority.

1. MODES OF INDIVIDUALISM

Non-individualistic theories of authority have often emerged in reaction to the perceived weakness of classical contractarian and consent-based doctrines, and that is how I shall approach them here. In Chapter 6, I discussed a number of possible general objections to consent theory, objections which centred on doubts about whether consent is ever given, and if so, whether it is ever free and informed. Our result was a qualified defence of consent. But even if that argument were unsound, the damage to consent theory would have been minimal. At best, it would have shown that the state has legitimate authority over few if any, and not that consent theory misrepresents what it would be for such authority to exist. Hence, these objections are perfectly compatible with the view that consent theory is the correct account of our relation to the state: an anarchist can be a consent theorist. For this reason, the arguments to which we now turn are more radical. They seek to establish that, even when the validity conditions for consent *are* fulfilled, the theory presents a misleading picture of the forms of commitment at stake.

Reacting against that strand of western political theory which regards political and sometimes even social life as artificial, some writers emphasize the social dimension of human existence and see the atomic individual as an artificial abstraction. The recent popularity of such views is not unprecedented; they echo an earlier line of criticism of market society found in thinkers as varied as Carlyle, Marx, and Durkheim, one which urges us to begin with the community and attempt to understand individual lives as necessarily constructed in that context. The uses to which such theories have been put are diverse. Here, I wish to consider only whether some such view might offer an alternative to the justifications for political authority which we have already discussed. More exactly, I shall examine some communitarian approaches to the problem of political obligation, namely, the thesis that everyone has an obligation to obey all the laws of his or her own state. In Chapter 8, I shall stipulate a distinction between theories of justified authority and theories of political obligation, but for present purposes this may be ignored.

A communitarian may begin with the correct observation that not all obligations are assumed voluntarily. (The obligation to keep promises, as Hume saw, obviously cannot be.) Consent theory, however, attempts to assimilate duties to one's state to commitments to a voluntary organization. A radically individualistic approach, it sets the threshold for rational commitment too high; it makes our attachment to a reasonably just state look weaker than it is by supposing that we must intentionally do something in order to become attached, something which has attachment as part of its aim. But underlying all this, the objector continues, is a suspect social metaphysics according to which the only morally significant relations between abstract individuals are external ones created by acts of will. Only in this peculiar context does the question of political obligation even arise. As one writer puts it: 'political obligation is an important concept for certain theorists only—in general, liberals, individualists, believers in the artificiality of society.'[1] Similarly, it is sometimes said that the plausibility of Socrates' very strong view of the duty to submit to the laws is tied to a classical conception of the person as much less individualistic and independent than the modern one; the questions that rive our public and private

[1] T. McPherson, *Political Obligation* (London: Routledge and Kegan Paul, 1967), 63.

commitments just do not arise for the polis-animal. And in a related vein, Hegel's distaste for contractarianism lies in the fact that it attempts to reduce the deeper unities of the state to a mundane mechanical combination of wills. As in marriage, the social relations between individual and state should be seen as internal and constitutive, not as external and instrumental. This family of objections poses a radical critique of the whole social theory underlying consent-based arguments. Rejecting individualism, it offers a counter-image of our moral predicament. Just what is at issue here?

When it is objected that individualistic assumptions render some accounts of political authority unsound and perhaps unintelligible, the acceptability of several different theses may be at issue, for individualism in a social theory may be manifest in different forms.[2] At the deepest, metaphysical level, one could be an *ontological* individualist, regarding only individual human beings as ultimately real. This would not preclude talk of societies, nations, groups, classes, and so on, although it would require a reductionist interpretation of them. Similarly, social relations could be retained, provided they were understood as external relations between independently existing and uniquely real persons.[3]

Individualism in that sense is to be distinguished from the family of views which go under the name of *methodological* individualism, that is, the doctrine that the only acceptable ultimate explanations of social phenomena are those couched wholly in terms of facts about individuals. The boundaries of this second theory are somewhat vague. As Lukes has persuasively argued, there is actually a continuum of so-called individual facts, ranging from purely physical descriptions to those richly detailed accounts which make reference to 'institutional facts' (such as 'casting a vote,' or 'obeying a law'). So far, explanations of social phenomena only seem to work if they admit at least some facts well along towards the institutional end of the scale: we can explain election results in terms of votes cast but not in terms of neurophysiology, and

[2] Following S. Lukes, *Individualism* (Oxford: Basil Blackwell, 1973).

[3] Cf. C. C. Gould, *Marx's Social Ontology* (Cambridge, Mass.: MIT Press, 1978), ch. 1.

nothing on the horizon suggests that this is about to change.[4]

Although sometimes confused, the methodological and ontological theses are logically independent. It may be that only individuals are ultimately real in some favoured metaphysical sense, but also that reductive explanations of social phenomena are untrue, unavailable, or not worth pursuing. This might be the case if social phenomena are systemically or functionally organized. An analogy may help clarify here. Arguably, the only ultimately real components of a computer are the hardware (under a purely physical description); however, any adequate theory of its operation will also need to make reference to the programme and the rest of the software. Moreover, how we ought to study some subject matter depends not only on the inherent nature of that thing, but also on our natures, including our limited capacities for receiving, interpreting, and processing data. A predictive model which could not be calculated in real time, for example, would be useless. This means that the sort of considerations supporting methodological individualism will need to be quite different from those supporting ontological individualism.

Finally—and this may be more obvious—both of these are logically independent of the third, and for our purposes most important, mode of individualism. Lukes divides *ethical* individualism into two variants:[5] the view that individual human beings are the object of all value, and the view that they are the source of all value in the sense that what is of value depends entirely on the nature of their choices, desires, and commitments. Here, I shall regard the latter thesis as more properly a theory of moral epistemology and not of first-order, or substantive, value theory at all. As to the former, it extends well beyond ethical egoism, the case considered by Lukes. It includes everything covered by McTaggart's view that only conscious beings and their mental states can be of ultimate value, i.e. of value as an end in themselves and not merely as a means.[6]

For anyone accepting a strong version of the fact-value

[4] For some interesting reflections on why not, see H. Putnam, *Meaning and the Moral Sciences* (London: Routledge and Kegan Paul, 1978), 66–77.

[5] S. Lukes, *Individualism*, 99–106.

[6] J. McT. E. McTaggart, 'The Individualism of Value', 109.

distinction, the independence of ethical from ontological or methodological individualism follows immediately. Naturally, there are historical, ideological, and other affinities among these views. But the relation is no stronger than that. One can view social classes as ultimately real features of the social world and deplore their existence, and one can regard the nation state as non-instrumentally valuable while subscribing to a reductivist explanatory account of it. Even if values must supervene on natural facts, it does not follow that these must be ultimate ones, such as matter and motion, rather than secondary ones. Thus, one can reject ethical individualism without adopting anti-individualistic ontologies or methods. And if the main objection to this sort of theory is (as it is often thought) that we must at all costs avoid the ontological slum of general wills and group minds, then we can reduce the domain of contention by providing a theory which admits ultimate values other than individual persons and their mental states, but which is compatible with a fairly sparse social ontology. There is therefore no need to reject non-individualistic theories a priori, in the way that certain philosophers still do, by supposing that methodological or ontological considerations rule them out from the beginning. The relative independence of the different modes of individualism frees up some space for a serious assessment of the alternatives.

2. THE CONCEPT OF MEMBERSHIP

One sort of anti-individualism reacts against consent theory with various conceptual claims about obligation and authority, including the argument that authority relations are transmitted through the very terms of political discourse. Hanna Pitkin, for example, says that it is a 'symptom of philosophical disorder',[7] to ask for the ground of our obligation to obey. There is, she claims, no theoretical explanation superior to the following point of 'grammar': 'It is part of the concept, the meaning of "authority" that those subject to it are required to obey, that it has a right to command. It is part of the concept,

[7] H. F. Pitkin, 'Obligation and Consent', *American Political Science Review* 59 (1965) and 60 (1966), repr. in P. Laslett, W. G. Runciman, and Q. Skinner, eds., *Philosophy, Politics and Society*, 4th ser. (Oxford: Blackwell, 1972), 75.

the meaning of "law", that those to whom it is applicable are obligated to obey it.'[8] Those, like the traditional consent theorists, who fail to see this are in the grips of what she calls 'a peculiar picture of man and society', an abstractly individualistic one which ignores that, 'It is only as a result of [society's] influence that he becomes the particular person he does become, with his particular interests, values, desires, language and obligations.'[9]

Pursuing a similar line of thought still further, Thomas McPherson comes to conclude that it is literally meaningless to ask for a general justification for political obligation:

> "Why should I (a member) accept the rules of the club?" is an absurd question. Accepting the rules is part of what it *means* to be a member. Similarly, "Why should I obey the government?" is an absurd question. We have not understood what it *means* to be a member of political society if we suppose that political obligation is something we might not have had and that therefore needs to be *justified*.[10]

These arguments simply shift the line of dispute in a way which highlights the inherent weakness of the linguistic approach to political theory. Even if the justification of authority can only be answered by reference to the fact of membership, we can still coherently ask whether it is justifiable to be a member of an association like the state, knowing that it brings with it the obligations that it does. Moreover, as we noted in Chapter 3, the options facing the conscientious citizen are not simply the acceptance of authority or revolt; she may choose to comply peacefully with the state, obeying often or always, though never for the reason that her obedience is required. Peaceful compliance is possible without membership, and thus without its obligations.

It is implausible that the normative issues can be resolved by lexicography, or even by appeals to philosophical grammar. Which are the words whose meaning establishes that peaceful compliance is not the appropriate relationship between the conscientious citizen and the state: 'member'? 'citizen'? One

[8] Ibid. 78.

[9] Ibid. 75.

[10] T. McPherson, *Political Obligation*, 64. Cf. T. D. Weldon, *The Vocabulary of Politics*, 57 for what may be the original source of these arguments.

would naturally have thought that the political dispute between those who affirm and those who deny the state's claim to authority simply includes a dispute about what those words mean. And suppose there were some term whose use was universally recognized as implying that one was obliged to obey; could we not then just refuse to play that language game, everything else remaining the same? So long as the concept of good citizenship remains a complex and contested one, political argument will infect every level of inquiry and the normative issues will have to be joined at some level. Chasing them along the road of grammar delays but does not eliminate the meeting point.

3. NO ARCHIMEDEAN POINT

Although unacceptable, the above argument can be restated in non-linguistic terms, as in the common idealist thesis, made notorious by T. H. Green, that, 'To ask why I am to submit to the power of the state, is to ask why I am to allow my life to be regulated by that complex of institutions without which I literally should not have a life to call my own.'[11] The argument is that there is no neutral, uncommitted point to which we might retreat and assess our obligations, as the consent theorist would have us do. One's very existence—and even more, the concept of one's existence as an independent individual with a life of one's *own*—depends on political institutions. And if individual lives are in this way deeply social, so is morality. To think of moral duties as self-imposed laws in the Kantian fashion is incoherent; laws, properly so called, are always imposed by others. Similarly, consent-based duties are purely abstract and not socially situated, and hence we can explain neither their content nor their motivating power. In contrast, the idealists direct our attention to a certain kind of community which, in its positive morality, expresses our duties as inherently social demands that are not merely products of our wills. Under certain conditions, which Hegel and Bradley among others purport to describe, the state can be understood as such a community. When it is, the duty of obedience becomes morally unproblematic.

[11] T. H. Green, *Lectures on the Principles of Political Obligation*, 122.

A related way of bringing in the social dimension is the neo-Wittgensteinian view that, as a normative institution, political authority essentially depends upon social practices and rules which provide the criteria for right and wrong ways of acting. Peter Winch once promoted a very strong version of this thesis. Beginning with the sound premiss that authority is not a causal relation between wills but an internal and normative one, he argued that the very idea of a right and wrong way of doing things essentially involves shared concepts of value. But one can have no such concepts unless one follows certain criterial social rules which constitute them. It is to these normative judgments that authoritative requests therefore appeal and, because they are so imbricated in the fabric of social life, we are unable to view our situation without them. It therefore makes no sense, he held, to suppose that we 'choose' to accept authority. Rather, 'the fact that one is a human social being, engaged in rule-governed activities and on that account able to deliberate and to choose, is in itself sufficient to commit one to the acceptance of legitimate political authority. For the exercise of such authority is a precondition of rule-governed activities. There would, therefore be a sort of inconsistency in "choosing to reject" all such authority.'[12]

What are we to make of such claims? Suppose it were true that our most central moral notions need public criteria for their application and intelligibility, and that there can be no Archimedean point from which we can at once judge all of these criteria. Surely some room for critical reflection would remain, however, for we could call into question some of the criteria without calling into question all of them; we could repair our ship at sea. What then licenses the final inference in the argument, from 'we must accept some social rules' to 'we must accept political authority'? Could we not use the inherently social criteria of, for example, religion or customary morality to evaluate political order? The leap from the necessity for a rule-governed outlook to the necessity for political regulation is unsupported, as Winch later came to accept.[13] In rejecting his earlier argument, however, Winch

[12] P. Winch, 'Authority', 105.

[13] Ibid. 110. And compare H. F. Pitkin, 'Obligation and Consent' with her *Wittgenstein and Justice*, (Berkeley: University of California Press, 1972), 199–204.

none the less maintained that social life would be impossible without some kind of authority, although not necessarily the authority of a specialized institution like the state. Yet even this does not follow. We must insist on a still finer analysis, and distinguish the necessity for a normative framework of rules and practices from the necessity for that special sort of normative framework which characterizes authority. That cannot be established by the sort of considerations to which Winch appeals.

These arguments, like those which purport to show that ethics must be socially situated, all fall to a fundamental objection: they fail to distinguish global and local criteria for the intelligibility of evaluation. If they are correct they apply globally, to all obligations, to all other moral concepts, and indeed to the possibility of all practical judgments. They do not apply in a distinctive and local way to the problem of political authority. In this respect they are, like meta-ethical claims, independent of the substantive issues and cannot therefore function as a critique of individualistic accounts like consent theory. At best they show that both consensual obligations and non-consensual obligations are intelligible only in a social context, that consent itself has constitutive criteria which are inherently social, and so on. Even if all that is true, however, it goes no way to establishing that consent is inferior to other socially constituted concepts as an account of the relation in question. More generally, no philosophical theory about the *status* of concepts like 'consent' or 'individual' is going to support or weaken the plausibility of any normative position, any more than the falsity of methodological individualism would entail the rejection of ethical individualism.

4. ATOMISM AND THE SOCIAL THESIS

The failure of the above versions of the communitarian thesis points to a significant, if sometimes neglected, truth about what sort of argument is needed here. If it is to be at all persuasive, communitarianism must isolate some value or first-order normative consideration which individualistic theories miss. If it attempts to remain above the political fray in the lofty realm of methodology or meta-ethics, it can too easily be neutralized by an individualist willing to concede that people are essentially social creatures and that moral and political life is a social achievement, while maintaining that the best life for these social creatures is one which best serves their socially constructed individualities. To block this, we must bring community back down to earth.

Charles Taylor begins to move in the right direction in an insightful essay which locates the errors of consent theory in a general philosophical stance he calls 'atomism'.[14] This doctrine is a complex network of ontological, methodological, and ethical positions. In political theory, Taylor takes its distinctive symptoms to be talk of a state of nature, the view that people can flourish outside society, that individual rights have primacy over other moral considerations, and that the only ultimately valuable goods are divisible ones. Although ideologically harmonious, these positions are logically distinct and it is a little difficult to find representatives of the atomist tradition in political thought who consistently held to all of them. This itself need pose no objection, however, for Taylor is not really offering a definition of 'atomism' but just seeking to describe a related family, or perhaps syndrome, of attitudes. In fact, his main concern is only with one particularly influential member of that family: the doctrine of the primacy of individual rights. A moral theory based solely on natural rights is indeed an individualistic one in the serious sense, for it counts as intrinsically valuable goods only the interests of individuals, and explains other moral concepts by their logical or justificatory relationship to individual rights. On a rights-based theory, moral obligations must be explained and justified in terms of rights and are thus of secondary importance. The state therefore has legitimate authority only as a correlate of individuals' obligations to obey which must in turn be derived from their exercising or taking measures designed to protect the exercise of their rights. Taylor presents an attractive argument against that view by investigating the ground of individual rights. Rights exist to protect and express respect for certain fundamental human capacities. But if these capacities are the ultimate foundation of rights then one

[14] C. Taylor, 'Atomism', in A. Kontos, ed., *Powers, Possessions and Freedom* (Toronto: University of Toronto Press, 1979), 39–61.

cannot exclude the possibility that they may directly give rise to moral obligations, including the obligation to belong to a community, if they are instrumentally necessary to, or a constitutive part of, a society which respects and promotes these capacities.

The idea of an obligation to 'belong' is, one must admit, a bit hazy. It presents a real challenge to individualists only if it is or includes an obligation to obey. Moreover, it is possible to conceive of human capacities in such a way as to bring them under the umbrella of individual interests and this suggests that Taylor's theory may not be as anti-individualistic as he thinks. But let that pass. Even under a favourable interpretation, the argument does not support the desired conclusion.

A communitarian political theory must show not merely that people are naturally *social* animals and can only flourish in a social context—what Taylor calls the 'social thesis'—but also that they are naturally political. Interpreted in its broadest form, it is not clear that any political theorist apart from Hobbes has ever rejected the social thesis. The battle between individualists like Kant and Mill and their critics like Hegel and Marx was never fought over that piece of territory but rather over what sort of social conditions encourage individual flourishing. One way of putting this point is to say that communitarians must either respect or give reasons for rejecting the common distinction between state and society. It is true that any form of social order from the family and tribe onwards is a theatre of conflicts of interest, exercises of power, legitimating ideologies, and so forth. In this weak sense all forms of human society are political. To concede this does not show, however, that any form of human society must incorporate those particular relations of subordination which we recognize as authority nor does it show that there is no difference in kind between, say, the family and the modern state. What then is the power of the social thesis? If sound, it creates a strong case for thinking that there are some moral obligations which are primary and not merely derived from rights. But it does nothing to prove that no moral obligations are secondary. The possibility therefore remains that while some obligations are not dependent on consent for their validity, others are and political obligations fall in the latter category. The crucial step for our purposes therefore remains to be taken. We need to establish, not just that the free individual is a product of a certain kind of society and therefore must support the social conditions of such freedom, but also that such support is not possible, or not complete, without conceding the moral authority of the state. This argument cannot proceed conceptually. As Taylor notes, anarchism is a possible account of the relation between a free citizen and the culture of freedom. For two reasons, however, he thinks that the odds are against it. First, 'it seems much more likely from the historical record that we need rather some species of political society. And if this is so then we must acknowledge an obligation to belong to this kind of society in affirming freedom.'[15] Secondly, 'men's deliberating together about what will be binding on all of them is an essential part of the exercise of freedom. It is only in this way that they can come to grips with certain basic issues in a way which will actually have an effect in their lives.'[16] Neither claim is sound as it stands. To concede that the conditions of human development require society is not to concede that they require authority, unless we repeat Hume's error of holding that the former is impossible without general recognition of the latter. Nor is the value of public deliberation essentially tied to deliberating about what our duties will be. We can conceive of a public order of mutual coercion which relies only on sanctions to promote the common good and in which sanctions are regarded merely as threats and not as duties.[17] In those circumstances, debate about which sanctions should be imposed would bring home in a lively way our common fate—but it would not be debate about duties. A gang of robbers can argue about their own policies without for a moment supposing that they are disputing their moral obligations. Hence, the social thesis does not provide sufficient reply to the consent theorist's objection that even if the conditions for human flourishing are social, they are not political in any sense that presupposes authority relations.

[15] Ibid. 58–9.

[16] Ibid. 59.

[17] On the difference between liability to sanctions and recognition of duties see, H. L. A. Hart, *The Concept of Law*, 79–88; and P. M. S. Hacker, 'Sanction Theories of Duty', in A. W. B. Simpson, ed., *Oxford Essays in Jurisprudence*, 2nd ser. (Oxford: Clarendon Press, 1973), 131–70.

5. CONSENSUAL COMMUNITIES

Thus far we have found nothing to dislodge the conclusion that only if individuals consent are they bound to obey the state and thus nothing to mitigate the individualistic rigours of that theory. But perhaps we have been looking in the wrong place. There is much more to the communitarian picture than the arguments for obedience which have just been criticized. Indeed, on two substantive points I think that communitarian objections are decisive. First, it is wrong to think of political life as purely instrumental in the way many consent theorists, contractarians, and conventionalists tend to do, to see it as the public means for securing essentially private ends. If there is anything worth preserving of the civic republican tradition it is the view that political life may have intrinsic value. Secondly, the consent theorist does tend to overestimate the role of the will at the expense of communal traditions in establishing those moral relations which are constitutive of political life. And these two faults in consent theory are not merely incidental; they are intimately connected with its main feature, the analogy between life in a state and a voluntary association. Descriptively, states are not like that for the scope of their authority is maximal and their jurisdiction compulsory. Normatively, the bonds of commitment appropriate to purely voluntary associations are qualitatively different from those in a flourishing political community. One's tennis club very rarely generates the same deep feelings of belonging combined with relative externality that one experiences in the state. Ideally, we would like to amend the individualist picture in such a way as to capture these truths while retaining the normative function of consent.

Consent theory is not only wrong but incoherent if it supposes that all obligations are self-assumed (the duty to keep promises cannot be the result of a promise). And it is wrong if it supposes that all self-assumed obligations are wholly creatures of consent. Fortunately, an acceptable version of it need make neither error. There are two reasons why the range of legitimate authority seems so limited according to consent theory. First, some people perform no actions that can be counted as consent of any sort. Secondly, the scope of the state's authority is so wide that some who do consent will not be thought to consent to *that*. They may intend, for example, to bind themselves to just laws only, and to reserve their own right to judge about cases of moral necessity or civil disobedience. But this ignores that the state purports to regulate such defences as well. To expand the range of the state's authority many have tried to weaken the nature of consent by extending it to cover notions of tacit or hypothetical consent. For reasons already given, that cannot succeed. A distinct possibility, however, is to expand the scope of the state's authority by widening the implications of consensual acts. If it could be shown that people need not consent to every detail of the state's jurisdiction, but only to a general social role of citizenship which includes an obligation to obey, then the consent-based argument will have been widened without undermining the normative foundations of consent. I approach the issue by considering some recent reflections on the most important of classical consent theorists.

With increasing frequency it is argued that Locke is not a consent theorist in the sense of Chapter 6 at all. Pitkin challenges the traditional view by examining those limits which Locke imposes on the validity of consent.[18] The difficulties in Locke's argument about 'tacit consent', she argues, do not go so far as to obliterate the distinction between legitimate authority and coercion, for the terms of the original contract are dictated, not by the will of the parties, but by the law of nature. The only intention we need impute to contractors is the aim for self-preservation; the law of nature guarantees that in pursuing that aim they cannot voluntarily become the slave of another. We lack absolute arbitrary power over our own lives and so cannot transfer such power to another. Pitkin thus reasons that for Locke, 'you are obligated to obey not really because you have consented; your consent is virtually automatic. Rather you are obligated to obey because of certain characteristics of the government—that it is acting within the bounds of trusteeship based on an original contract.'[19] Thus, consent appears to cast only the faintest hypothetical shadow over Locke's theory: political authority is

[18] H. F. Pitkin, 'Obligation and Consent'. [19] Ibid. 56.

a matter of what rational people could be supposed to agree to, not what duties they have created for themselves. 'For now the Lockean doctrine becomes this: your personal consent is essentially irrelevant to your obligation to obey, or its absence. Your obligation to obey depends on the character of the government—whether it is acting within the bounds of *the* (only possible) contract.'[20] Similarly in John Dunn's influential work on Locke, consent is demoted from the status of a duty-generating practice to a mere limiting condition on legitimacy. In an important article, he argues that Locke means by consent little more than uncoerced acceptance of some practice: 'where a practice is legitimate and a role involves participation in the practice, consent to do so and hence consent to its responsibilities is axiomatic—all potential doubts are resolved in favour of the practice.'[21] But the legitimacy of the practice does not itself flow from consent. Locke was too much a theist to think of human consent as generating moral duties *ex nihilo*. Often, 'men's psychological reach exceeds their juristic grasp';[22] they freely and deliberately form the intention to undertake duties which violate the law of nature. But that law is independent of our will and cannot be amended or repealed by our consensual acts. Thus slavery contracts are void *ab initio*. Now, this is not the view of one who celebrates the unfettered human will as a mode of creating duties. To suppose that it is is to substitute our concerns and our metaphysics for Locke's. The *Two Treatises* should therefore properly be read, not as an account of how such obligations can be generated by a sheer act of will, but as an argument for limitations on the possible scope of political obligation.[23] As might be expected from a moralist who has a fundamentally theological world view, Locke's theme is human dependence, not independence.

These powerful arguments have a common strength and a common weakness. They usefully remind us of the historical and theoretical limitations of the view that consent is

[20] Ibid. 57.

[21] J. Dunn, 'Consent in the Political Theory of John Locke', in his *Political Obligation in its Historical Context* (Cambridge: Cambridge University Press, 1980), 52.

[22] Ibid. 33.

[23] J. Dunn, *The Political Thought of John Locke* (Cambridge: Cambridge University Press, 1969), 143.

essentially a duty-creating act. Why would people wish to create duties out of nothing; and how could they do it? Consent theory should not be seen as a celebration of the value-creating power of the human will. It is in order to express or secure certain values that we have the practice of consent. The limitation of these arguments is their assumption that if consent is not a duty-creating act it is irrelevant, at best a limiting condition on the legitimacy of a practice established in some other way. This ignores other important alternatives. Consent can also be seen as a device not for generating duties out of nothing but the will of the parties, but for determining the conditions of application or varying the content of pre-existing, socially (or for Locke, divinely) constituted duties.

Consider again the institution of marriage and the duties it entails. Here, I am not thinking of cohabitation contracts, or other devices by which couples desiring to enter a relationship of legally recognized and enforceable monogamy can do so without getting married, but of the standard case where they avail themselves of an independently existing institution which is partly constituted by a set of publicly recognized rights and duties. Now, whether one thinks of the form of that institution as being set by social convention or divine sanction, it is certainly not a product of the agreement of the parties. In this respect, it is very unlike a contract which creates duties in a morally empty universe. The content of the duties is external to the will of the parties, but they apply to particular couples only through their own consent. In these circumstances, consent is something less than a duty-generating device or an expression of an omnipotent individual will which alone is competent to bind itself. The sovereignty of the will is hedged in by social convention over which it has applicative but not creative power. This is plainly the case in the traditional institution of marriage, for this feature often attracts radical criticism. Yet although marriage is not fully responsive to the will of the parties, it would be equally wrong to characterize it as a situation in which consent is 'essentially irrelevant' or 'axiomatic', a mere limiting condition on a practice whose validity is independently established. For the institution of marriage would have little value if consent were not essential to its application to a particular couple; not merely for the obvious reason that monogamy would go less well among pairs who do not agree to it, but more importantly because consent is a constitutive feature of the relationship they seek to establish. And yet at the same time, their consent does not go all the way down to ground level: the normative contours of the institution are relatively external to their wills, although its application and value for them is not. This suggests that one may have a two-part explanation of consent-based duties: an account of their structure and content, subject to the social thesis, and an independent account of their validity and application subject to consent.

We should, I think, accept the communitarian critique in so far as it suggests that much of contemporary consent theory is in the grips of an odd, strangely individualistic picture of human nature and its moral powers. It is wrong to think of our most important duties as being consequences only of our own wills; this is to drain them of the social dimension which explains their form and content. In this respect, our duties will be subject to the social thesis. The duties incumbent on the good citizen, then, are those which constitute citizenship in his community. To attempt to step back from these, and ask, from the point of view of nowhere at all, whether they are really his duties is perhaps to ask the unaskable. They are constitutive of his identity as a citizen and in this sense, but only in this sense, are prior to his particularities. The scope of consent may therefore be extended somewhat, to cover those individuals who willingly assume the role of citizen and thus its constitutive duties, but in whose psychological history we can locate no acts or intentions which create those duties. If we can explain the value of such role-bound consent, we may be able legitimately to extend the doctrine without relying on the fiction of tacit consent or on the unacceptable theories of hypothetical consent. But as we have seen, calling attention to this fact cannot itself explain how the duties constitutive of our roles come to bind. At this point the normative force of consent must still take over, not as a device to explain the structure of our moral worlds, but to explain our own positions within them. The fact that the duties of a citizen are my duties is still a question which depends inherently on whether I have consented to occupying the role which they constitute.

6. SHARED GOODS AND CIVIC LIFE

This revision of consent theory has certain affinities with Bradley's view that the realm of obligation cannot adequately be understood in either purely consequentialist or Kantian terms but only as 'the objective world of my station and its duties'. It adds to that theory the provision that at least political stations, including citizenship, are to be occupied only by consent.[24] Such a hybrid view is vulnerable to attack from both sides. In this section I defend it from the radical consent theorist who argues that consent should go all the way down to the ground floor and include the nature of stations. In the next section I defend it against the communitarian who holds that the objectivity of duties must extend all the way up, and include an immediate obligation to belong.

If we value consent as a means of acquiring obligations then why not extend it to the nature of the obligations themselves? Even if the so-called natural duties of fidelity, charity, and so on resist an account as being will-constituted, the duty to obey may none the less seem a likely candidate. One might reconsider the earlier analogy with marriage. If we value consenting as a means of making monogamy go well, or expressing mutual trust, would a more perfect expression of that not be a monogamy contract whose terms were exhaustively set by the parties involved? Why should a socially given cluster of rights and duties be treated as any more than a default option, available to those unable to or uninterested in designing their own, in the way that intestacy laws bind only those who do not create a will? To establish the difference one must show that there is some intrinsic value in a common public status, such as being married, which value would not be realizable, or would only be realized to a lesser degree, under a regime of individualized private contracts.

One might be tempted to pursue an instrumental explan-

[24] '[A]lthough within certain limits I may choose my station according to my own liking, yet I and everyone else must have some station with duties pertaining to it, and those duties do not depend on our opinion or liking.' F. H. Bradley, *Ethical Studies*, 2nd edn. (Oxford: Oxford University Press, 1962), 176.

ation for this, to understand it as a means of economizing on the time and effort needed to tailor social relations precisely to one's individual circumstances or as a means of providing a standard form of relationship in order to simplify and stabilize interactions with others by creating reasonably reliable grounds for social expectations. No doubt this is part of the story. But it is unlikely to be fully satisfactory in the present context. In recognizing the authority of the state as a set of standard, boiler-plate terms of a social contract, too much is at risk over interests that are too vital, and the security of expectations can be attained in too many other ways. Moreover, this is not how such common social forms are understood by their members; those who approve of our familiar system of monogamous marriage do not regard its general framework of rights and duties as second-best to an ideal individually negotiated contract. They regard it as essentially constitutive of the relation itself. This suggests that the instrumental explanation is too simple and that we should search for an alternative.

Let us return to the distinction introduced in Chapter 5 between an ordinary private good and a public good in the economist's sense. In its pure form, the latter is jointly supplied and inexcludable—co-operation is needed to produce it, but once the good is available for some then all can benefit from it. This causes well-known problems because such goods are difficult to price, and markets for them are not generally efficient. Typical institutional solutions to such problems include enforcement mechanisms to ensure supply and exclusion devices to control consumption. But these are imperfect and work, when they do, by partially transforming the good into a private one, such as when we sell gas masks to allocate clean air, or charge admission to a public beach. And yet those who value public goods prefer the presence of these imperfect devices to their absence. This shows that the public nature of such goods is not part of their value, but rather an obstacle to be overcome. Now, not all goods with a communal aspect are public goods in this sense. In some cases, to privatize a good is to transform it in a way which changes its value. There can be no market in friendship so it is not a private good, but neither are its external effects (reciprocity, mutual respect, trust, etc.) mere externalities whose presence confounds its production: they are essential to it. Thus, friendship is not a public good in the above sense. Rather, it is a *shared* good which can be enjoyed only in a form of association which itself partly constitutes the good shared.[25]

It seems likely that, for some people anyway, the pleasures of civic life are shared goods. In a reasonably just society the status of citizen is something of value in part because it is a common one. All those who value social solidarity for its own sake are likely, in the context of the modern state, to see civic ties as providing a common nexus linking those who share little else. The status of citizenship is in part constituted by our political obligations and to assume it is to assume them, not as a matter of linguistic propriety or as a tool instrumental to securing the public good, but as an element of an inherently valuable relationship. Now we are on the threshold of a more acceptable version of the organic view discussed in Chapter 6. It is not so much that consenting to obey expresses a valuable feeling of belonging to one's society, but that it concretely instantiates a form of association which may be regarded as a shared good. But a final step is needed to explain the role of authority relations in such an association.

Most valuable things are good in different respects or, as we might say, contain goods of different sorts. One can value an unspoiled forest as a resource for the pulp and paper industry, as a recreational area, or as intrinsically valuable for its natural beauty. This is equally true of human associations. Some of them have public aspects—inexcludable and non-rival dimensions of instrumental value—as well as shared aspects—inherently valuable relationships. A racially tolerant society, for example, promotes the public goods of security and the efficient use of human capital, but it also expresses valuable associations among people. We might say that it is a good with at least two very different aspects. These can on occasion give rise to practical conflicts: on the one hand, in its guise as a public good it provides a justification for free-riding (a general atmosphere of tolerance does not depend on my contribution), while on the other its shared aspect gives

[25] Cf. D. Réaume, 'Individuals, Groups and Rights to Public Goods', *University of Toronto Law Journal* 38 (1988), 1–27.

reason for participation (one cannot share in the valued relationship if one is a free-rider). From one point of view, the communal aspect of the good is a burden, from another it is a benefit. In some cases, this conflict can be resolved in the standard way: one weighs the benefit against the burden and decides whether, on balance, it is worth it. In other cases, the shared aspect of the relationship is jeopardized by this very calculation. Close friendships, for example, are unavailable to those who treat all conflicting reasons as potentially negotiable against the value of the relationship. For that reason, friendship is often recognized as a paradigm of the sort of commitment shared goods can generate. The natural expression of the attraction of such goods is to regard the relationship as obligation-imposing, as putting at least certain competing claims out of consideration at all. Many organic theories of the state have suggested that political relations can sometimes be understood in this way, as *philia politike*, civic friendship. No doubt this is extremely idealistic. And civic friendship may conflict with other loyalties. But where it exists it is of value, and it survives because its norms are regarded as binding. They provide a common framework or structure for a shared good.

This is the primary reason why some would value a system of many different private contractual arrangements less than a common social contract. Only the latter would express civic friendship. Note that this argument does not seek to establish that one must view political life in this way, that it is impossible, immoral, or inherently unfulfilling to reject it. Nor is it claimed that this view is common in the modern state; on the contrary, the decline of the public realm is well documented. It only seeks to show that such a view is intelligible and that it can figure in a sound argument extending the scope of legitimate authority to those who consent to the social role of citizenship even if they have not created the set of duties which are constitutive of it.

7. SOCIAL ROLES AND IDENTITY

In that way the communitarian thesis can and should modify consent theory. But most modern communitarians would not be satisfied with the concession that the social thesis applies to the nature and content of our duties because they feature in the shared goods of citizenship, but not to their incidence. They would see this as half-hearted, giving up the social thesis just where it begins to have bite and would argue, not merely that individual consent is not sufficient to be bound, but that it is not necessary either. In this, they tend to share Hegel's view,[26] that when we understand our political obligations as socially situated in the realm of objective ethics, we can no longer see them as optional in the way that the consent theorist does. The concession that they are not optional all the way to ground level is not for them adequate, for it still admits the possibility that the subject of a reasonably just state may lack the duty of obedience. Indeed, if taken seriously, such obligations must bind few citizens of modern states who usually view citizenship as a private or public good or as a shared good to which they do not themselves subscribe (just as one can see the value of friendship which one does not share). A full-blooded communitarian will want to argue that the social reality of obligation requires that it be, fundamentally, non-optional.

To establish this the communitarian characteristically appeals to the social thesis. As argued above, that cannot succeed: even if our moral nature depends on institutions which nurture our essential capacities, that does not show that we cannot support such institutions without accepting their claim to create duties for us, and thus without acknowledging the authority of the state. Other avenues remain open, however. The communitarian might instead try to weaken the role of consent by reminding us that some social roles generate duties even when they are not voluntarily assumed.

In some cases, it is unclear to what extent the assumption of a given role is voluntary. It seems reasonable to suppose that, if one agrees to assume a certain risk of occupying a role, then one's occupying it is voluntary if the risk materializes. Someone who agrees to draw straws for a dangerous mission cannot be said to have been selected non-voluntarily. Perhaps that analysis can be extended to cover a number of other

[26] G. W. F. Hegel, *The Philosophy of Right*. §§ 75, 75A (pp. 58–9, 242).

social roles commonly thought to be non-voluntary (e.g., juror, army draftee, etc.). There remains, however, a range of cases which is less easily accommodated. For example, a famous athlete who becomes a role-model for children may acquire certain duties of good conduct which he neither voluntarily assumed nor willingly undertook the risk of; a woman who becomes pregnant as a result of a rape and who could not terminate the pregnancy without serious risk to her health is an involuntary mother and may yet have some duties towards her infant. Now, in such non-voluntary roles, it is not the occupancy of the role itself which justifies holding their incumbents to be under the duty. Such institutions have an identificatory function in showing which duties their incumbent has, but they have no justificatory function in grounding those duties.[27] For every role-based duty it is possible to give a role-independent explanation of why the duty binds. But that explanation need not rest on the claim that the role was voluntarily assumed. It is a matter of controversy which non-voluntary roles do generate valid duties, and also what the ground of their validity is. There are, however, two conditions which make it more likely that the duties are binding. First, the attendant duties may not be very onerous. One rarely becomes an uncle or aunt voluntarily, but the minor obligations which that role brings generally require little beyond the demands of natural duty. Secondly, the duties, although more substantial, may secure a very great benefit for those who are themselves non-voluntarily dependent on their performance. Non-voluntary parenthood, for example, plausibly brings at least the duty to ensure that the child is cared for. Now, when it is true both that obligations are slight and the benefits great, as in the duty of an athlete to set a good example for children, the case in favour looks quite powerful.

To what extent can a communitarian follow this route in attempting to disestablish consent? Not, I think, very far at all. Consider the social role of citizenship. It cannot be said that the duties it brings are slight. The state claims supreme authority over vital concerns; at the very least it includes the

[27] The distinction is due to M. Stocker, 'Moral Duties, Institutions, and Natural Facts', *Monist* 54 (1970), 605.

liability to taxation and military service. These alone may at times require substantial sacrifice of what would otherwise be one's legitimate interests. What about the benefits which result from holding people non-voluntarily to be under such duties? Concede for the sake of argument that they are substantial. But what needs to be shown, and what this approach cannot show, is that unless occupiers of the role of citizen recognize that they are duty-bound to act in these desirable ways, they cannot be relied on to do so. Once again, the proposal founders on the fact that peaceful compliance with the law will be sufficient to protect the interests of other citizens. No one except the officials of the state will be harmed if people fail to regard it as authoritative.

It seems then that we cannot abandon consent as a validating condition of the political role. But instead of defending role-bound duties, the communitarian may attack the assumptions about moral personality which underpin the whole idea of consenting to occupy a role. Who is it that does the consenting? Michael Sandel's criticisms of Rawls register a sceptical note. He says that the individualism of modern deontological liberals, whose moral theory assigns priority to the right over the good, incorporates an incoherent view of the self as prior to all of its merely contingent ends.[28] Not only is this said to be a philosophically unsatisfactory position, but it is also held to promote a morally undesirable form of individualism by devaluing the rich communal—but merely contingent—fabric of our lives. It is not clear to what extent this last charge holds good. Rawls could reply that the mutual disinterestedness of parties to the social contract does not prejudice life in actual societies in favour of individualistic habits in which people pursue their own plans of life without valuing the good of others (although respecting their rights and liberties). Rawls foresees a diversity of actual motivation and levels of concern and his political theory seeks to describe a framework within which free communal association is a possible value. Sandel believes that this misses the point. Of course the abstract self can accommodate community in this diminished form. What it cannot accommodate, he says, is a

[28] M. J. Sandel, *Liberalism and the Limits of Justice* (Cambridge: Cambridge University Press, 1982), esp. 59–65.

form of community constitutive of the very bounds of the self. One consequence of always standing at a distance from those interests and concerns which are only contingently its own is to 'put the self beyond the reach of experience, to make it invulnerable, to fix its identity once and for all. No commitment could grip me so deeply that I could not understand myself without it.'[29] The Rawlsian metaphysics is thus alleged to support a politics of interests, not a politics of identities: 'It rules out the possibility of a public life in which, for good or ill, the identity as well as the interests of the participants could be at stake.'[30] The same charge can be brought against the present proposal. In accepting the social thesis with respect to the content of our obligations but rejecting it with respect to their incidence, I have presupposed that we can coherently talk of a self which gives or withholds its consent to these arrangements and I have excluded the crucial claim that these commitments are not merely constitutive of the station of citizenship, but also of the identity of the citizen. And that is simply to ignore the charge that Hegel, Green, and the other idealists bring. Thus we return to the objection that there is no Archimedean point from which to assess our obligations.

Is this view about the constitution of our identities really a coherent one? There can be no doubt that as a matter of fact they are socially constituted in the way the thesis suggests. Of course, not all of one's projects are constitutive of one's identity; it may not even be true of such vitally important concerns as one's vocation. (It is a sure sign of middle-class professionalism to think that most people have no conception of themselves as persons which does not include their jobs.) Yet there is no doubt that many people cannot conceive of themselves apart from at least some of their merely contingent, 'morally arbitrary', social characteristics, such as gender, religion, ethnicity, fundamental moral values, and so on. However, what we regard as identity-constituting characteristics tends to change over time: religion was once so treated in the political sphere and hence conflicts between religious groups were seen, not as conflicts among interests, but as conflicts among identities. To compromise an interest was

[29] Ibid. 62. [30] Ibid.

seen as selling out one's essential personhood, to secure a right as establishing it. In some modern states, ethnic nationalism continues to play a similar role. Whether or not we should welcome the politics of identity is a very complicated issue. Here I merely wish to suggest why it poses no threat to this compromise between consent and community.

To challenge the thesis that consent is necessary for justified authority it is not sufficient to prove that *some* of our morally arbitrary, accidental characteristics are identity-constituting. For suppose that gender has this role. That would not weaken the claim that men and women have an obligation to obey only if they agree to do so. For it to do the work expected of it, we would have to show that *political obligation* is constitutive of one's identity as a person. If that were true it would indeed make no sense to ask whether we are bound by our consent, because if we were not so bound we would be different people. Now, political obligation involves the acceptance of authority relations, that is, acceptance that the requirements of one's state create moral duties. Can these be identity-constituting? It is not impossible that this should be so, although it does seem much less plausible than the claims of religion, values, or ethnicity. It is important to note that a consent theorist is not committed to the unlikely position that one's nationality is not part of one's identity. In so far as such questions are intelligible at all, perhaps it does make sense to say that if one had been Italian rather than Scots one would have been a different person. But this has little to do with the authority states claim. After all, what would it mean to say that outside authority relations one had no conception of oneself as a person? It would mean that at the core of one's very self-understanding lie the commands of another. This is much more than the normal surrender of judgement characteristic of any obedience to authority. There, an independently constituted subject surrenders his judgement, usually for limited time and purposes. In the political communitarian view, however, the person has lost any conception of himself apart from what others tell him to do. I do not know how common that attitude is, but it is hard to imagine why it should be thought to have any moral value. The great obstacle for modern communitarians is finding some way to give the theory critical edge, of allowing for evaluation of the identity-constituting communities to which people belong (some way of approving Bruderhof while denouncing Salem Massachusetts), and of allowing for the competing commitments which each person feels.[31] It is, of course, possible to follow the classical idealist route and posit some transcendental or historical standpoint from which to adjudge communities as good or bad, say by the extent to which they help realize the idea of the state, or freedom, or human perfection. But that move, common to thinkers like Hegel and Green, finds little favour among modern communitarians, who are drawn to the warmth and local colour of community precisely because they are sceptical of any transcendental standpoint. They may propose instead that all criticism begin internally, as must the criticism of a social practice, in Alasdair MacIntyre's view.[32] But if the community's authority relations are constitutive of our very identities, even this edge gets dulled. To begin to transform one's community would not simply be an exercise in self-discovery or the first tentative kick at the ladder upon which we have ascended; it would be a violation of duty. An identity constituted by authority relations is communitarianism at its least appealing. It is no accident that many communitarians have seen the ideal social order as being non-authoritarian and that some have found the appeal of anarchism hard to resist. One may perfectly well hold that ethics must be socially situated and reject the view that there can be no coherent self-understanding apart from authority relations. Moreover, both the transcendental and the internal critical stances misunderstand what is at issue. To show that good communities can be distinguished from bad ones is not sufficient to the task at hand. It does not establish the authority of good communities any more than being able to distinguish good parents from bad ones secures their authority. No one can have legitimate authority if they use it unjustly; but some just people and institutions can none the less lack it.

[31] For an excellent introduction to these problems, see A. Gutmann, 'Communitarian Critics of Liberalism', *Philosophy and Public Affairs* 14 (1985), 308–22.

[32] A. MacIntyre, *After Virtue* (Notre Dame: University of Notre Dame Press, 1981), 175–89.

8. THE COMMUNITY OF COMMUNITIES?

Underlying much of modern communitarianism are certain classical doctrines which have found their way into the civic republican tradition. These have coalesced around the rejection of political instrumentalism. The original text puts the point as well as any of its modern supporters:

> a polis is not a mere society, having a common territory, established for the prevention of wrong-doing and for the sake of exchange. These are conditions without which a polis cannot exist; but all of them together do not constitute a polis, which is a community of families and aggregations of families in well-being, for the sake of a perfect and self-sufficing life.[33]

The polis is thus a community of communities and, because it is uniquely self-sufficient, it provides the paramount forum for human development. The instrumental justifications for association, such as those offered by conventionalists and contractarians, at most touch the necessary infrastructure for political life.

The weaker thesis, that political life has non-instrumental value, has been accepted here. The common status of citizenship may indeed have intrinsic value. But the above passage also suggests a stronger and less attractive thesis that political life is the highest form of social existence. Whatever the truth concerning the polis, it is difficult to accept that the modern state is a complete community, sufficient for its members' material and moral needs. Not even the largest and most wealthy of our states can be self-sufficient. Ecological interdependency has become a real constraint on their actions; citizens' wants have expanded to include goods which their own states do not or cannot profitably produce, leading to economic interdependency; and, most important of all, the changes in the technology of warfare have irreversibly altered almost every state's capacity to guarantee the security of its own citizens. In view of such changed circumstances, it would be very odd to continue to insist that the state is a complete form of community. Nor can its status be underwritten by

[33] Aristotle, *Politics*, 1280^{b} 30–5, trans. B. Jowett (amended) (New York: Modern Library, 1943).

appeal to that other famous Aristotelian argument: 'If all communities aim at some good, the polis, which is the highest of all, and which embraces all the rest, aims, and in a greater degree than any other, at the highest good.'[34] That is to confuse the common good with the highest good. It may be that the all-embracing goods which civic association provides are in fact merely the lowest common denominators amongst a wide range of diverse values. The claim that these common goods have non-instrumental value does not establish that they are goods of the highest value.

The relevance of these strands of traditional civic republicanism to the moral situation of modern citizens is therefore somewhat limited and, despite their prominence in communitarian thought, they do not advance the present argument. The rejection of political instrumentalism need not incline us to accept that the state is the unique or paramount arena for pursuing the common good. Indeed, those communal forms of association which are now felt to have the greatest importance are narrower ones like families, trade unions, and ethnic and religious groups. These do tend to be identity-constituting and they impose serious obligations on their members. Indeed, when the political order is viewed as external and anonymous, their demands will be felt to be particularly important and will often give rise to conflicts of duty. There is nothing in the nature of the state which guarantees that these conflicts will always be resolved in its favour. Here, at least, the pluralists' picture seems the most plausible: 'no man's allegiance is, in fact, unique. He is a point towards which a thousand associations converge; what then we ask is that where conflict comes we have assurance that he follows the path of his instructed conscience.'[35]

None of this means that commitment to civic life as one's primary locus of loyalty must be irrational. Far from it: there remain many contingent factors which make political community and its shared goods reasonable as primary commit-

[34] Aristotle, *Politics*, 1252^a 1–5, trans. B. Jowett. See the discussion in S. I. Benn and R. S. Peters, *Social Principles and the Democratic State*, 268–77, and in M. Walzer, *Obligations* (Cambridge, Mass.: Harvard University Press, 1970), 19–20.

[35] H. J. Laski, *Authority in the Modern State* (New Haven: Yale University Press, 1919), 92.

ments. It might be, for example, that people have a yearning for middle-range attachments, broader than most other associations in the political system but stopping short of the human race or the Kingdom of Ends, which help them partly transcend the claims of their particular ethnic, religious, or partisan group, but which are more intelligible and easily accommodated than the requirements of complete community. Simply as a decision problem, it is often easier to obey the law than the moral law: its requirements are often (though not necessarily) clearer and thus provide a publicly recognized standard of aspiration. In a reasonably just state they will normally coincide with the requirements of morality and will thus tend to produce the same ends by other means. And to this mundane thesis we might join a more speculative claim. T. H. Green suggests that, 'the love of mankind . . . needs to be particularized in order to have any power over life and action. Just as there can be no true friendship except towards this or that individual, so there can be no true public spirit which is not localized in some way.'[36] The human condition being a finite one of limited intelligence and sympathies, it may be that we can only participate in the ideal of complete community in partial and incomplete ways. A reasonably just state may provide a realistic and reachable forum for the wider forms of friendship. But none of these considerations is powerful enough to sustain the conclusion that rational persons *must* have as their primary locus of loyalty the civic order, for they cannot show that the shared goods of civic life are always dominant. At best, they show that such commitments may be rational and justified, and that they can figure in a sound theory of legitimate authority. Perhaps we cannot fairly expect a stronger conclusion from arguments at this level of generality.

Thus it appears that the radical consent theorist and the radical communitarian both offer inadequate conceptions of what is at stake in the problem of political authority. The radical consent theorist is wrong to think that consent can only function to create duties *ex nihilo* and wrong to think that there are no indivisible goods which are intrinsically valuable.

[36] T. H. Green, *Lectures on the Principles of Political Obligation*, 175.

The radical communitarian is wrong to think that the social thesis justifies treating the state's requirements as authoritative, and wrong to think that authority relations partly constitute our identities. The truth of the matter is best understood by seeing that each of these addresses a different aspect of our problem: the communitarian the structure and content of our duties, the consent theorist their incumbency. A suitably socialized extension of consent theory will therefore provide an adequate justification of political authority, one superior to the classical conventionalist, contractarian, and consent-based accounts, and without the unattractive features of full-blooded communitarianism. It is clear, however, that its scope will still be narrower than any of those theories, for it is unlikely to be able to deliver the conclusion that everyone is so bound. It offers a picture of the state in which authority is justified over some perhaps, but not over all. In the next chapter, we consider whether this should be counted as an objection.

8

THE POSSIBILITY OF POLITICAL OBLIGATION

THE authority of the state is justified, according to the view defended here, when citizens consent to it. Typically, however, their consent is not to a list of duties, nor even to an explicit procedure for generating such duties, but only to a certain social role which includes obedience as a constitutive element. Consent theory is therefore tempered with a social dimension; consent remains an individual action, although one whose justification may be based on values which are neither instrumental nor wholly individualistic. Contrary to the anarchists' view, political authority is therefore justifiable. But it will not have escaped notice that conditions under which it is justified are fairly stringent. The state must, of course, be reasonably just; but beyond that a further element is needed, the creation of a kind of social relation absent in conventionalist and contractarian theories. Many will feel that this is hopelessly demanding. Let us explore some of the consequences of such a view. Certain questions immediately spring to mind: Does it follow then that there is no obligation to obey the law? What is the relationship between the problem of authority and the problem of political obligation as classically understood? These are the issues for the present chapter. The concluding chapter considers the wider implications of these views for the role of obedience in political life.

1. PROBLEMS OF POLITICAL OBLIGATION

We have thus far been speaking quite casually and indifferently about the state having authority or its citizens being under an obligation to obey. Political theorists generally regard these as being two sides of one coin. And to this point nothing has turned on any distinction that might be drawn between them.

But when we come to consider the import of the justificatory arguments, we must be more precise. Any sensitive student of the subject will note that, for all the alleged centrality of the problem of political obligation, there remains little consensus even within the democratic tradition as to what exactly the problem is. A whole family of questions seem to be implicated: What is the foundation of the state's authority? What could justify its right to coerce? What is the source of the citizen's duty to comply? What is the value of government? What makes government legitimate? Indeed, this is one of those cases where fair-minded historical investigation might even call into question the existence of any such abiding issue as 'the problem of political obligation'—a case where we might be led to conclude, with Collingwood, that, 'the history of political theory is not the history of different answers given to one and the same question, but the history of a problem more or less constantly changing, whose solution was changing with it', and that to think otherwise is 'merely a vulgar error, consequent on a kind of historical myopia'. [1] Certainly *Crito*'s problem is not that of *Leviathan*, nor *Leviathan*'s that of the *Social Contract*. Is it not therefore misleading to speak as if there were a single continuing research problem?

As a matter of history, it probably is. With shifting conceptions of the relationship between self and non-self, between individuality and community, there have been changing views of the nexus between citizens and the state, including changes in the language in which the relationship is expressed. On the other hand, we should not be blind to that degree of continuity which is guaranteed by the unity of a philosophic tradition which shares, if little else, a canon of widely read texts. The diversity we find is thus diversity within a tradition of argument, no doubt including shared and perpetuated misreadings and misunderstandings.

A quick survey of the modern literature will, I think, reveal two main clusters of views about the problem. It has been said that the theory of political obligation is 'an attempt to provide the elements of an answer to the political agent's "what should

[1] R. G. Collingwood, *An Autobiography* (London: Oxford University Press, 1970), 62, 60–1.

I do?"'[2] or that it examines the question of 'whether the state has ethical claims which no other association possesses and whether these are paramount',[3] or that it seeks to identify 'those moral obligations we have because we are citizens'.[4] These are representative of what I shall call the *broad* conception of political obligation: the view that it concerns both the responsive and active components of good citizenship, not merely the duty to obey the law, but also duties of participation, support for the government, and so forth. In contrast, those who favour the *narrow* conception of political obligation limit its scope to the responsive side and, in particular, to the duty to obey the law: 'Why, or under what conditions and circumstances, ought we to obey the law?'[5] or 'Why *ought* we to obey the government?'[6] are its characteristic formulations. Which view one takes will have an influence on whether one thinks such obligations exist or not. The demands of the broad conception are greater, requiring of the citizen not merely the passive response of obedience, but also the time and effort required in genuine participation in the public life of the society. It is a more high-minded view, but one currently in less favour among citizens of states where private life is often thought to be the central focus of meaning and value. The narrow view tends to remove the active side of citizenship from the sphere of obligation and to regard it as meritorious but supererogatory behaviour. It is of course possible to subscribe to the narrow view and to hold that laws are preferable when they result from the input of citizens.

This division among conceptions of political obligation marks a dispute of a particular structure. Political obligation is, after all, the requirement-oriented side of *good citizenship*, a value-ascribing concept which is internally complex, consciously contested within a tradition of argument, and whose dispute may plausibly be thought to promote and preserve

[2] J. Tussman, *Obligation and the Body Politic* (New York: Oxford University Press, 1960), 15.

[3] A. C. Ewing, *The Individual, the State, and World Government* (London: Macmillan, 1947), 211.

[4] R. M. Hare, 'Political Obligation', in T. Honderich, ed., *Social Ends and Political Means* (London: Routledge and Kegan Paul, 1976), 2.

[5] P. Singer, *Democracy and Disobedience*, p.v.

[6] T. McPherson, *Political Obligation*, 4.

that cluster of ideals which form it: because the contest is part of the essence of the concept itself, we can say that it is an essentially contested concept, in the strict sense of the term.[7] The problem of political obligation itself incorporates a contest over the different facets of citizenship, what they require of us, and which are the most important. The broad conception, however, includes the narrow one, since it includes at least the duty to obey the law. This is not to say that it is simply the sum of this duty and others, because in a context of active participation regarded as a moral duty, the nature of the state's requirements will be seen in a different light; they will be self-imposed laws. But on either view, if there is no duty to obey the law, then there is no political obligation, so that is the thesis we will examine here.

2. AN INSOLUBLE PROBLEM

There are many good reasons for obeying the law which have nothing whatever to do with the claim that it is obligatory to do so. Political obligation, if that idea is to serve any useful argumentative function, must be meant to strengthen these other reasons by adding a further general consideration in favour of obedience. The problem then is this: once we have taken all the other ordinary reasons for obedience into account, what is left over to ground the obligation? I wish to show that there is generally nothing left over and thus that there is no such obligation.

It is important to notice that this is an issue which will not be settled just by discovering the truth or falsity of certain general claims in legal theory. There is a long-standing dispute between those who assert that the existence and content of legal obligations can be ascertained without recourse to moral argument and those who deny it. Legal positivists take the former stand and view the existence of law as a matter of social fact. But if they are correct it does not

[7] I take an essentially contested concept to be one, not merely the essence of which is contested, but the contest about which is part of its essence. I believe this accords with the original use of the term. See W. G. Gallie, *Philosophy and the Historical Understanding* (London: Chatto and Windus, 1964), 157–91. Cf. my 'The Political Content of Legal Theory', *Philosophy of the Social Sciences* 17 (1987), 1–20.

show that there is no moral obligation to obey the law. For it might be true that the existence of law has certain general consequences which argue in favour of recognizing an obligation to obey it. Thus there is, for example, no inconsistency between Hobbes's positivism and his view that there is an obligation to obey. One might, after all, take a positivist view of promises according to which their existence and content can be determined without recourse to moral argument while also holding that there are sound moral principles which sustain the conclusion that everyone ought to keep their promises.

How then can the sceptical thesis be established? We might begin by trying to identify a fairly complete list of reasons for obeying the law, including all the general prima-facie obligations of fidelity, veracity, beneficence, justice, gratitude, and so on, and then ask whether, over and above those appearing on the list, there is a further, distinct obligation to obey the law. The project, of course, is greatly hampered by the inherent controversiality and possible incompleteness of any list we might draw up. We could never be sure that an apparent obligation to obey is not merely required by some general consideration which we neglected to include on the list. But there is a still more serious error in this approach. It assumes that the obligation to obey the law is in some sense a basic one, on a par with the other enumerated prima-facie obligations. Why should we make that assumption? Suppose there is a sound general argument which establishes that everyone has performed some action which amounts to a promise to obey. Surely we would not then wish to object that this is not really evidence of an obligation to obey the law, but merely of an obligation to keep one's promises. The obligation to obey may be a specification of one or more of the basic obligations and yet be sound for all that. Indeed, virtually every writer from Plato to Rawls has supposed that political obligation is in fact an application or special case of one or more of the commonly recognized obligations. The sceptical argument must therefore proceed in another way.

Instead of looking for a distinctive obligation to obey, I shall articulate certain conditions which any argument purporting to ground political obligation must meet, and then attempt to show why none can succeed. These conditions are derived simply by considering what it would take to establish the conclusion in question: that every citizen has a duty to obey all the laws of his or her own state. Any argument to that effect must satisfy the following parameters:

(1) Morality: It is trivially true that we all have a legal obligation to obey the state: that is a mere reflection of law's nature as a normative system which purports to impose duties on its subjects. It is less trivial but equally uninteresting that most of us do in fact obey the law; we might even be able to state some low-level sociological generalizations about why this is so. Neither of these establishes the existence of political obligation, which is a moral reason for action and which therefore has whatever formal and material features a requirement must have in order to be moral. It is beyond the scope of this book to consider this issue, but I shall adopt the commonplace view that it is something more than direct prudential reasoning. The first requirement thus excludes arguments to the effect that certain threats, offers, or considerations of self-interest mandate compliance.

(2) Content-Independence: This has been discussed at some length in Chapter 2. The core idea is that the fact that some action is legally required must itself count in the practical reasoning of the citizens, independently of the nature and merits of that action. We ought to refrain from assaulting people even if it were not a crime, and we ought to keep our promises, whether the law of contract so requires or not. In political life as elsewhere we have at least those general duties which bind irrespective of social and political institutions. One who believes in political obligation accepts more than this platitude: he or she accepts that the fact that the state requires something of us itself changes our moral position by giving us further duties or giving existing ones a new source of validity. All of this is perfectly consistent with the law having only prima-facie force. But it must at least in principle be capable of making some difference to our moral reasoning, a difference which does not depend on the nature of the action prescribed. Now, because it is a requirement of justice that the duties which the government imposes reinforce, or at least not

conflict unacceptably with, general moral duties, it will be difficult to tell, as an empirical matter, what motivates citizens, particularly if they are already inclined to do what the law requires of them and to abstain from what it forbids. Our ability to discern what is actually going on will therefore turn on our capacity to make judgements about complex counterfactuals involving what citizens would do if their motives or the state's requirements were different. This complexity makes descriptive political science extremely difficult. But the idea of content-independent force is a coherent and necessary one in any argument purporting to establish the existence of a political obligation. It serves to rule out any arguments which cannot show how politics makes a difference to what people ought to do.

(3) Bindingness: Together with (2) this condition specifies more narrowly what sort of moral reason is expected, along the lines already defended in Chapter 2. It aims to capture the common view that some actions are obligatory which do not, however, seem to be of special weight and importance. According to (3), they are special because they exclude from consideration certain otherwise valid reasons for non-performance of the action—usually, and at a minimum, weak considerations of ordinary self-interest or convenience.

Together, (2) and (3) pick out a subset of all the possible reasons for complying with the law as being of special interest: they offer a partial analysis of what it is to have an obligation. Though severally necessary, however, they are not jointly sufficient for one to have a moral obligation because they specify this in purely formal terms: some things satisfying (2) and (3) are not moral reasons of any sort. Every legal obligation, for example, also has this structure. Not all moral theories, it is fair to say, place special importance on obligations. A pure act-utilitarian, for reasons discussed earlier, would not accept the proposed distinction between praiseworthy and obligatory actions. Thus, if one insisted on (2) and (3), this would rule out such arguments from the beginning. As we shall see, however, it will in the end make no difference to the success of utilitarian theories whether we do or not, for there are other requirements which they cannot meet.

(4) Particularity:[8] Citizens are normally bound only to the laws of their *own* state. This condition seeks to capture the directionality common to political obligation and other special obligations. Just as promising creates duties to particular persons only and not to the world at large, political obligations bind them to certain states only. In the standard case, this means to the state of which they are citizens. But this is not necessarily so. Where the source of the obligation is promissory, its direction follows that of the promise. A visitor, for example, may be required to promise to obey the law in order to be granted an entry visa or a work permit. Moreover, even in the standard case there is a little difficulty in specifying exactly what is meant by one's 'own' state, and different theories of obligation do this in different ways. Citizenship is both a moral concept and a legal one, so it is little help by itself: the law claims to determine both the content and the liability of obligations. Sometimes residence is taken to be the appropriate indicator, but it is not wholly satisfactory either for it is also commonly held that citizens stand in a special relationship to their own state in a way that resident aliens do not. There is no implication here that such aliens, or tourists in foreign countries, have no reason to respect the laws of the land in which they find themselves. On the contrary, to do so is generally courteous, prudent, and morally required. But it is felt that the existence of political obligations marks a further, special, relationship. Locke appealed to the metaphor of the family to explain this through his idea of full membership in a political community: the duties of a permanent house guest may be the same as those of members of the family, but their ground and duration differ. Some theorists, like John Rawls, try to side-step this issue by speaking of the duty to comply with those just institutions which 'apply to us'; but this explains nothing.[9] We normally regard political institutions as applying to us only if they either exert real control over our lives or if we stand in a relation of moral obligation to them. But the latter is the very problem at issue, and the former renders senseless the thought

[8] I owe the term to A. J. Simmons, *Moral Principles and Political Obligations*, 31.

[9] J. Rawls, *A Theory of Justice*, 334. Cf. A. J. Simmons, *Moral Principles and Political Obligations*, 143–56.

that there is some special, directional relationship involved. The political institutions of many countries exert substantial control over us through the interdependent world economy and strategic alliances. Yet only in the rare circumstances of dual citizenship and the like do we think that people owe allegiance to more than one country.

The consequences of (4) are wide-ranging, for most ordinary moral reasons do not respect the boundaries of states in the appropriate way. While they might be able to explain duties to humanity in general, they can make little sense of narrower, more particular bonds. On grounds of justice and utility, for example, South Africans may be more tightly bound to the laws of Sweden than to their own. Americans benefit from many of the pollution control regulations of Canada. But we none the less feel that political obligation, if it exists at all, stops at borders in ways that these other considerations do not. We must not overstate the point. The claim is not that it is paradoxical or impossible for individuals to owe duties to more than one country. Some obviously do. Apart from difficulties in cases of conflict of duty (especially in wartime), the reason for rejecting such a view is just that it is not at all what classical and modern writers defend in defending political obligation. While the condition of particularity need not be understood as excluding plural obligations, it does exclude general ones. Political obligation is not just some general duty to humanity which requires compliance with governments, but rather a special moral relationship between a citizen and the state. Those who deny the existence of such a bond deny that any such relationship makes sense. They assert that persons are, in the moral sense, stateless.

(5) Universality: Political obligation purports to bind all citizens to all laws and is in that sense doubly universal. It is not in dispute that some people have moral reasons to obey some laws. It is very likely that there are some people who have obligations to obey all the laws (for example, those public officials who have taken an oath to do so). And it is certain that there are some laws which all of us ought to obey: that is true of every prohibited act which, like assault and murder, is in any case morally wrong. It is not worth

discussing any of these weak claims, for they are not at the centre of the problem of political obligation. The important question is whether it is true of all citizens that they are bound to obey all their laws.

According to the theory of political obligation, obedience is a virtue for all, not just for some; and its menu of requirements is *table d'hôte* rather than *à la carte*. This aspect of universality is related to (2) above: if law has content-independent force, then it has it *qua* law, and that will underwrite the obligation to obey all the laws. Is this too demanding? Aren't there cases of necessity, or infractions *de minimis*, in which one is entitled not to obey certain valid laws? Indeed there are, but the state purports to regulate these exceptions as well. Like a universal law of nature, the thesis of political obligation cannot withstand a single counterexample. In a just state, there can be no valid laws which are morally inert. To suppose otherwise is just to concede that there is no obligation to obey the law as such.

This final condition has the consequence of ruling out any arguments which are merely based on the systematic character of law, for example, on the fact that a legal system being in force provides certain goods of social co-operation. These benefits result from the general effects of the legal system as a whole, from the way it co-ordinates and secures expectations. Because their source is systematic, they are threatened only by disobedience which threatens the existence of the legal system or which substantially weakens it. Despite the familiar harangues of law-and-order ideologues, however, it is just false to think that there are no laws whose disobedience the system can survive, and false to think that there are no people whose compliance is unnecessary. Hume thought that 'exact obedience' to the magistrate is a necessary condition for the existence of the political system, and grounded his view in common sense. Yet common sense actually supports only a much weaker conclusion: there must be general, but not perfect, obedience. This is not to deny that widespread disregard of certain laws (e.g., fundamental constitutional provisions, or those governing the administration of justice) would bring the system down; nor that certain opinion leaders (e.g. Gandhi) can be very influential in mobilizing general disobedience. It is just to remind us of the platitude that most laws and most people are not that important.

If we now consider the net effect of these five conditions, it will be seen that none of the most popular theories of political obligation satisfies all of them. Prudence fails to pass (1); it offers no moral reasons of any sort, nor can it extend to cover all persons and all laws, so it fails (5) as well. Indeed, there are often prudential reasons to break the law. And where prudence applies it does so without regard to boundaries: visitors to foreign countries have strong prudential reasons to comply, flowing from both the threat of sanction and informal social pressure. Utilitarianism fails, as we have already remarked, to satisfy (3), and for related reasons will fail to generate particularized obligations of the right sort: (4). While it is generally true that one's actions have more important consequences for those nearby than those more distant, this is not always true and the obligation to obey is not thought to vary in proportion to the extent it is. If one waived these objections on the ground that it is part of the utilitarian programme to reduce or, in more revisionist versions, eliminate all fundamental obligations, one would still have difficulty with (5); any direct version of utilitarianism will notoriously counsel breaking some of the laws, some of the time. It is more difficult to speak with confidence about the fate of indirect utilitarian theories since they come in many forms. If they rely on conventionalist arguments, then the objections set out in Chapter 4 tell against them too. If they rely on claims about motivational or informational imperfections in order to justify a general policy of obedience, then they cannot succeed where well-informed and well-motivated people correctly judge that utility would be maximized by disobedience. What about the view that obedience is fair return for benefits received? This may generate obligations of the right form, satisfying (1) to (3), but they are inadequately particularized, since there is no less reason to deal fairly with foreigners than with one's fellow citizens. No doubt most continuing contexts of reciprocity exist within rather than between states, but there are too many exceptions for (4) to be secure. Nor are obligations of fairness likely to be universal in scope: (5) Not all laws promote social co-operation or a fair distributive scheme, and some people are regularly excluded from enjoying the benefits of those that do. Of all the common theories, only consent satisfies the conditions of morality, content-independence, bindingness, and particularity. But its failure is notorious: not everyone does something which can reasonably be interpreted as consenting to the authority of the state.

This surely creates a very strong presumption in favour of the sceptical view that there is no general obligation to obey the law. This view is not part of the mainstream of the democratic tradition, although it is commonplace among anarchists of various sorts. Yet recently a number of moderate democratic theorists who are not anarchists have defended similar conclusions.[10] And among those who do retain some faith in the moral bonds of allegiance it usually comes in a highly attenuated and qualified form: while admitting a natural duty to support and comply with just institutions, even Rawls concedes that 'There is . . . no political obligation, strictly speaking, for citizens generally.'[11]

All of their arguments proceed inductively, as I have done above, by assessing and rejecting the popular theories and then inviting us to suppose that no other theory can fare any better. Such a strategy cannot fully persuade, however, for it does not show what it is about political obligation that makes it unlikely that a sound argument will be discovered tomorrow, or next year. Given the wide range of theories which have failed, we may begin to suspect that it is not merely a lack of imagination or diligence which is at fault. It raises the suspicion that there is something about the joint demands of these conditions which makes it especially unlikely that any new alternative will succeed. I shall now try to show that this is indeed the case.

[10] R. A. Wasserstrom, 'The Obligation to Obey the Law', *UCLA Law Review* 10 (1963), 780–807; M. B. E. Smith, 'Is There a Prima Facie Obligation to Obey the Law?' *Yale Law Journal* 82 (1973), 950–76; A. D. Woozley, *Law and Obedience* (London: Duckworth, 1979); J. Raz, *The Authority of Law*; A. J. Simmons, *Moral Principles and Political Obligations*; J. Feinberg, 'Civil Disobedience in the Modern World', in J. Feinberg and H. Gross, eds., *Philosophy of Law*, 3rd edn. (Belmont, Calif.: Wadsworth, 1986), 129–42.

[11] J. Rawls, *A Theory of Justice*, 114.

3. WHY THERE IS NO OBLIGATION TO OBEY

Strictly speaking, political obligation is impossible only if the demands of conditions (1) to (5) above *cannot* simultaneously be met. If we interpret that to mean that there can exist no moral principle whose application would yield these features, then it can easily be established that political obligation is possible, for the principle of consent could satisfy them all. If everyone promises to obey all the laws, then every citizen has an obligation of the appropriate form. But this is not, I think, the most interesting interpretation of the problem. While it asks whether there *could be* such a thing as political obligation, democratic theorists have normally asked whether *there is* such a thing. We should therefore think of it in the traditional way, as establishing an existential proposition about such obligations. It puts the question of whether such obligations now exist, anywhere. For obvious reasons consent theory cannot show that: there is no state whose citizens have all made such a promise or its equivalent. Pateman has suggested that this is no accident, because the structure of actual liberal democratic states is such that citizens could not even succeed in obligating themselves if they tried, for the opportunities for real self-commitment are too few.[12] She contemplates the possibility of a radically participatory political order which would provide the necessary social background and institutional resources for commitments of the right sort. However, certain general considerations cast doubt on the universal value of such commitments, even in a participatory society.

Although they are logically consistent, there is a deep normative tension among the five conditions which can best be explained in this way. The role of particularized obligations in moral theory is a special one. Not all theories will have room for them, because not all theories give sufficient weight to the sorts of value which make them important. Act-utilitarianism is the most familiar example of one which does not. Why should we be willing to recognize permissions to assume special obligations which may get in the way of the agent-neutral maximization of value? Many reasons have

[12] C. Pateman, *The Problem of Political Obligation.*

been suggested to explain this: a concern for individual freedom, for self-expression, for autonomy, for integrity, and so forth. In different ways, these all acknowledge a special concern for the circumstances of individual lives and how the ways in which they can go well or ill may depend on the aims which the agents have assumed. Particular obligations are justified when, for one or more of these reasons, we feel that the moral demands on someone should also be individualized.

Now it is an obvious but significant fact that people differ in their needs, interests, desires, and aspirations in ways which make it extremely unlikely that the same set of particular obligations will apply to each: they have their own abilities, families, biographies, and so on. And for that reason it is very unlikely that they will all have equal reason to bind themselves to obey the state. They will have other loyalties which are for them equally or even more important. This might seem to go against the argument of Chapter 7 that a common, public status of citizenship, constituted by its various duties, may be of intrinsic value. The emphasis on the particular circumstances of individuals seems to favour the position of radical consent theory according to which we have all and only the duties we have specifically agreed to. But in fact there is no contradiction here, for that argument was only meant to establish that a common status is coherently valuable, not that all do so value it. Indeed, I took pains to argue that for many people other statuses and loyalties will be more important than their political ones. Now consider the other side of the coin: What sort of considerations are likely to apply with sufficient generality that they will cover all persons? For the same reasons it is manifestly unlikely that they will be special obligations. They may be considerations of utility which do not impose obligations in the strict sense or considerations of fairness which are not sufficiently particularized. There is therefore something, if not contradictory, at least highly unstable in a set of principles like (1) to (5): they aim to create special moral ties which bind all persons in circumstances where the value of such ties is dubious. This is not to say that it is of the nature of particular obligations that they are unlikely to be universal among some social group. Members of a family or church may all share a common set of particular obligations. But this is because the social circumstances of those institutions are such that the diversity of interests and situations is more limited than it is in the state. When an institution claims supreme authority over everyone within its territory the variability of circumstances is inevitably greater.

The simplest way out of such a problem is to abandon some of the conditions. No doubt readers will find some of them too stringent. It is relatively easy, as we have seen above, to find principles which satisfy four of them, so we might make the adjustment almost anywhere. We might look for non-moral principles, or ones which are not particularized. But since the conditions are not arbitrary but aim to describe the traditional problem of political obligation, such an amendment must be principled. There must be something unsatisfactory about the requirement that we choose to abandon, apart from the mere fact that it is hard to satisfy. I am going to suggest that we give up (5), not because it cannot easily be satisfied, but because, although traditionally central to the idea of political obligation, it distorts our understanding of the moral situation of citizens of the modern state. The result will be offered not as a theory of political obligation, but as an alternative to it. It will allow that some people in a reasonably just state have political obligations, while denying the existence of a general political obligation binding on all.

4. OBLIGATION AND AUTHORITY

To deny political obligation is to deny that all persons have duties to obey all the laws of their own states. It may therefore seem that if one has a sound general conclusion of the sort sketched above, then the detailed analysis of arguments seeking to justify the authority of the state is otiose. For the state has authority only if citizens have an obligation to obey; the above argument shows that there is no such obligation, and hence, by contraposition, there can be no legitimate authority. The impossibility result looks too powerful.

Whether the absence of political obligation entails the illegitimacy of authority depends both on the analysis of authority and on the relation between authority and obligation.

It is usually suggested that they are *correlative* in the way that claim rights are correlative to obligations. A promisee's right to five dollars is the other side of the promisor's obligation to pay: both are simply logically correlated results of a valid promise which justifies each. In such cases, we can regard an obligation-based and a rights-based statement of the moral relationship as notational variants: there is no causal, temporal, or justificatory priority of one over the other. It has been claimed that the authority of the state and the obligation to obey are related in this way. D. D. Raphael, for example, holds that it is a formally correct, though empty, explanation of the duty of obedience that it is correlated to the state's authority: 'It follows logically that if the State is authoritative, i.e. has the right to issue orders to its citizens and the right to receive obedience from them, the citizens are obliged to obey those orders. The recipient right of the State to be obeyed by the citizens, and the obligation of the citizens to obey, are simply two different ways of expressing one thing, the metaphorical tie or bond between the two parties.'[13]

It is, as Raphael says, empty to point to the legal obligation to obey in order to justify the state's claim to authority. This is just because legal obligations can be created only by such authority. As a general thesis, however, it is less certain that statements referring to authority and those referring to an obligation to obey are logically interchangeable. There is, in the first place, the somewhat technical point that the logical correlates involved in authority relations are often not, in Hohfeldian terms, 'right' and 'duty', but rather 'power' and 'liability'. Anyone who has authority has the normative power to change the position of another and those subject to that authority are liable to have their positions changed. This may take place through the imposition of duties, but it may also involve the waiving of duties or the creation of liberties. The correlation between a right to rule and a duty to obey is distinctive only of the case of political authority. Secondly, and more importantly, whether the right to rule and the duty to obey are simply logical correlates depends on substantive questions of political theory, and not on the analysis of

[13] D. D. Raphael, *Problems of Political Philosophy* (London: Macmillan, 1976), 78.

concepts. It is important to keep in mind the identities of the two parties tied by the metaphorical bond to which Raphael refers: they are the state on the one hand, and the citizens on the other. But if we view that state as the creature of its citizens, as the instrument of their aims and whose purposes it should serve, then we would no longer see this correlation as purely a matter of logic; we would say that the authority of the state *follows from* the existence of their obligations not in the weak sense that they are logical correlates, but in the strong sense that the existence of the obligations is the ground of its authority. Alternatively, if one put the priority the other way round, as in a primitive monarchy perhaps, citizens might think that their obligations were normative consequences of independently justified authority. In assuming correlativity we usually rely on a substantive rather than analytic thesis about the state, namely, that it is properly the instrument of its citizens' aims. In that case, the relationship between authority and obligation is not one of notational variants.

The issue here is similar to that of whether there can be a substantial difference between rights- and duty-based moral theories, or whether rights and duties are merely two interchangeable expressions of one relationship. Priority can be assigned to one of the two correlates only if it reveals a distinction in the point of the theories, or in the way they are taken to be justified. Ronald Dworkin notes that, 'there is a world of difference in saying that you shouldn't lie because you have a duty not to lie and saying you shouldn't lie because I have a right not to be lied to.'[14] The former, he thinks, puts moral codes and the value of obedience at the centre, the latter, the individual agent and her interests. Similar differences in emphasis will be found between those political theories which explain the obligation of obedience by the existence of political authority, and those which see authority as a normative consequence of obligations. The latter was the view of all the classical consent theorists and contractarians who saw the state's right to rule as nothing more than the sum of those rights transferred to it by people in the state of nature.

[14] R. Dworkin, *Taking Rights Seriously*, 171.

Either way, however, the correlation between authority and obligation seems to be liable to the sceptical argument against authority. If obligation justifies authority, then denial of obligation will undercut the latter. If obligation is a necessary consequence of independently justified authority, then its absence will also count against it. It may seem that the only hope is to deny the correlativity thesis in any form. This is the line taken by Rolf Sartorius. Political obligation, he says, involves the question, 'Under what conditions, if any, may the citizen lie under a prima facie obligation to obey those who claim political authority?' whereas the problem in the justification of authority is, 'Under what conditions, if any, may those in power claim to rule as a matter of moral right?'[15] He then argues that since the justification for political authority is precisely that rational individuals in the state of nature would not voluntarily co-operate to enforce rights (because rights enforcement is a general Prisoner's Dilemma) and since genuine obligations must be voluntarily incurred, the justification for authority *undercuts* the conditions for political obligation. Hence he concludes that the government only holds a trust, that is, 'the right and responsibility to act in certain ways for the benefit of its citizens.'[16] Sartorius's argument thus tries to free authority from scepticism about obligation by showing that the former has a different justification from the latter. The failure of voluntary co-operation in the state of nature is at once the condition justifying authority and the condition explaining why there is no obligation.

The claim that such arguments can justify authority has already been rejected in Chapter 5. Here, I wish only to consider whether this move does indeed sever the correlation between authority and obligation. For that to be so it must be shown that the justification for the state's authority does not *include* a right to obedience, for if the state has a right to obedience, then we have a correlative obligation to obey. But consider Sartorius's actual justification for authority: life is enormously inconvenient in a state of nature in

[15] R. Sartorius, 'Political Authority and Political Obligation', *Virginia Law Review* 67 (1981), 3.

[16] Ibid. 4.

which voluntary respect for rights is impossible. These inconveniences are just those due to private rights-enforcement: as Locke saw, it will be partial, uncertain, and unreliable. But a coercive monopoly remedies this only if it largely excludes private enforcement in favour of public. In that case, however, the state has rights to enforce which individuals lack, and its determinations in private disputes claim to bind the parties by right, and so to obligate them. The claim that rational parties in the state of nature would not *agree* to such a scheme does not show that once it is imposed no obligations would follow. If anything, it rather suggests that agreements are not the only way of generating moral obligations. This is surely compatible with any sound voluntarist view of the distinction between obligations and moral reasons of other sorts. If the only commitments considered voluntary were those unilateral ones it was rational to make in the absence of assurances of general compliance, then even ordinary contracts would generate no obligations, for they too are irrational unless it is reasonable to expect that the other party will abide by the terms. Since these are the very paradigm of obligation on the individualistic voluntarist view, we cannot accept Sartorius's argument against correlativity.

The surprisingly popular view that all moral obligations must be voluntarily assumed cannot, I think, withstand examination. It rests on a tendentious distinction between obligation and duty which is not regularly recognized in ordinary language and which has but weak foundations in moral theory. The source of the view is a false inference from the directionality of obligations: in contrast to many natural duties and general moral reasons for acting, obligations are typically owed to some particular person or group. Voluntary undertakings are a common and central way of creating such obligations; but they are not the only way. Social roles like that of parent or teacher also bring with them directional obligations even in some cases when the role is not voluntarily assumed. To insist in the face of this that such obligations are really 'duties' or some such equivalent is to engage in pointless verbal legislation. The weakness of non-voluntary grounds for the obligation to obey has nothing to do with the nature of obligations; it results from the nature of the state.

There is a final difficulty with this attempt to disconnect obligation and authority. Even if sound, it cannot justify a *claim-right* to rule, for there is no attached obligation; at best it only establishes the existence of a *liberty*. It is crucially important, however, that this is not what states in fact claim. They do not claim a liberty to regulate human behaviour in the way that other associations in a pluralistic society do: they claim supreme authority over many people. Raphael puts the point well: 'The authority to issue commands is not simply a right or permission to do something, as is a licence (or being authorized) to drive a car; it is also a right against those to whom the commands are addressed that they should do what they are commanded to do. It is a right to receive obedience, and it corresponds to an obligation on the part of the others to give obedience.'[17] No doubt there are some authorities whose normative powers do not extend so far as to include the imposition of obligations on their subjects, but the state is not among them.

It is of the nature of obligations that they are binding, content-independent moral reasons and thus conditions (1), (2), and (3) seem quite secure; we could not abandon them without abandoning part of any satisfactory analysis of political authority. Yet it has another related feature: the obligations it imposes are thought to be directional. A state will itself determine who are the addressees of its laws: everyone within a certain territory, everyone of a certain ancestry, or even everyone in the world. But each political obligation which a person might have is owed to a particular state, and that secures (4) also as a necessary condition.

None of these arguments suffices to show that there can be authority without obligation, and thus they cannot save authority from the sceptical argument advanced here. The correct response to it in fact lies in another, simpler, direction. Fortunately it is unnecessary to deny the correlativity thesis, for it is a thesis about the nature of the state's *claims*, not about its *existence conditions*. A state may exist even when some of its claims have no justification. A state cannot exist unless it claims authority with some success and general compliance.

[17] D. D. Raphael, *Problems of Political Philosophy*, 69.

But equally it may have some failures: it may claim authority over some people over whom its authority is not justified. Recall that the denial of political obligation does not entail any of the following: (1) some people have no reason to obey the law, (2) no one is obligated to obey the law, or (3) there are no laws which everyone is obligated to obey. These statements might be true, but the denial that everyone has a moral obligation to obey all the laws of their own state does not establish that they are.

In one way, then, political obligation is narrower than authority, since it purports to apply to all persons, whereas authority is explicitly relational in form. In Chapter 2, we characterized it as a three-place relation among an authority, a subject, and a range of action. It is readily conceded that there are limits to the third variable: for any given authority there are some things which it cannot legitimately require of the subject. We should concede as much about the second variable: there are some people over whom it does not have authority at all. It therefore appears that (5) is the culprit and should be abandoned. This will allow us to stipulate a verbal distinction: political obligation is the relation justified by an argument satisfying conditions (1) to (5); political authority is justified by an argument satisfying (1) to (4). Where such authority is justified, there are indeed correlative obligations to obey; but there need not be any general political obligation.

5. DENYING UNIVERSALITY

Let us now consider which of these two concepts, political obligation or justified authority, is the more useful in understanding the moral situation of citizens of modern states. The state itself purports to determine all the limits there are to its own authority; but our arguments suggest that this is one aspect of its self-image that we cannot share. Instead, I propose that we reject political obligation in favour of justified authority as the central organizing concept, for it does not tempt us to false generalizations about the relations of obedience. If we expect that the moral relationship will be the universal one contemplated by traditional theories of obligation, we may be tempted to stretch or expand the grounds of allegiance; that is often the motivation for theories of tacit consent and hypothetical contract which aim to show that all are bound. Perhaps it would be better simply to reconsider the value of that aim, and admit a more nuanced approach to the relations between citizen and state. There may be resistance to this view, and not only because it is such a great departure from the standard assumptions of the democratic tradition. It is not possible to prove that we should cease thinking about political allegiance in a universal way; and the urge to do so has deep roots. In this section, I can do little more than explore some of the sources of this resistance, and attempt to weaken them.

5.1 *Social Order*

Perhaps the most powerful consideration in favour of universality is one which was often also used to justify the necessity for absolute authority. Harold Laski writes, 'From the threshold of the seventeenth century what the state demands is the whole of the man's allegiance lest, in seeking less, it should obtain nothing.'[18] If the state conceded the legitimacy of the demands of other organizations, its claim to supremacy would collapse. Likewise, we might suppose that to concede that some people are not bound by its laws is to sow the seeds from which lawlessness and disruption will spread, thus supporting Hume's thesis that the unconditional obedience of all is a necessary condition of the state's existence as a valued institution.

Not only is this thesis false on the facts, as argued above, but it also underestimates the sources of stability in political society. We began this book by distinguishing between authoritative and stable social orders, and noting that legitimate authority is only one source of social order. The state may also coerce, persuade, and bribe people and generally guide their behaviour in many other ways which do not involve relying on the specific techniques of authoritative guidance. Moreover, a just state is one which encourages its citizens to do those things which ought on independent moral grounds to be done: such as to respect rights, strive for the

[18] H. J. Laski, *Authority in the Modern State*, 23.

common good, aim at self-perfection. These aims all have intrinsic appeal and it would be wrong to suppose that no one will follow them unless ordered to do so. The just state is not the fragile entity that the objection contemplates: it is fairly robust and has sources of stability quite distinct from its exercise of authority.

5.2 *The Assurance Problem Revisited*

Questions of stability can arise, however, in another way which we have already touched on in Chapter 6. Rawls's objections to consent theory have obvious application here as well. If it is uncertain whether all are bound to obey, or if it is certain that some are but not known who, then some desirable forms of social co-operation will fail because people otherwise willing to do their duty will not if they feel insecure that others will do theirs. The possibility that some are not bound by the state's authority can only complicate the assurance problem.

Many of the objections to the first argument from stability apply here also. The assurance problem only requires for its solution the presence of considerations which make it reasonable to expect that others will do their duty; it does not require any particular *source* of that expectation. Provided that enough of those prudential and moral considerations still apply, the absence of a general obligation to obey will not be excessively damaging. Moreover, the existence of a general political obligation would not in any case be sufficient to solve the assurance problem on its own. There is such an obligation if there is a sound argument supporting the conclusion that each person has a moral obligation to obey the law, but that argument does not itself ensure that all will behave as they ought to, nor does it ensure that the range of acts they are obligated to perform is uncontroversial. Assurance problems are therefore liable to break out at other points too.

5.3 *Outlaws and Coercion*

Another common source of the appeal of universality is the belief that if some people have no obligation to obey then they cannot rightfully be coerced by the state, thereby creating within civil society dangerous regions of normative vacuum inhabited by independents who remain in the state of nature.

Yet the security of all those who have obligations is dependent on relations among all people in the territory and not only among others who are bound.

It does not follow, however, that the state may not coerce those over whom it has no authority.[19] Consider an analogy. Parents have authority over their children, which includes limited power to punish or coerce them. This power extends only to their own children. Yet there are circumstances in which parents may legitimately coerce the children of others, for example, when they attack their own children. This power also is limited, and may even be subject to more stringent regulation. But there are cases in which it is justified, and yet in those cases the justification is not that they have authority over the other children. Related arguments may establish that the state can legitimately coerce those over whom it has no authority in order to protect those over whom it does. It will be a complex matter to decide how far this power extends, but that it exists to some degree is unlikely to be disputed. It may be said that this argument will not succeed unless it can be shown that the state has the *same* degree of legitimate coercive power over those who are not obligated as it has over those who are. But why should this be so? Is it because of the problems which may arise due to jurisdictional uncertainties? Any justification for the state's coercive power must, however, take these consequences into account in the first place. If we regard voluntary obligations as especially serious or important we come to the view that those who promise to obey are indeed bound more tightly to the state than those who do not. Whether one might object precisely to this feature is a question to which we now turn.

5.4 *Civic Union*

The arguments from stability and assurance each make what are by now fairly familiar errors, and can be answered by considering the range of reasons for obedience that are available even in the absence of legitimate authority. Not so with the final objection. The view that to abandon universality

[19] As A. J. Simmons also notices: *Moral Principles and Political Obligations*, 36–7. See also the discussion in Chapter 3 above of the difference between authority and justified coercion.

is to distort fundamentally the nature of the civic union raises a more complex, and more controversial, issue.

It may be useful to approach this question by considering it in the context of Rawls's theory of political allegiance. Recall that he supposes that even in a reasonably just society, only a minority of citizens will have political obligations in the strict sense. This follows from his view that all obligations properly so called flow from the principle of fairness: that those who accept the benefits of a scheme of social co-operation for mutual benefit ought to do their fair share to support such a scheme. It is unlikely, however, that many citizens voluntarily accept these benefits in any important sense. In the state, the benefits of security, law and order, and the like are almost unavoidable fall-out of the scheme of co-operation. Only comparatively few occupying special positions in the political system can be said willingly to accept the benefits and only they have obligations in the strict sense. Thus, he says, there is 'another sense of *noblesse oblige*: namely, that those who are more privileged are likely to acquire obligations' and this minority is mainly composed of those who 'are best able to gain political office and to take advantage of the opportunities offered by the constitutional system.'[20] The others are also bound to obey, but by principles of natural duty rather than obligation, principles which apply regardless of voluntary action on one's own part and which require citizens to support and comply with just institutions which apply to them. The justification for principles of natural duty is that they would be acknowledged as binding in the original position in order to gain the benefits of social stability and avoid the assurance problem.

The bifurcated ground of allegiance is somewhat puzzling in Rawls's theory, for it appears as a blot on his contractarian conception, which otherwise aims to bring political order as close as possible to a voluntary scheme of co-operation. For the vast majority of citizens, however, the fundamental principles of legitimacy have no foundation whatsoever in their voluntary acts and are grounded only in the purported requirements of social stability. This compromise with volun-

[20] J. Rawls, *A Theory of Justice*, 116, 344.

tarism is too near the centre of things, too fundamental to be dismissed as a minor aberration. Pateman has argued that it reveals the shallowness of Rawls's commitment to voluntarism and his unjustified willingness to regard the liberal democratic state as inherently rational and its authority as axiomatic. (In this, she detects a Hegelian note in Rawls, though in fact the idea of divided allegiance has affinities to a source much closer to the mainstream of the liberal tradition: it is in some ways related to Locke's distinction between express consenters who are 'members' of the commonwealth, and tacit consenters who, though bound to obey it, are not.) In Pateman's view, Rawls's distinction between obligation and natural duty is a way of 'institutionalizing the non-voluntarist status of child-bride citizens and the moral proletariat.'[21] Thus, the central worry is that this opens a fissure in the civic union, a moral caste system in which the better-placed are bound by obligations while the majority are bound by natural duty.

What precisely is the force of this objection? It cannot be that it is *better* to have obligations than duties. Consider the analogy with Locke's claim in the Second Treatise (§ 121): express consenters are 'perpetually and indispensably' obliged to obey, whereas tacit consenters who are bound only by their enjoyment of the benefits of civil society have a duty which 'begins and ends with the enjoyment'. If this is a moral caste system, it is ordered the wrong way round. If anything, express consenters seem worse off than do tacit consenters. Nor is it even true that those who have the obligations lack the natural duties, for it is a defining feature of the latter that they apply to everyone irrespective of any voluntary action on their part. Why then should anyone object to the distinction? The worry is that it marks a distinction between two kinds of person. For anyone tempted by Rousseauan visions of the organic unity of the political order, any such division would be intolerable. Should the fundamental principles of social unity be irreducibly plural, the meaning of the political order and the value of its requirements would differ for different people. Not everyone would view it as self-legislated commands; only those who were voluntarily committed to it would see it as an

[21] C. Pateman, *The Problem of Political Obligation*, 118.

extension of their own wills and thus only they would regard it as consistent with the demands of autonomy. For those who acquire their duties involuntarily, the state would always seem in some measure an external, brute fact and one fears they might for that reason feel less loyal to it.

In one straightforward sense, however, it is not correct to think of this distinction as marking the difference between two kinds of person. First, as noted above, everyone is in fact subject to the natural duties; they are no indignity and, if part of the moral law, might be equally susceptible to a hypothetical voluntarist interpretation, perhaps along Kantian lines. In any case, even the most committed voluntarist needs some independent explanation of why voluntary undertakings bind, and whatever that explanation is it may be the archetype for a form of argument which would apply directly to non-voluntary cases as well. (Suppose, for instance, the principle of detrimental reliance explains why we should keep our promises; then it may also explain the duty to tell the truth.) Secondly, there is no one who is constitutionally *disabled* from assuming obligations to the state. Any member of the 'moral proletariat' may enjoy upward mobility, if that is what it is, simply by promising to obey. The reason that it is the better-placed members of society who are likely to have full-blooded obligations is that they are more likely, under the sociological conditions imagined by Rawls, voluntarily to enjoy the fruits of the system or to assume leadership roles. Now, one might coherently object to this as unjustifiable élitism, and thus to the whole theory of justice whose weakly egalitarian difference principle permits large inequalities of wealth and condition provided only that they do not interfere with equal civil liberties and that they have some small trickle-down benefits even to the worst-off. But in that case one should tackle the theory of justice directly, rather than blame the divided conception of allegiance for creating a moral proletariat.

Perhaps none of this proves that our allegiance to the state does not have the universal form suggested by the traditional idea of political obligation. But it does, I think, make it seem less strange to suppose that it may not. Some of us have natural duties to obey, others duties of consent, still others may have only weak prudential ties, and some may have none at all. None of these principles will fulfil all five requirements of a theory of political obligation, but some will satisfy the first four, in which case the state will enjoy legitimate authority. This authority is unlikely to extend to everyone, although that does not preclude the state regulating their affairs on different grounds. The resulting picture is more complex—but more realistic—than the traditional theory of political obligation. Indeed, fair-minded inquiry suggests that there is no such thing, for the requirements of the theory stand in deep tension with one another. Legitimate authority resists this scepticism, for it does not suppose that each citizen is bound, but only that some are. The complexities of individual lives and the diversity of needs and interests all suggest that it is not useful to demand of a theory of allegiance that it explain how our political bonds can be moral, content-independent, binding, particular, and universal. The last requirement should be dropped, and with it the idea of political obligation as usually conceived. Political obligations will remain, here and there, as correlates of justified authority. But the idea of a general obligation to obey, binding all people to all laws, will have lost any explanatory or ideological value it may once have had, and the old arguments purporting to establish such an obligation will finally be put out of their misery.

9

OBEDIENCE AND CIVILITY

If political obligation is not a realistic possibility, and if the state's authority extends to some but not others, it may seem that anarchy cannot be far away. If people came to accept that political bonds in the modern state are more complex and more attenuated than traditional theories suggest, would it not weaken their tendency to obey and support just institutions? We all know how fragile the commitment to do one's duty can be, how easily people are distracted by self-interest and shortsightedness. In view of the near universality of these human failings, how could the tendency to obey just institutions be anything other than a virtue? Whatever the merits of our arguments as matters of abstract political theory, some may feel that, taking people as they are, the practical consequences of accepting the views defended here would be malign. In this, they might even find an ally in J. S. Mill, who, for all his devotion to liberty and individuality, held that a society of freedom must none the less be deeply rooted in the habit of obedience, what he called 'the first lesson of civilisation'.[1] There is not much to be said for it: it does not ensure the development of human potential, but obedience to one's rulers is none the less an absolutely necessary condition for all further progress. The limitations of government, the checks and hedges that bind the public exercise of power, are vital too, but they occupy a historically and logically secondary position. Limited government is after all a form of government, the security of which is impossible to guarantee without a general habit of obedience. Combine that with an argument to show that cherished values and human rights cannot be secure without some form of government, and it seems that one has at least a plausible case for the view that obedience is a virtue. English political thought in Hobbes,

[1] J. S. Mill, *On Representative Government*, ed. R. B. MacCallum (Oxford: Blackwell, 1946), 154.

Hume, Bentham, Austin, and the two Mills continually returns to the deep theme that it is on regular and therefore regulable behaviour that civil society is founded, and that without this the rest cannot last. Just as the foundations of the most attractive buildings are rarely a pleasant sight, they are essential, and bear the weight of the rest of the structure.

1. NO DIFFERENCE?

One might resist this practical conclusion by appeal to a line of argument purporting to show that the sceptical view will in fact make no difference to the character of political institutions. It has been a constant theme of this book that the authority of the state should be seen as a specific and distinct problem about the nature of social relations in political society, and not merely an instance of some generic problem of social order. Authority is a social relation of a particular kind, and its justification must show why that kind of relation is of value. It follows directly that, although foundational, the problem of political authority does not exhaust the theory of the state. The classical problem of political obligation often presents the issue as if it were otherwise; it 'represents the citizen as confronted by a single absolute choice between obedience and resistance, between conformity and treason.'[2] When the issue is embedded, as it often was, in the context of absolute government versus the right to revolution, then the choices may seem so stark. Our concerns, however, are different. We do not generally look to theories of civil disobedience or political obligation to determine the boundaries of legitimate revolutionary or insurrectionist activity. It is recognized that these doctrines only have a significant role in the context of limited constitutional government and that they are not attuned to the issues relevant to complete overthrow of the system. Moreover, we always think of the claims of the state as imposing at best prima-facie obligations: able to be overridden though not ignored. Because they recognize the binding force of many other moral duties, most modern sceptics therefore share John Simmons's view that, 'from a

[2] A. Quinton, ed., *Political Philosophy* (Oxford: Oxford University Press, 1967), 13.

conclusion that no one in a state has political obligations *nothing* follows immediately concerning a justification of disobedience. For political obligations are only one factor among many which would enter into a calculation about disobedience.'[3] If this is correct then sceptical arguments may make no difference to the viability of constitutional government.

This view rests on two groups of assumptions: about the specificity and limited nature of obligations as a single component in the complete structure of moral reasoning, and about compliance as the primary issue of importance. The first group of assumptions are plausible, widely shared, and have been defended here. They serve to narrow the question so that whether we have political obligations is not just a matter of whether there are grounds for a fairly robust allegiance to the authority, but whether there are moral grounds of a certain kind: obligations correlative to the state's authority. But these are not the only considerations which should bear on the attitudes and behaviour of thoughtful citizens. And if the reach of our obligations does not exhaust the scope of what we ought morally to do (let alone the scope of prudential rationality), then the denial that there is a general obligation to obey but only patchy and variable individual obligations will not suffice to show that we have no rational grounds for allegiance. This is another way of explaining what once might have been put in the idiom of natural law: even if there are no *political* obligations binding us to obey, let us say, the criminal law, we are none the less not at liberty to commit murder for there is no escaping the background requirements of natural duty. Murder is wrong irrespective of the particular institutional arrangements in our society. If we add to such considerations the requirements of prudence, we may account for many of the feelings of allegiance and loyalty (at least the openly discussable ones) that we actually have. Specifically political ties are thus prima facie in character, and are set apart for reasons of theoretical convenience and moral importance. They do not exhaust rational allegiance and to be sceptical about them will not, without more, be destabilizing.

[3] A. J. Simmons, *Moral Principles and Political Obligations*, 193.

Not everyone, however, accepts the reassuring view that the absence of a general obligation to obey makes no difference. According to A. M. Honoré,[4] for example, the consequences of such scepticism would be profound and undesirable. In morally hard cases, individuals' decisions about what to do will often turn on their views about the burden of proof, about the nature of the background presumptions to be defeated. One who accepts that there is a prima-facie obligation to obey will obey when morally in doubt, whereas the sceptic will disobey whenever the costs of obedience outweigh his estimate of the general benefits. Because much moral reasoning takes place under conditions of widespread uncertainty about facts and principles, scepticism will on the whole produce less obedience than is desirable. Moreover, it opens the door to manipulation by the self-interested who will try to exploit uncertainty to their own advantage.

Some might say that we should not bother meeting such an argument on the ground that it does not challenge the theoretical denial of the obligation to obey, but only the practical consequences of believing in it. Suppose we had a conclusive argument to show that there is no God, and someone objected that, in view of the well-known human tendency to act selfishly when retribution is unfeared and the need to feel that the meaning of life has some transcendental guarantee, we should not believe our conclusion. Even if sound, that argument would be unlikely to budge the atheist who would instead maintain that we should aim not to accommodate these weaknesses, but to overcome them in the name of a coherent, humanistic morality. Could we resist Honoré's challenge in a similar way? I think not, for the sceptic's doubts centre on the validity of an obligation, not the existence of some entity. A given obligation is valid only when there is good reason for holding people to be under the duty in question. Honoré's claims about the consequences of scepticism are relevant to establishing the existence and weight of those reasons in a way that the social or psychological consequences of atheism are not relevant to establishing the

[4] A. M. Honoré, 'Must We Obey? Necessity as a Ground of Obligation', *Virginia Law Review* 67 (1981), 39–61.

existence of God. We need to assess his argument about the burden of proof more directly.

Whether it is considered sound or not partly depends on how one understands the notion of a prima-facie obligation. There is no philosophical consensus on the concept, and it is so fraught with problems that there is a case for a moratorium on its use. Commonly, it is taken to mean an obligation we have, other-things-being-equal, in contrast to an obligation all-things-considered, that is to say, a sound moral consideration which may none the less not be conclusive about how one ought to act. A prima-facie obligation to tell the truth, for example, is one which may be outweighed by a more important moral reason, but which cannot simply be ignored. Characteristically, a defeated prima-facie obligation still leaves some moral trace even its breach. We may lie to save a life, but still owe a duty later to apologize or explain to the deceived party. That is perhaps the commonest use of the term, and the existence of such an obligation is what is denied by the sceptical view advanced in the last chapter. Honoré, however, uses the notion in a more stringent legalistic sense to mean a consideration which can be outweighed only if a clear and persuasive case can be established against it.[5] This admits of two interpretations. If the case need only be clear and persuasive to the person contemplating disobedience, then recognizing such an obligation will increase the burden of proof only in a limited number of cases. If, on the other hand, the test is an objective one, it seems very demanding indeed. Either way, it commits us to holding that prima-facie obligations bind presumptively in the face of uncertainty. It follows from that conception, however, that in view of the many hard cases in moral reasoning, such a strong case for disobedience will rarely be established and the burden of proof rarely satisfied. Thus, his prima-facie obligation to obey is in fact a substantial presumption in favour of obedience, perhaps even approaching an absolute requirement to obey. Yet the argument from uncertainty and the deficiencies of human nature does not secure so strong a conclusion. Suppose

[5] I owe the objection to D. Lyons, 'Need, Necessity and Political Obligation', *Virginia Law Review* 67 (1981), 63–77. Honoré modifies his position in *Making Law Bind* (Oxford: Clarendon Press, 1987), ch. 6.

that this exigent view of prima-facie obligation is in fact acceptable. Why is such heavy artillery needed to defeat the risks of moral uncertainty and disagreement? We must remember that the rest of moral reasoning is still in place. Even under uncertainty, reasons of beneficence and prudence are still to get their full weight in the decision about whether or not to comply. If disobedience would harm the legitimate interests of others, or if it would set off a chain reaction of unjustified dissent, then these should weigh heavily in our reasoning about what to do. So the absence of a presumption in favour of obedience is still not a presumption in favour of disobedience.

These thoughts bear only on the first group of assumptions underlying the neutralization of scepticism: they show that it is correct to insist that political obligations are only one set of moral reasons among others and that to deny their force is not to prescribe disobedience. This much we should accept. However, there is lurking in the argument another assumption which also goes to sustain the no-difference view. If we hold that it makes no difference whether there is a general obligation to obey provided that compliance is secured by independent moral and prudential considerations, then we are assuming that the practical consequences of accepting these views are to be assessed only in terms of *how much* compliance results from them. For this argument is couched in terms of stability and seeks to meet the objection by pointing out that in view of other legitimate considerations a political morality which excludes the obligation to obey could secure as much stability as could one including it, or at least that it could secure a level of stability above the minimum threshold necessary for an orderly existence.

But is this all that matters? Suppose we come to believe of some state that the authority it claims over its citizens is unjustifiable, and also that they can none the less be reliably expected to obey for fear of the secret police. We would not feel that the most significant feature of that political system is that it manages to secure as much compliance as one in which stability is secured by the justified belief in its legitimacy. Of at least equal importance is the nature of the reasoning which generates public allegiance. A population whose compliance is largely underwritten by fear of sanctions participates in a fundamentally different form of life than one whose compliance flows from the belief that the law is morally binding: that is the truth in Weber's analysis of legitimacy. And obedience based on the belief that one has an obligation to obey differs again, though more subtly, from calculated compliance based on consequentialist reasoning. The whole point in distinguishing the realm of authority and obligation was to acknowledge its descriptive and moral significance in understanding life in the modern state. To take a sceptical position about the state's claims to authority and then seek to neutralize the consequences of the view by insisting that it may make no difference to the quantum of compliance which results is to subvert the very rationale for investigating the problem of authority in the first place. We began by distinguishing the problem of social order from problems of social relations, arguing that authority was among the latter. To defend political obligation is not just to approve a certain measure of stability in political institutions. It is to prescribe a particular form of social relations: the willingness of citizens to take the state's requirements as binding, content-independent reasons to act. To show that such reasons have a more restricted application than is always claimed or often thought is to call into question their value.

Thus we must refine our understanding of the consequences of scepticism. It is of course true that the lack of a general obligation to obey is not a licence to disobey; it is only the absence of one element in the assessment that the conscientious citizen must make. When all other considerations are finely balanced, however, its absence will make a difference. But its significance is not limited to such, possibly rare, cases of equipoise. More importantly, the sceptical view entails that we can never rely on the claim that all have a moral obligation to obey in order to justify compliance. That this is not a small thing can be seen by considering how often we have heard the appeal to such an obligation to justify compliance in circumstances in which we think that resistance is called for. Obviously, given the significance of serious and public disobedience of the law, many other factors must also come into account. One should never disobey lightly, not because that would violate a prima-facie obligation to obey, but because public acts of disobedience may have serious consequences which it is always wrong to ignore. Whether or not circumstances and motivations are such that the truth of the sceptical thesis makes any difference to public order, it does make a difference to the nature of social relations even in a reasonably just state. The sceptical thesis establishes that whatever bonds of obligation there are among citizens generally, whatever network of duties covers them all, they are not the product of the law and the other authoritative requirements of the state. Even if it leaves intact the gross external features of stability and compliance, scepticism therefore changes our view of political order from the inside; it forces us to reassess its moral basis and significance.

2. IS OBEDIENCE A VIRTUE?

An attitude of obedience, a willingness to accept the authority of the state, cannot be shown to be obligatory. It is, however, certainly permissible. Some have preferred Thoreau's view that 'The only obligation which I have a right to assume, is to do at any time what I think right.'[6] But the weakness of that position has already been exposed in Chapter 2. If the state is reasonably just, then one does no wrong by assuming or expressing a commitment to it. One might be tempted to leave the conclusion at that, and then press on with the aim of providing a theory of the limits of authority, or the scope and methods of justifiable disobedience. But this would, I think, give too little weight to the considerations which motivate positions like that of Honoré. They are not simply mistaken theoretical views or expressions of an ideology of deference to law. On the contrary, they respond to serious issues which demand the consideration of anyone interested in non-utopian political theory, that is, in political theory which aspires to convince in social and economic circumstances reasonably similar to our own. If one wishes to speculate about the institutions and attitudes appropriate to beings more nearly perfect than ourselves, then one might drop the issue. Utopian

[6] H. D. Thoreau, *Walden and Civil Disobedience* (New York: New American Library, 1960), 223.

political theory has its own traditions from which much may be learned. But my aims in concluding this book are more modest. I am interested in whether there is some way to reconcile the platitudes about human limitations with the view of authority defended here, some way that meets rather than ignores what is sound in the objection.

The nerve of that objection is, to repeat, that in the context of uncertainty and imperfect motivation the rejection of political obligation and the insistence on the limited scope of legitimate authority will lead to an unacceptable quantum of disobedience, and that we should therefore recognize a general obligation to obey. That argument fails because other factors determining this quantum are left in place by the sceptical argument and thus the dire consequences will not come to pass. But need one proceed in this way at all? Why argue for an *obligation* to obey? There are admirable traits of character which have nothing to do with the realm of obligation. Given the common frailties of human nature, and the uncertainty of accomplishing our most cherished plans and projects, almost everyone needs a certain amount of courage. It is of value, deserves praise, and should be inculcated in the young. Yet it is not obligatory to be courageous. The zoologist who spoils his research career because of an unjustified timidity about travel in the wilderness has not just for that reason failed in his moral obligations. He may have such obligations, but the value of courage does not establish them. His failing, though real, is not of a sort which would warrant either punishment or the most serious forms of criticism which our moral practices provide. However, it is not only permissible but also admirable and valuable to show courage, and because it answers to a common human need and makes human life go better we can with confidence give it the traditional title of a virtue.

This avenue might be more promising than that of attempting to establish that obedience is obligatory. Modern moral philosophy too often gets trapped within the narrow view of morality as primarily a matter of rights and duties, and thus ignores or undervalues considerations which cannot be so expressed. Some who are inclined to concede this point might none the less maintain that it applies to personal morality only and that the political fragment of morality is essentially a matter of rights and duties. But there is little profit in such a stipulation. If political life would be intolerable or much less valuable without certain virtues then they may fairly be counted as political virtues on the ground that they are necessary conditions of political morality. Whatever we decide to call them, we should not make the error of assuming that if obedience is not among the citizen's obligations or the state's rights, then it is a matter of moral indifference. One goes about arguing for the existence of a virtue in a different way, by showing the value of the character traits in which it inheres. Can we take seriously not only that obedience is the first lesson of civilization as Mill says, but also that it ranks among the first virtues of the civilized?

It is, of course, only a virtue in certain circumstances, those of reasonable justice. We deplore rather than praise obedient Nazis. This is no special obstacle, however, for the same is true of many other virtues. Courage in a Nazi is equally problematic. But obedience does have one difficulty which courage or prudence do not. These virtues clearly benefit their possessors; in some general sense their lives will go better with them than without. This is not to deny the existence of other-regarding effects: it is better to be in the trenches with the courageous or prudent than with the timid or reckless, but we regard these as secondary to the main value of the virtues. This is less clear in the case of obedience. In certain cases it is beneficial to the agent to obey just laws, particularly those which provide facilities for private action such as the law of trusts or of contract. But these are admittedly special cases. At least on the surface, many laws will require the agent to sacrifice his own good for the good of others. Few if any of the redistributive tax regimes in most modern states could be justified to the agent in purely self-regarding terms. Like justice, obedience seems to be inherently other-regarding. This is not the place to open the large and venerable question of whether by some complex, indirect argument justice can be shown to be of benefit to its possessor, or whether the virtues can be extended to the other-regarding class as well. I shall simply assume a favourable answer, and investigate the virtue of obedience in that context. If this can be shown to be wrong, then it will only strengthen the sceptical case.

In arguing for a virtue, we must clearly specify what it is allegedly needed for. Consider the traditional theological virtue of faith. I take it as given that faith cannot be shown to be a virtue unless certain theological arguments are sound; if there is no God then we do not need faith as normally understood. But suppose there is a God who has revealed His will in certain historical events. Would we then need faith? Geach points out that it depends on what for:[7] faith can quite easily be shown to be necessary to help us hang on to belief through illness, momentary doubt, political repression, temptation, and even in the face of some counterarguments whose glamour is greater than their persuasive force. But that is not the really difficult question. It is: Do we need faith to generate or justify belief? Showing that, even for a theist, is a much more difficult matter. Certainly we cannot appeal to faith itself to ground belief in God's existence or our confidence in the Biblical claim that we need faith. That would be viciously circular. Obedience is, in some ways, in a similar position. It cannot be that the fundamental principles of political morality are to be grounded in obedience to the state's requirements; we cannot support constitutional government on the ground that our constitution requires it any more than we can regard the state as authoritative because it claims authority. Each requires an independent foundation. Thus, the role of obedience must also be a secondary one, at most an additional security for a form of government which we know on independent grounds to be worthy of our support. It needs this additional security, not just because of the controversial character of judgements about justice, but because of our weaknesses in living up to its demands. Obedience may be a valuable corrective to our standing temptation to do wrong; it cannot be a source of primary commitment to do the right thing.

What, more precisely, is obedience needed to remedy? The proposal is that it is needed to remedy the common failures of imperfectly motivated people who must act in cases of uncer-

[7] P. T. Geach, *The Virtues* (Cambridge: Cambridge University Press, 1977), 37–8.

tainty. That our motivation is imperfect needs no elaboration: illegitimate self-preference and excessive demands for assurance that others will behave as they ought are painfully familiar. But the nature of uncertainty is more complex. In political life we are constantly confronted with uncertainty about facts, causal relations, and the likely consequences of our policies. Uncertainty is often exaggerated and exploited as an excuse for inaction (such as President Reagan's claim that it is uncertain whether acid rain is caused by industry or by trees) but principled people must also confront genuine doubts about the social world: the deterrent effect of criminal penalties and the relation between crime and media violence are only two of the well-known examples. Generally it is not possible to delay action until the facts are finally in, and to do so would in any case be to decide for the status quo. Conscientious citizens and officials therefore need policies to deal with factual uncertainty.

That problem is complex enough, for there is no fully satisfactory theory of how we should decide under uncertainty even when our goals are clear and well ordered. But even that is nothing like as difficult as normative uncertainty, that is, doubts about the requirements of political morality. Few can be entirely sure that abortion should be permitted on demand, or that private ownership of radio frequencies is justifiable, or that free speech should not protect the expression of racial hatred. And even a true believer on any of these issues must, if honest, concede that there are informed citizens who conscientiously and sincerely hold opinions to the contrary. This is not, or need not be, an expression of moral scepticism; about some matters there may be no doubt. It is a reflection of intelligent humility and the willingness to regard other citizens as our equals.

The problem of disobedience is sometimes thought to be most serious when a law is clearly unjust. That is not quite right. Only when a law is thought to be unjust does the problem arise, but the really difficult cases are those in which moral and factual uncertainty make it controversial whether or not the law is just. It is easy to miss the fact that our attachment to the state takes different forms and is grounded in different principles in these various cases. The traditional theory of political obligation binds us to just laws only. The theories of utility, consent, fairness, and so forth all seek to account for our attachment to just institutions; none of them provides a direct argument for the support of unjust or even deeply controversial policies. If we regard controversiality as imposing the risk of injustice, then we may treat the central problem as one of grounding the duty to obey laws which are unjust or possibly unjust. What could explain such a duty? Some particularly rigoristic moralities may deny that anything does, especially if they admit strong deontological prohibitions against doing evil that good may come. All but the most stringent deontologist, however, will concede that there is sometimes a duty to obey unjust laws by relying on a familiar institutional argument.[8]

In Rawls's language, constitutional democracy in any of its familiar forms is an imperfect procedure with respect to justice. Unlike the competitive market, which under ideal conditions guarantees attainment of efficiency, the best constitutional order can only tend towards justice. The explanation for this difference is uncomplicated, for the market makes only very weak demands on human motivation. Self-interested, well-informed agents trading rationally in the market will always promote efficiency; but political institutions require an element of good faith and a sense of justice on the part of citizens and officials in order to have any chance of success. One problem of institutional design (with which the classical utilitarians were keenly concerned) lies in finding ways to keep this requirement fairly low, especially by linking the self-interest of politicians to the common good. But the demands of justice can only be lowered; they can never be eliminated. Moreover, any feasible rule for social decision, including majority rule, is liable to produce unjustifiable results from time to time. Even if the majority should always rule, it cannot be that the majority is always right. It therefore follows that in any non-utopian theory, some injustice is inevitable.

Now, on no plausible theory could citizens be expected to tolerate any degree of injustice whatever, to give absolute

[8] I follow J. Rawls, *A Theory of Justice*, 350–62.

commitment to the outcome of majoritarian decision procedures. A suitably articulated theory of justice will specify certain limits beyond which all bets are off. It is not possible to discuss the arguments for such limits here. I will assume, with Rawls, that they include at least the distributive restriction that there be no entrenched minorities, that is, no individuals or identifiable groups whose interests are continually being harmed by the political system, and an absolute restriction on the amount of harm that is to be tolerated in any one case. I ignore the controversial question of whether harm to certain classes of interests, such as civil liberties or equality of opportunity, is to be regarded as more serious than harm to interests in social and economic welfare. (These priorities flow from the particular conception of justice in play and not from the general doctrine of disobedience.) For our purposes it is enough to accept a second conclusion: that there is a degree of injustice which is in principle tolerable.

In Rawls's argument, these two conclusions figure as premisses in the justification for obeying unjust laws. Constitutional government is highly desirable, yet is certain to produce at least occasional injustice. There is, however, a range of tolerable injustice. This is therefore to be seen as a fair price to pay for the benefits of a constitutional system. The arguments for the natural duty of justice (and also fairness) thus indirectly warrant obeying unjust laws, for they commend allegiance to a system which can sometimes do wrong. Now, we might use this observation to make the following proposal: in view of the imperfections and uncertainties of politics, and inadequate motivation, we should regard obedience as a virtue, a modest one perhaps, but a virtue none the less. We have an argument to show that some injustice should be tolerated, and secure knowledge that common human failings make it likely that we will be less tolerant than we ought. Together these are taken to support the view that we should seek to inculcate an attitude of obedience, understood as the habit of not making one's compliance with law always conditional on one's own view of its justice, and of regarding the procedure of majority rule as excluding certain otherwise valid reasons for disobeying.

First, I should underscore that this is not another argument for a general obligation to obey the law. The burden of Chapter 8 was to establish that there is no such thing. It is not claimed that the present argument will apply to all persons, or bind them to all laws. Just like courage, there are circumstances and people which do not call for the virtue in question. And those who continue always to act on their own best judgement do not violate any general obligation to obey. Yet for those to whom these considerations do apply, majority decision procedures will have justified, though limited, authority. By arguing for the virtue of obedience, we will have established the legitimacy of political authority in certain familiar forms.

Before we accept even this conclusion, however, we must ask whether the proposed remedy is suited to the defects. Is it, first of all, sufficient to the task? It will certainly succeed in restraining disobedience in cases falling within the boundary of tolerable injustice for it will be a general attitude of taking all the requirements of the state on trust, because they are its requirements. He may have doubts about the justice of a certain system of income taxation, but the obedient citizen will pay none the less, so long as the perceived injustice falls within the bounds of tolerability. The habit of obedience will therefore have to be, in some sense, a discriminating one, for it must not encourage acquiescence in the face of serious injustice. But how could a character trait be discriminating in this way? One is obedient only if one is willing not to make one's compliance conditional on one's own view of the merits of the case. How can we square this with reasonable security that the habit of obedience will not carry us over the limits of tolerable injustice? Only on one condition: if it is possible to identify these limits in a content-independent way. Suppose that the bounds of tolerability could be determined only by assessing the substantive issues at hand. If that were so, then one's compliance would be conditional on one's own view of the merits. No habit of obedience could be conditional in this way; it would not be an attitude of obedience at all. So for the habit of obedience to be discriminating we need a way of testing for the limits of injustice which does not require an assessment of the merits of each case, one which does not require an appeal to the very values at issue. Suppose, for instance, that all tolerable injustices arose from some well-known procedural defects in legislating, say, from bills passed when the house was inquorate, or when members have failed to take the appropriate oath of office, or when they purport to legislate *ultra vires*. If that were so, we could identify the range of tolerability without engaging in a full-blown analysis of the case at hand, and thus without making our obedience conditional on the results of such an analysis. A test of pedigree would suffice. But of course it is wildly implausible that the range of tolerability can in fact be identified in a content-neutral way. The very rough criteria stated above, that injustices not bear too heavily on a single individual or group and that in no given case may they be too serious, require first-order moral judgements. This is perhaps obvious in respect of the absolute condition that it not be too serious, but it is even true of the seemingly more formal distributive condition. What constitutes a fair spreading of the burdens of injustice may depend on the aims and nature of the policy in question. Some actuarial categorizations, such as age, may be justifiable grounds of liability in social insurance decisions; others, such as race or gender, may not. The decision about which should be permitted cannot be made on content-neutral grounds. There is therefore no avoiding substantive judgements about the bounds of tolerable injustice. We could not take on trust the government's claim that these bounds have not been exceeded by a certain legislative programme any more than we could take the veracity of the Bible on faith. It follows then that obedience cannot be the virtue we seek, for it cannot be discriminating in the right way. We can never suspend judgement about the bounds of tolerable injustice. If not limited, a habit of obedience is undesirable; if limited it is unattainable.

3. THE VIRTUE OF CIVILITY

It may seem that having rejected the virtue of obedience we must return to the view that, although permissible, there is nothing positive to be said for those attitudes which most citizens of constitutional regimes typically feel towards their governments. This would not in itself be a decisive objection.

In the area of group loyalties, our unreflective feelings may not be especially reliable guides to sound moral principles. Nor would it leave us without a plausible theoretical account of the functions of such attitudes. Emile Durkheim posed a question about seemingly irrational religious beliefs which might also serve here: 'If the peoples themselves have been the artisans of these systems of erroneous ideas, at the same time that they were their dupes, how has this extraordinary hoax been able to perpetuate itself throughout the course of history?'[9] This was not intended as a *reductio ad absurdum*: he was not trying to show that religion could not be a hoax in the purely cognitive sense, but inviting us to speculate about what social functions it might have. Durkheim doubted that the social practice of religion could persist and be such an important feature of most societies if it was completely empty. A social practice may, of course, misrepresent itself. From the sociological point of view, the transcendental claims of religion are hollow; but its real significance may lie elsewhere, perhaps as a mechanism for promoting social solidarity or class rule. Political sociology is not a very advanced science, but already it has provided plausible answers to Durkheim's question as translated to politics. After all, citizens are not the sole artisans of their loyalties. States actively inculcate loyalty, often with great success. The theories of socialization and ideology provide the beginnings of an adequate explanatory account of our tribal feelings. So the sceptical thesis might be taken as a prelude to political sociology. However, without either foreclosing that option or belittling these explanations, we might still pause before rushing to their embrace. Our objections to the virtue of obedience were that it is a case of overkill. Perhaps it is possible to moderate and refine the virtue somewhat, without reverting to the position that one should simply judge each law as it comes, and obey only when conscience so counsels.

What precisely is at risk if we take a neutral attitude? The worry is that in so doing we will weaken a form of government which, though imperfect, is thought to be best among the feasible alternatives. What we need then is precisely the virtue

[9] Cited in R. Aron, *Main Currents of Sociological Thought* (Harmondsworth: Penguin, 1967), ii. 56.

of not taking advantage of these imperfections. Now, if we assumed a general obligation to obey it would indeed have that effect but, as we have seen, it would be too wide-ranging. There is, however, logical space between the alternatives of complying only when the merits of the case demand it and taking all the state's requirements as binding directives. We may instead appeal to what Rawls has called our 'natural duty of civility not to invoke the faults of social arrangements as a too ready excuse for not complying with them, nor to exploit inevitable loopholes in the rules to advance our interests.'[10] Rawls's argument for this duty is, of course, that it would be acknowledged by the rational, egoistic but uninformed parties to a constitutional convention. He regards it as completing the theory of allegiance: obligations of fairness and natural duty bind us to obey just institutions; the natural duty of civility extends the scope of that commitment to unjust outputs of those institutions where the injustice is both tolerable and inevitable. If, however, there is no general obligation to obey, then we cannot ground the virtue of civility by arguing that it is a necessary extension of that obligation. It must instead be shown to stand on its own.

An important contrast between the virtue of civility and that of obedience is that the former at no point requires a surrender of judgement. On the contrary, it demands as a first reaction to perceived injustice an immediate assessment of its seriousness. Then only if the injustice is found to be both within the bounds of tolerability and not easily avoided does civility counsel compliance. This is not to assign content-independent moral significance to law; it does not amount to the claim that we must obey the law because it is the law or because, in the absence of compelling reasons to the contrary, there is a presumption in favour of obedience. Civility does, however, prescribe a weaker form of commitment: the conservative one of self-restraint. It commends a willingness to deliberate about the character of injustice before disobeying and condemns those forms of rigorism which will tolerate nothing but perfection in human institutions. Why is such restraint a virtue? To some extent it does contribute to the

[10] J. Rawls, *A Theory of Justice*, 355.

stability of constitutional government in the way that Rawls suggests: in circumstances of imperfect motivation and moral uncertainty it helps to sustain valuable institutions. If people took every perceived deviation from the requirements of justice as warranting disobedience, then perhaps the system could not survive and trust and mutual confidence would break down. If that spectre causes some to fear scepticism then they may find in civility the reassurance they seek. It cannot finally allay all worries, however, because the uncertainty of human judgement must enter at some point. Like justice itself, the idea of tolerable injustice is inherently controversial. Moreover, we have learned by now not to invest too much trust in arguments based on a supposed need for stability. The sources of order are many, and conscientious citizens will never lightly disobey the law. But there is a further, less instrumental, value which is also captured by the virtue of civility. It expresses a kind of reciprocity and is thus one component of social solidarity and a public conception of justice. Mutual tolerance of minor and occasional injustice is an essential part of a shared commitment to political institutions. All such institutions are imperfect, and civility is essential if any are to exist. But a given group of people share certain particular institutions, and their commitment to *these* ones, to making them better rather than cutting loose and reorganizing, is partly expressed through political restraint. Limited mutual forbearance is part of what it is to belong to a political community, sharing a common fate. For all that, however, it is not obligatory to be civil. Those throughout history whose stringent ideals condemned reform in favour of revolution, or motivated them to rend the civic bond and to begin again in new utopian communities, violated no obligations. It may be said that the fallibility and insecurity of their new constructions attests to their failure, but if so it is a failure of a different kind. It is not one which should attract punishment or condemnation; it represents a lack of wisdom and not of moral fibre.

Civility itself has bounds, as given by the best conception of justice. But on any conception, it will be recognized as a substantial political virtue, lying between the vices of rigorism on the one hand and complacency on the other. So understood, it fulfils the role often wrongly assigned to other principles. Even a sceptic about political obligation, one who holds that the state's authority over its citizens is qualified and incomplete, can regard civility as a primary virtue in political society. It may be said that civility will in certain circumstances generate obligations, particularly if others are induced to rely on our self-restraint. That is no doubt true, although those bonds will be weaker than what has traditionally been contemplated by democratic theorists. In combination with the general requirements of justice, and the special obligations acquired through consent, they pretty much exhaust our political duties. The state and other citizens cannot expect more. Or less.

INDEX

Printed in Poland
by Amazon Fulfillment
Poland Sp. z o.o., Wrocław